My
Daily
Huddle

There is nothing more powerful than starting your day off with Jesus.

Joe Pettigrew

My Daily Huddle

ISBN 9798303464346

Published by ITZ Publishing

Book Design and Photography:
    Paul Jackson
    Holly Rhodes

Printed in the United States of America

My Daily Huddle will empower you (of whatever generation you represent) to understand that God's Word is just as applicable today as it ever was! You will discover the power of spending time in His Word each day. Explore a transformative journey through scripture, devotion, and meditation with this 52 week devotional and meditation guide. It will provide daily reflections and meditations that will deepen your faith, enhance your spiritual growth, and cultivate inner peace. Each day features a carefully selected Bible verse, thoughtful devotional insights, and guided meditations designed to inspire and uplift readers.Alongside timeless wisdom this book offers a blend of biblical teachings and universal truths to enrich your spiritual practice. The Daily Huddle is a daily devotional that has been sent out each morning for seven years. They are read more than 3,000,000 times each year to   individuals in all 50 states and 40 countries. Whether it's a full plate or a heavy heart, don't let whatever you're walking through today keep you from tasting God's goodness. You were created to be nourished daily by the sweet and satisfying love of God. I hope you enjoy what has been prepared for you.

Joe

Acknowledgments

My Wife:

Trudy Pettigrew

My Children:

Ashley McBroom (Daniel)

Tara Roberts (Paul)

Tyler Pettigrew (Jackie)

My Grandchildren:

Conner Roberts

Stella McBroom

Posy McBroom

Heidi Pettigrew

Daphne Pettigrew

Josie Pettigrew

Birdie Roberts

Special Benefactors:

Peter and Mary Katherine Mascolo

Hugh and Jill Freeze

Jim and Linda Shoemaker

Matt and April Rocco

Rick Moore

Glenn Family Foundation

My Church:

First Presbyterian Church

Brownsville, Tennessee.

What People Are Saying About
My Daily Huddle

Go on a journey with your heart to ask yourself questions every person wants to ask but is afraid no one has the answers. But God's Word does have the answers, and My Daily Huddle devotional talks to you about important issues of life.
Author and Pastor, Dr. Tony Evans, TX

Everyday My Daily Huddle is bringing us inspiration that lifts our soul and provides direction for our best life. That is why I subscribe. Hope you will join us.
Author and Pastor, Randy Frazee, KS

My Daily Huddle is a practical and challenging book that helps us see the scoreboard more clearly and ensure we win when the final gun sounds. In the time it takes to listen to the sports recap, you can spend a life-changing few minutes to keep a score that counts.
NFL Quarterback, Colt McCoy, TX

No matter what stage of life you find yourself, My Daily Huddle will give you the perspectives you need to get the most out of everything you do.
Fox News Mike Huckabee, DC

God calls us to have faith and integrity, show sacrifice and leadership, and carry a strong legacy. My Daily Huddle is a geat read.
Chick-Fil-A Former CEO, Dan Cathy, GA

My Daily Huddle is a practical and fun read. I enjoyed how Joe weaved in some fascinating stories with takeaway biblical truths that challenge me to be a better follower of Christ.

American Family Association President, Tim Wildmon, MS

My Daily Huddle is a solid, Biblical approach to many of today's most pressing problems. I look forward to reading it each morning.

Exibit A CEO, Don Furr, TN

How do you balance your life; how do you stay in the zone? You stay strong in your Christian beliefs and make them the focal point of your life. I highly recommend My Daily Huddle; you won't be sorry. Don't miss it!

ESPN College GameDay, Lee Corso, FL

Christians are looking for something that fits the bill like this. With everything happening in America today and fewer people attending church, this will fill a tremendous void. I read The Daily Huddle each day.

The Oak Financial Group CEO, Rick Moore, TX

The Daily Huddle can be done alone, with an office group, or of course, with a small church group. It is extremely relevant today.

FedEx Former Senior Executive, Mike Glenn, TN

My Daily Huddle is an uplifting instrument that inspires me each morning to know I am not alone and life can be a mission accomplished!

ESPN Sports, Chris Mortensen, NY

This is a great read. Written to regular people about real issues grounded in Scripture.

CEO Duck Dynasty, Phil Robertson, LA

Thanks for your good work and blessings on this new book. I give Jesus Christ the advance credit for you and My Daily Huddle.

NFL, NASCAR Owner, Joe Gibbs, NC

I have been subscribing to Dr. Joe's The Daily Huddle devotional for many years. Dr. Joe has always communicated his messages based on sound biblical principles and practical application. My Daily Huddle is one of Dr. Joe's best efforts.

Etech CEO, Matt Rocco, TX

Thanks for sharing My Daily Huddle. I look forward to reading the devotional every day. I have enjoyed The Daily Huddle for many years.

Auburn Football Coach, Hugh Freeze, AL

January 1

WHAT'S THAT IN YOUR EYE?

In Matthew 7:3-5, Jesus teaches us the importance of introspection and humility with the imagery of trying to remove a speck from someone else's eye while ignoring the plank in your own. This passage is a powerful reminder to focus on our shortcomings before criticizing others. It's easy to fall into the habit of noticing the faults of those around us. We judge quickly, feeling justified in our opinions, but Jesus calls us to look inward first. Our eyes are often clouded by the planks of pride, envy, and self-righteousness, which distort our perception of others and ourselves. Consider what it means to see others through the eyes of love and grace. This doesn't mean ignoring wrongdoing but approaching it compassionately and acknowledging our flawed nature. By removing the planks from our own eyes, we open ourselves to clearer sight and understanding. Ask yourself today, What planks are in my eyes? Is it a lingering resentment? A hidden prejudice or a habit of speaking without understanding? Whatever it may be, bring it before God. Seek His wisdom and healing, and invite the Holy Spirit to transform our hearts and minds. When we do this, we improve our relationship with others and deepen our connection with God.

You hypocrite, first take the plank out of your eye, and then you will see clearly to remove the speck from your brother's eye.
Matthew 7:5

GOD KNOWS YOUR NAME

With the world bustling with people and noise, it's easy to feel insignificant and overlooked. Yet, the Bible tells us something profoundly comforting and reassuring—God knows your name. He sees you, understands you, and cares about every detail of your life. When Isaiah penned the words of God in Isaiah 43, he spoke to a people who felt forgotten and forsaken. Through this verse, God assured them of His intimate knowledge and deep love for each of them. Just as He called Israel by name and claimed them as His own, He knows you personally and treasures you as His beloved child. Your name is not just a label—it represents your story, struggles, and triumphs. God knows the path you have walked and the burdens you carry. He knows your dreams, fears, and heart's deepest desires. This knowledge is not distant or impersonal. It is filled with love and compassion, offering you comfort and strength. Whenever you feel lost or alone, remember that God knows your name. He is with you in every situation, guiding and supporting you. Trust in His promise and take solace in the fact that you are known and cherished by Him. Just think about it: God knows your name!

But now, this is what the Lord says—he who created you, Jacob, he who formed you, Israel: Do not fear, for I have redeemed you; I have summoned you by name; you are mine.
Isaiah 43:1

January 3

THE GOD OF SURPRISES

Our God is a God of surprises. In the tapestry of life, with its ups and downs, twists and turns, God often reveals Himself in unexpected ways. We sometimes forget that God is not only a God of order but also a God of surprises. He delights in blessing us beyond our expectations when we least anticipate it. Consider the story of Joseph, who went from pit to palace. Sold into slavery by his brothers, Joseph's life seemed to be on a downward spiral. Yet, God had surprising plans in store. Joseph rose to become the second most powerful man in Egypt through a series of unforeseen events, ultimately saving his family from famine. God used what others meant for harm to position Joseph for greatness. Trust God's hidden hand and His divine surprises. When we face trials or uncertainties, we can rest assured that God is working behind the scenes. His surprises are not mere coincidences but are woven into His sovereign plan for our lives. Have there been moments where God surprised you in ways you never imagined? It could be a closed door that led to a better opportunity or a setback that paved the way for a new beginning. Today, count on the God of surprises. Trust that His plans for you are good, and filled with hope and a prosperous future. Remain open to His unexpected blessings.

For I know the plans I have for you, declares the Lord, plans to prosper you and not to harm you, plans to give you hope and a future.
Jeremiah 29:11

January 4

YOU MATTER TO GOD

It's easy to feel insignificant and overlooked. However, the truth is that you matter deeply to God. He intricately designed you with purpose and intention, molding every aspect of your being. The verse from Jeremiah assures us that God has a divine plan for each of us. It's a reminder that we are not just random beings in a vast universe but dearly loved children crafted by our Heavenly Father. His plans are not for harm, but for our benefit, filled with hope and a promising future. Consider the artistry God used in creating you. Each talent and trait you possess is lovingly chosen and given to you for a reason. Your life is a piece of His grand design; every thread contributes to His beautiful masterpiece. When doubts creep in or you feel undervalued, remember that the Creator of the heavens and the Earth has set His gaze upon you. Your worth is not defined by worldly measures but by the immeasurable love of God. He values you immensely—enough to send His Son, Jesus, to redeem you. Take a moment today to reflect on how much you mean to God. In prayer, ask Him to reveal how He wants you to fulfill His purpose. Remember, you are irreplaceable and eternally cherished. You matter to God.

For I know the plans I have for you, declares the Lord, plans for welfare
and not for evil, to give you a future and a hope.
Jeremiah 29:11

January 5

REPRESENTING JESUS

You have the opportunity to be an ambassador for Christ today. This role is both an honor and a responsibility, as it requires you to live in a way that reflects Jesus' teachings and love. In a world often filled with challenges and distractions, how do we effectively represent Jesus? We can start by cultivating a personal relationship with Him. We deepen our understanding of His character and teachings through prayer, scripture reading, and meditation. This relationship forms the foundation of our faith and equips us to share His love with others. We should strive for authenticity. Being genuine in our actions and words ensures His light shines through us. When people see our sincerity, they are more likely to be drawn to the message of Christ. Lastly, love is our most powerful tool. Jesus instructed us to love our neighbors as we love ourselves (Mark 12:31). This love should be evident in our interactions as we extend kindness, patience, and understanding to those around us. We become living examples of His grace and compassion. Each day presents new opportunities to embody the teachings of Jesus. Living transparently and lovingly makes His presence known in the world. Let's commit to being His hands and feet to those we encounter.

Therefore, we are ambassadors for Christ, as though God were making His appeal through us. We implore you on behalf of Christ, be reconciled to God.
2 Corinthians 5:20

ARE YOU CONTENT?

In a world constantly pushing for more success, more possessions, more acknowledgment—it's easy to lose sight of contentment. Yet, we are called to find satisfaction not in the abundance of things but in the presence of God and His promises. The Apostle Paul introduces us to the profound secret of being content. He experienced both abundance and scarcity, yet his peace did not falter. His contentment was rooted in Christ. Are you seeking fulfillment in temporary things, or do you rest in God's eternal love and presence? True contentment arises not from external conditions but from an internal reliance on God's strength. We must ask Jesus to help us find contentment not in our possessions or status but in our relationship with Him. We must count on His strength, to be grateful for His provision, and to trust in His plan for our lives. Challenge yourself today to pause and consider the areas where discontentment creeps in. True contentment is found not in possessions or circumstances but in a relationship with Christ.

I am not saying this because I am in need, for I have learned to be content, whatever the circumstances. I know what it is to be in need and what it is to have plenty. I have learned the secret of being content in any and every situation, whether well-fed or hungry, whether living in plenty or want. I can do all this through him, who gives me strength.
Philippians 4:11-13

FOLLOW THE LEADER

Following Jesus is an active, daily commitment. It's about aligning our actions, thoughts, and intentions with His teachings and example. His path was not laden with ease or comfort but was marked by sacrifice, service, and unwavering faith in God's plan. When Jesus invites us to follow Him, He calls us to a life that may challenge our comforts and redefine our vision of success. Following Him means we put aside our ambitions and instead focus on His kingdom's values—love, compassion, humility, and truth. Reflect on the current state of your life and priorities. Are there areas where you need to shift focus from self-centered desires to Christ-centered living? Jesus' call is universal but intensely personal. It invites us to examine where we are in our spiritual walk and make conscious choices that align us more closely with His path. This may involve letting go of past grievances, extending forgiveness, or pursuing justice for others. Remember, this is not a solo mission. We are part of a community of believers, the Church, all on this same pilgrimage. Lean on your brothers and sisters in Christ for support, wisdom, and encouragement as you endeavor to follow the leader. In doing so, you will find strength and joy in the shared journey.

Then Jesus said to His disciples, If anyone desires to come after Me, let him deny himself, and take up his cross, and follow Me.
Matthew 16:24

DO YOU BELIEVE?

Have you ever paused to reflect on what it truly means to be identified as a Christian? More than a label or a routine, Christianity is a call to live out the teachings of Jesus Christ in every aspect of our lives. It's a life-transforming relationship with the Savior, marked by a deep and abiding love for others. It's all too easy to fall into the habit of simply going through the motions—attending Church, participating in activities, and reciting prayers—without genuinely embodying the spirit of Christ. But Jesus reminds us that the hallmark of a faithful Christian is love. Love that is patient and kind that doesn't envy or boast that isn't proud or rude, that forgives and always hopes (1 Corinthians 13). Take a moment to examine your life and interactions with those around you. Do your actions and words reflect the love of Christ? Being a Christian means being a light in the darkness and offering grace and compassion to all. It means standing firm in faith, even when faced with trials, and sharing our hope in Jesus with a world in desperate need. Today, as you do your daily tasks, challenge yourself to demonstrate love in practical ways intentionally. Through a kind word, a helping hand, or a listening ear, show those you encounter that you are a follower of Christ—not just in name, but in action.

They will know we are Christians by our love.
John 13:35

DON'T UNDERSTAND?

There are moments in our Christian walk when confusion clouds our hearts and minds. We sometimes struggle with perplexing situations that test our faith and question our understanding. These are the times when we find ourselves saying, I don't understand. Yet, as believers, it is in these very moments that we are called to deepen our trust in God. The Scripture in Proverbs 3 reminds us that our understanding is limited and fallible. We are encouraged to trust the Lord, who sees the bigger picture and knows what is best for us. This act of trust is not passive; it requires us to submit our ways to Him and rely on His guidance, even when the path is unclear. In moments of uncertainty, take comfort in knowing that God is sovereign and His plans for us are filled with hope and a future. While we may not always understand His ways, we can rest assured that His wisdom surpasses our own. Today, reflect on areas where you need clarification. Surrender these concerns to God, trusting IIc will guide you through them. Write down the situations you struggle to understand, and ask God to reveal His purpose in those areas.

Trust in the Lord with all your heart and lean not on your own understanding; in all your ways submit to him, and he will make your paths straight.
Proverbs 3:5-6

DON'T LOOK BACK

Don't Look Back resonates deeply within the Christian life, as it encourages us to trust God's plans and have faith in His direction. Life often presents us with moments where the past seems alluring or more comfortable than the uncertain future. Yet, as Christians, we are called to fix our eyes on Jesus and the path He has set before us. Dwelling on our past mistakes, regrets, or even successes can hinder our spiritual growth and our ability to engage with God entirely in actions in our lives. Consider the Israelites during their exodus from Egypt. Despite witnessing God's miracles, they longed for the familiarity of their past bondage. Like them, we can be tempted to look back when facing difficulties or changes. Paul the Apostle also speaks to this in Philippians 3:13-14, where he emphasizes the importance of forgetting what is behind and straining toward what lies ahead. This forward-looking mindset is crucial for our spiritual development and the collective progress of the body of Christ. Today, reflect on what may be holding you back. Are you clinging to past habits, relationships, or fears? Release them to God and step boldly into the future. Looking back, it is never as fulfilling as the promises God has ahead.

But Jesus said to him, No one, having put his hand to the plow, and looking back, is fit for the kingdom of God.
Luke 9:62

BILLY GRAHAM-HIS IMPACT

Few people will debate the influence of Rev. Billy Graham on our world. There were rallies at football stadiums where thousands and thousands of people gave their lives to Jesus. He was a personal friend and confidant to 11 US Presidents, and for 15 years, was voted by the Gallup organization as one of the 10 Most Respected Christian Leaders in the world. We are humbled at best when we place our lives next to his. It says in Scripture there will be more joy in Heaven over one sinner repenting than over ninety-nine righteous men who need no repentance. Don't you wonder what Heaven was like the day Dr. Graham changed his address? On Dr. Graham's 90th birthday, he sums up his perspective on eternity:

Someday, you will read or hear that Billy Graham is dead. Don't believe a word of it. I shall be more alive than I am now. I will just have changed my address. I will have gone in the presence of God.

We talk about what would happen if we died tonight. Billy Graham knew beyond a shadow of a doubt where his next address would be. Do you?

I tell you that in the same way, there will be more joy in Heaven over one sinner who repents than over ninety-nine righteous persons who need no repentance.
Luke 15:7

DON'T GROW UP

"The disciples came to Jesus and asked, Who is the greatest in the Kingdom of Heaven? He called a little child to Him and placed the child among them. And He said: Truly I tell you, unless you change and become like little children, you will never enter the Kingdom of Heaven. Therefore, whoever humbles himself like this child is the greatest in the Kingdom of Heaven" (Matthew 18:1–3). We must approach Him with a childlike attitude to do great things for God. We can learn a lot from watching little children. They find a way to enjoy whatever they're doing wherever they are. They're quick to forgive an offense. They're fighting over something; the next moment, they're playing happily together. And trusting comes easily to them. Children don't worry about mortgage payments, meals, or making ends meet because they implicitly trust that we will provide what they need. What is Jesus teaching us?

- Have simple faith.
- Pray simple prayers.
- Be quick to repent.
- Reach regularly for God's help.

When we forgive children, they don't run around feeling guilty; they forget it and move on. How can we be more like children?

Unless you change and become like little children, you will never enter the kingdom of Heaven.
Matthew 18:3

WHY WORRY?

Worry can often feel like a sport. Yet, we are encouraged to cast our anxieties on God. This passage reminds us that worry is not the path God has planned for us. Instead, we are invited to bring our concerns to Him, trusting that He will provide peace beyond our understanding. The word "guard" in this Scripture paints a vivid picture of protection, as if God Himself stands sentinel over our hearts and minds, shielding us from the turmoil of anxiety. Consider how birds, as mentioned in Matthew 6:26, neither sow nor reap yet are fed by our Heavenly Father. They don't fret about their future needs because they rely entirely on God's provision. Reflect on the countless times God has been faithful in our lives and the lives of others. Gratitude for His past provision can fuel trust in His future care. Take a moment to focus on His promises, knowing that His plans for you are good and His love is everlasting. By doing so, we'll find that not only does worry diminish, but your faith grows stronger. What did you worry about last week? Did your worrying help?

Do not be anxious about anything, but in every situation, by prayer and petition, with thanksgiving, present your requests to God. And the peace of God, which transcends all understanding, will guard your hearts and minds in Christ Jesus.
Philippians 4:6-7

WHO ARE YOUR FRIENDS?

Remember what your mother used to say: The company you keep will profoundly influence your thoughts, actions, and spiritual growth. The Bible frequently highlights the importance of choosing our friends wisely. This verse emphasizes the value of surrounding ourselves with those who inspire and uplift us in our Christian walk. When we evaluate our friendships, we must ask ourselves if these relationships are pushing us closer to God or pulling us away. Are our friends encouraging us in our faith, providing godly counsel, and holding us accountable to biblical principles? Or do they tempt us and distract us from our spiritual goals? We should strive to build friendships rooted in love, mutual respect, and shared values. Paul reminds us, "Do not be misled: Bad company corrupts good character." Are there areas where you can foster deeper connections with those who share your faith? Perhaps there are opportunities to mentor others or to be mentored by someone more mature in their walk with God. In pursuing godly friendships, it's important to remember that Jesus is our ultimate companion. Maintaining a close relationship with Him gives us the wisdom to discern who should be part of our inner circle.

Walk with the wise and become wise, for a companion of fools suffers harm.
Proverbs 13:20

A DAY THAT MATTERS

Every day holds the potential to transform our lives in significant ways. Consider the story of Esther. In Esther 9:1, we read, "On this day, God's chosen people triumphed over their enemies," illustrating how swiftly circumstances can change when we align ourselves with God's purpose. Just as Esther went from an orphaned girl to a queen who saved her people, each day presents us with divine intervention and blessing opportunities. While initially her situation seemed dire and without hope, Esther's faith and courage led to a dramatic shift—not just for her, but for an entire nation. In our own lives, we often face challenges that seem impossible. Yet, as Christians, we are reminded that God can use any day to bring about change. A single moment can alter our trajectory, open new doors, or close ones that lead us astray. Our role is to remain faithful, vigilant, and ready to act when called. It can be as subtle as a changed perspective, a renewed spirit, or an unexpected blessing that turns our difficulties into triumphs. God's timing is perfect, and His plans are far greater than ours. Each day is a gift, an opportunity for growth and change. Trust in God, stay the course and remember that today might be the day that makes all the difference.

Why, you do not even know what will happen tomorrow.
James 4:14

MOVING FORWARD

Moving forward is a crucial yet sometimes challenging concept in our faith. Life often feels like a series of hurdles, each one higher than the last. But as believers, we have a unique advantage—trust in God's promises. Paul's words here provide both encouragement and a strategy for moving forward. Acknowledge the past, but don't dwell on it. Whether it's past successes or failures, they're past. Instead, Paul advises us to focus on the present task of pressing forward with purpose and perseverance. Moving forward requires active participation. It might mean forgiving someone who has wronged you or letting go of regrets that weigh heavily on your heart. It could involve pursuing a dream or calling you've hesitated to chase. In whatever form it takes, moving forward is an act of faith. Consider how you can apply Paul's strategy in your spiritual and everyday life. What are the things you need to forget? What goals lie straight ahead? God calls us to grow and advance in His plans for us. Reflect on these words as you take steps toward your future. Trust that God is with you.

Brothers and sisters, I do not consider myself yet to have taken hold of it. But one thing I do: Forgetting what is behind and straining toward what is ahead, I press on toward the goal to win the prize for which God has called me heavenward in Christ Jesus.
Philippians 3:13-14

TALKING THE TALK

The words we choose can either build others up or tear them down. James reminds us of the power of the tongue—an often underestimated tool that can bring blessings and curses. This duality reflects the struggle we face as Christians, striving to live out our faith in actions and words. Consider how often your words reflect your faith. Do they align with the love and grace we aspire to embody as followers of Christ? Words, once spoken, cannot be taken back. They echo in the hearts of those who hear them long after they have been said. It is crucial, then, that we speak with intention and kindness. Reflect on a situation where your words have fallen short of the love and encouragement you aim to spread. Instead of guilt, feel conviction—a call to transform this area of your life. As you go about your day, remember the immense power of your words. Choose them carefully, ensuring they reflect the teachings of Christ. May each interaction be an opportunity to share God's love, turning conversations into pathways of understanding and unity. Ultimately, talking the talk is about proclaiming our faith and living it consistently through our speech and heart aligned with God's will.

With the tongue, we praise our Lord and Father, and with it, we curse human beings who have been made in God's likeness. Out of the same mouth come praise and cursing. My brothers and sisters, this should not be.
James 3:9-10

January 18

YOU CAN'T TAKE IT WITH YOU

The Apostle Paul's words to Timothy remind us that the possessions we accumulate in this life have no eternal value. Consider this image for a moment: when we enter the world, our hands are empty, and when we leave, they are empty still. All the wealth, achievements, and possessions we gather are temporary. They bring neither fulfillment nor spiritual growth and certainly don't accompany us into eternity. Instead, our focus should be on nurturing what truly matters—our relationship with God and the people He has placed in our lives. Intangible treasures like love, kindness, and faith enrich our souls and align us with God's kingdom. These are what endure and influence our eternal destiny. This week, take time to evaluate your priorities. Are you investing too much time and energy in acquiring material possessions that will eventually fade away? Reflect on how you can shift your focus toward building treasures in Heaven, as Jesus taught in Matthew 6:20. Challenge yourself to practice generosity and contentment. What can you do today to share your blessings with others? This selfless action extends God's grace beyond your immediate circle, fostering a legacy that pleases Him.

For we brought nothing into the world, and we can
take nothing out of it.
1 Timothy 6:7

IT'S NEVER TO LATE

We often feel pressured to achieve goals or milestones. However, the Bible reminds us that God's timing is perfect, and it's never too late to pursue His purpose in our lives. Consider the story of Abraham. At 75 years old, God called him to leave his homeland and begin a new chapter (Genesis 12:1-4). It was an age when many would have settled into a comfortable routine. Yet, Abraham's faith in God's promises set him on a remarkable path that would impact generations. Similarly, Moses began his mission to lead the Israelites out of Egypt at 80 (Exodus 7:7). Despite his past and initial hesitation, Moses became a pivotal figure in God's plan for His people. These stories remind us that God's purpose does not diminish with age. Our timelines do not bind his plans for us. Instead, God equips and empowers us at every stage of our lives. The Apostle Paul, too, experienced a significant life change. Once a persecutor of Christians, Paul encountered Jesus on the road to Damascus and became one of the greatest apostles, spreading the Gospel to nations (Acts 9). His transformation shows that God's grace can turn our lives around even when we feel we've strayed too far. Take heart in knowing that with God, it's never too late to start anew or to fulfill His calling.

I was afraid I would lose your money, so I hid it in the Earth.
Matthew 25:25

KEEP SOWING SEEDS

It's easy to lose sight of the small actions that shape our future. The Bible teaches us a profound yet simple truth about sowing and reaping. Every action we take is like a seed planted in the soil of life. Whether it's a kind word, a humble act of service, or time spent in prayer, these seeds grow and yield fruit over time. Consider a farmer who diligently plants seeds, nurturing them with water and sunlight. Though the results aren't immediate, the harvest is abundant. Similarly, we are called to sow seeds of faith, love, and righteousness in our Christian walk. Remember that God is faithful even when the ground seems barren, or the wait feels long. He sees the seeds you plant; in His perfect timing, they will grow and bear fruit. Perhaps you've been serving in ministry, pouring your heart into others, yet seeing little return. Or you're investing in your spiritual growth, but progress feels slow. Keep sowing. Trust that God is cultivating something beautiful beneath the surface. The assurance found in Galatians is clear: "the seeds you plant will not return void." Keep sowing seeds of grace, kindness, and truth. Trust in God's promises and His timing. Your steadfastness will lead to a harvest of blessings, not just in your life but in the lives of those around you.

Then Nathanael exclaimed, Rabbi, you are the Son of God — the King of Israel.
John 1:49

FORGIVING OTHERS

Forgiveness is a profound act of grace and a fundamental test of our Christian faith. We often encounter situations that test our patience and challenge our capacity for forgiveness. But holding onto resentment and anger can weigh heavily on our spirits, hindering our spiritual growth and peace. Ephesians 4 reminds us that forgiveness is not just a suggestion; it's a transformational process commanded by God. This Scripture encourages us to shed bitterness and anger, replacing them with kindness and compassion. The call to forgive isn't just for the benefit of the person being forgiven; it's a liberating gift to ourselves, freeing us from grudges and emotional pain. Take a moment to reflect on your relationships. Has someone hurt you, whether recently or in the past? Consider what forgiving them means, not necessarily for their sake, but for yours. Forgiveness doesn't mean forgetting or excusing harmful behavior but releasing bitterness's hold over your life. Remember that just as we have been forgiven through Christ's sacrifice, we are called to extend that same grace to others. Today, identify someone you need to forgive.

Get rid of all bitterness, rage and anger, brawling and slander, along with every form of malice. Be kind and compassionate to one another, forgiving each other, just as in Christ, God forgave you.
Ephesians 4:31-32

DO YOU HAVE A HERO?

We often find ourselves looking up to someone for inspiration and guidance. Whether it's a family member, a public figure, or someone from our community, admiration can significantly shape our values and actions. But as Christians, it's essential to reflect on who holds the ultimate place of admiration. The Bible is filled with individuals whose stories offer valuable lessons for us. However, it is crucial to remember that they all point to the singular figure we should admire above all—Jesus Christ. Hebrews 12:2 encourages us to "fix our eyes on Jesus, the pioneer and perfecter of faith." By focusing on His life and teachings, we gain a deeper understanding of the path we are called to follow. Admiring Jesus and His qualities, such as compassion, humility, and unwavering faith, sets a solid foundation for our spiritual growth. While it's natural to admire the strengths and achievements of others, our ultimate admiration should be reserved for Jesus. Today, reflect on who you admire and ensure your admiration aligns with your faith's principles. Let Jesus' qualities shape your character.

Do nothing out of selfish ambition or vain conceit. Rather, in humility value others above yourselves, not looking to your own interests but each of you to the interests of the others. In your relationships with one another, have the same mindset as Christ Jesus.
Philippians 2:3-5

LIFE IS NOT FAIR

Life can often seem unfair, leaving us frustrated and disappointed. Yet, these moments present an opportunity to deepen our faith and trust in God. The Bible offers profound wisdom for times when life doesn't go our way. Today's verse reminds us that enduring hardships with grace and faith is an act of worship that pleases God. While the challenges we face may not always result from our actions, how we respond to them is a testament to our faith. The key is to maintain a heart aligned with God's will, trusting Him even when things are difficult. Consider Joseph's story in Genesis. Despite being sold into slavery by his brothers and later imprisoned unjustly, Joseph remained steadfast in his faith. Eventually, God used his trials to elevate him to a position of authority where he could save his family during a famine. Joseph's story illustrates that even when life's circumstances seem unfair, God has a more fantastic plan beyond our understanding. In moments of perceived injustice, seek comfort in God's promises and His greater purpose for you. Remember that while life on Earth may not always reflect perfect fairness, God's justice prevails. Keep your eyes on Him, and you will find peace and strength to endure. Reflect on how you can trust God's sovereignty in your life today.

But if you suffer for doing good and you endure it, this is commendable
before God.
1 Peter 2:20

ARE YOU A COMPLAINER?

Complaining is something we all find ourselves doing from time to time, but we must be mindful of its impact on our faith. Complaining often reveals a lack of trust in God's plan and provision. When we focus on what we perceive as missing or wrong, we overlook our blessings and God's grace. Paul reminds us in Philippians to avoid grumbling and arguing, urging us to be blameless and pure. When we abstain from complaining, we set ourselves apart, shining like stars in a negativity-filled world. This brightness comes not only from our words but also from our attitudes and actions that reflect our faith. Consider reflecting on your own life. Are you quick to voice dissatisfaction, or do you pause to find gratitude in your daily experiences? Instead of focusing on challenges, try to see them as opportunities for growth and trust in God's greater plan. Shifting your perspective opens you to more profound peace and joy. Take time today to acknowledge where you might be prone to complain. Remember, with each grateful thought, you draw nearer to His presence and reflect His love more brightly to those around you.

Do everything without grumbling or arguing so that you may become blameless and pure, children of God without fault in a warped and crooked generation. Then you will shine among them like stars in the sky.
Philippians 2:14-15

DOES GOD SEND TEXTS?

Throughout the day, you may receive a lot of text messages. Most of them consist of the things we need to accomplish. Every once in a while, we will receive a brief message conveying how much we are loved, and that does wonders to boost our day. A quick text, however, can only accentuate what has already been established through hard work in our relationships. To expect our relationships to thrive on texts alone would not only be foolish but would speak volumes about the value we place on intimacy. Prayer is our means of communicating with Jesus. If prayer is perceived as a requirement, it can quickly become work. As a relationship can falter when communication becomes forced, it is also true that our relationship with Jesus can become awkward if we don't understand how to communicate. Prayer should be more important than telling God what we want. When we expect Him to answer our cries for help and respond with a quick text message, our concept of prayer becomes small and self-serving. Our lives are busy. There is more on our to-do list than time to do it. Have you found a way to spend the time with Jesus in Prayer you want? It's up to you; the world is not going to help you. God may not text message us directly, but His messages are found in Scripture, prayer, and daily interactions.

My heart has heard You say, Come and talk with Me. And my heart responds, Lord, I am coming.
Psalm 27:8

KEEP YOUR WORKS SILENT

I'm an exhibitionist, said one NFL rookie. Life is too short to remain unnoticed by my fans. The same well-known athlete released a video about his greatest plays, which he frequently played for his friends and guests. The desire for praise is never far from any of us. We want people to notice our qualities and achievements. Applause-seeking can be ugly when it's tied to our faith. In Jesus' day, prayer, fasting, and charity were central to Jewish piety. Jesus saw how easily they could be wrongly used for personal attention. He said. "Don't do your good deeds publicly when you pray. Don't be like the hypocrites who love to pray publicly on street corners. And when you fast, don't make it obvious." Jesus' reason was apparent: When such spirituality is done to make us look good, the applause we receive will be our only reward. The One whose praise matters most will turn a blind eye. Jesus said that actual acts of faith would be hard to hide, as a city on a hill can't be hidden. We should keep quiet about our deeds and let our lives speak for themselves. In a world focused on recognition, remember Matthew 6:1. Perform your acts of kindness and charity quietly, seeking God's approval over human applause. Leave people guessing; your work is between you and God.

Give your gifts in private, and your Father, who sees everything,
will reward you.
Matthew 6:4

DO YOU HAVE DOUBTS?

Doubt can often feel like a shadow that never entirely leaves. It whispers questions into our hearts, shaking our confidence in God's promises. But doubt is not the enemy of faith; instead, it's an opportunity to deepen it. When we face moments of uncertainty, we are invited to lean closer to God's truth and promises. James reminds us in his epistle that when we ask God for wisdom or guidance, we must do so with a heart full of belief, not doubt. This doesn't mean we will never experience uncertainty. On the contrary, experiencing doubt can catalyze spiritual growth if we confront it with faith and perseverance. Consider the story of Peter walking on water. His doubt caused him to sink, but his faith got him out of the boat in the first place. Jesus didn't condemn Peter for his moment of fear. Instead, He extended His hand and lifted him, showing us that He will steady us when our faith wavers. Reflect on your life today. Are there areas where doubt is clouding your faith? Take these doubts to God. Ask Him for the wisdom and strength to overcome them, and trust that He can use even our uncertainties to strengthen our relationship with Him. Remember, faith isn't the absence of doubt; it's choosing to trust God despite it.

But when you ask, you must believe and not doubt, because the one who doubts is like a wave of the sea, blown and tossed by the wind.
James 1:6

WHO CAN YOU TRUST?

For Christians, the ultimate source of trust is God, whose faithfulness is unchanging and everlasting. This passage encourages us to trust God's wisdom rather than relying solely on our limited human perspective. Throughout Scripture, we see countless examples of individuals who placed their trust in God and were rewarded for their faith. From Abraham, who left his homeland without knowing his destination, to Moses, who led the Israelites out of Egypt, these stories illustrate the power of trusting in divine guidance. When we put our faith in God, we align ourselves with His perfect plan, even when we don't fully comprehend it. In our daily lives, we are often faced with decisions that challenge our ability to trust. Whether it's trusting others, ourselves, or the future, it's important to remember that God's understanding surpasses our own. We can find peace amid life's uncertainties and strength to face any circumstance by placing our trust in Him. Ultimately, while human relationships may falter, God's love remains constant. Scriptures remind us that His plans are for our good, and His faithfulness endures forever.

Trust in the Lord with all your heart and lean not on your own understanding; in all your ways submit to him, and he will make your paths straight.
Proverbs 3:5-6

January 29

YOUR WORST POSSESSION?

C. S. Lewis wrote in Mere Christianity, There is one vice of which no man in the world is free; everyone in the world loathes when he sees it in someone else. No fault makes a man more unpopular, and no fault that we are more unconscious of in ourselves. And the more we have it in ourselves, the more we dislike it in others. Can you guess what it is? Pride. Watching sports on television and listening to player interviews is only possible by being taken aback by the arrogance and pride some display; however, if we could play like those individuals, we may act the same way. What issues with pride are you encountering in your life? How can you keep your pride in check? You just may be more prideful than you believe that you are. Pride blinds us to our weaknesses, hindering spiritual growth. Let's seek humility in Christ, daily recognizing our need for His grace and guidance. Pride is a subtle yet powerful force that can lead us away from God. Proverbs 16:18 warns, "Pride goes before destruction, a haughty spirit before a fall." Reflect on your actions and thoughts today. Are they guided by humility or pride? Seek to cultivate a humble spirit that honors God and strengthens your walk with Him.

You have been deceived by your own pride.
Obadiah 1:3

HAVE YOU EVER FAILED?

Falling is not the end of our story. It's a reminder that failure is not about the fall itself but how we rise after falling. The righteous may fall but are resilient, drawing strength from their faith to stand up again. Even the most faithful individuals can find themselves facing defeat or making mistakes, but the persistent pursuit of God's path defines true righteousness. Consider Peter, one of Jesus' closest disciples, who famously denied Jesus three times before the crucifixion. Despite this significant failure, Peter went on to become a foundational leader in the early Church. His story illustrates that failure does not disqualify us from God's plans. Instead, it can be a powerful catalyst for growth and deeper reliance on Him. In moments when you feel like you've failed, remember that God's love and purpose for you remain unchanged. Allow your setbacks to become stepping stones, drawing you closer to the strength and wisdom in His word. Failure is a part of life. Remember, failure is not the end through Christ but a stepping stone to His greater plan. Trust and grow in Him. Let failure be a teacher, guiding you to rise, learn, and trust God's unfailing grace more deeply.

For though the righteous fall seven times, they rise again, but the wicked stumble when calamity strikes.
Proverbs 24:16

WHO'S COMING FOR DINNER?

When it comes to hospitality, the Bible provides us with a profound example through the story of Martha and Mary. In Luke 10:38-42, Jesus visits the home of these two sisters. Martha is busy with preparations while Mary sits at Jesus' feet, listening intently. This scenario presents a powerful lesson about priorities and presence. The essence of hosting isn't about the perfection of your home or the complexity of the meal but rather the quality of your presence with those you invite in. In our fast-paced lives, like Martha, we often get caught up in the busyness of preparing. We want everything to be perfect for our guests, but sometimes, we miss out on what's truly important—the opportunity to connect and share moments with them. Jesus' gentle correction reminds us that opening our homes and hearts is about more than physical preparation; it's about spiritual readiness. It invites us to pause and reflect on what truly matters — being present and focusing on the relationships we are cultivating. Next time you're preparing for a guest, remember to balance the tasks with the joy of connection. Choose, like Mary, to focus on what is better—the presence of those around your table.

Martha, Martha, the Lord answered, you are worried and upset about many things, but few things are needed—or indeed only one. Mary has chosen what is better, and it will not be taken away from her.
Luke 10:41-42

IT'S NOT A GOOD HOBBY?

It's easy to fall into the trap of worrying about the future, our families, our jobs, and many other things. For many, worrying has become an unintentional hobby, occupying their thoughts and stealing their peace. But is this what God desires for us? The Bible reminds us in Matthew 6:34, "not to worry about tomorrow." Jesus' teaching invites us to live in the present, trusting that God will provide for our needs. When we worry, we often attempt to control what feels uncontrollable, yet we're reminded that God sees the bigger picture. Worrying can become a cycle, like a hamster running on a wheel but never reaching a destination. It's mentally exhausting and spiritually draining. It takes our focus away from God and places it on our circumstances, often magnifying problems rather than resolving them. Instead of letting worry consume us, we are encouraged to cast our cares upon the Lord. 1 Peter 5:7 tells us to give all our worries and cares to God, for He cares for us deeply. This surrender opens our hearts to faith and allows us to experience the peace that surpasses all understanding.

Therefore, do not worry about tomorrow, for tomorrow will worry about itself. Each day has enough trouble of its own.
Matthew 6:34

DO YOU HAVE A SECRET?

Secrets carry a certain allure. For many, the things concealed from others—hidden talents, undisclosed dreams, or even unconfessed struggles—define the most cherished aspects of life. Yet, in our spiritual walk, the secret to a thriving relationship with God often lies in what we do behind closed doors. When Jesus spoke about prayer, He emphasized the importance of privacy. The secret place is where we meet God without the world's distractions. In this intimate setting, we can be honest and vulnerable, sharing our deepest fears and aspirations with the One who knows us best. It's in these moments that our faith is not just expressed but also fortified. The world might not see or understand the strength you draw from your secret time with God, but the evidence will manifest in your life. Like a tree nourished by hidden roots, your spiritual vitality will appear in the fruit you bear. Patience, love, and peace will reveal a heart deeply connected to its Creator. Ultimately, the secret to our spiritual strength and resilience isn't found in public displays of faith but in the quiet, consistent communion with God. Remember, a powerful life of faith begins in a secret place. What's your secret?

But when you pray, go into your room, close the door, and pray to your Father, who is unseen. Then your Father, who sees what is done in secret, will reward you.
Matthew 6:6

ARE YOU KIDDING ME?

We may not love God like we should, but we should be determined to try harder. We may not love our friends the way we should, but we should intend to work at it. We may not love our neighbor as we should —but we should keep trying. But love our enemy? Now, that seems impossible! Enemies scheme, back-stab, subject us to mental distress, and can even cause you bodily harm. If we could truly love them, they wouldn't be our enemies, would they? Jesus says, "Love your enemies" by doing good to them. Love is not mere emotion—it's the decision to do what's right and good for another person. Choose love over hatred today. No occasion justifies evil for evil; no injustice warrants unjust behavior. Instead, we can follow God's leading by loving our enemies. What's keeping you from loving your enemies? Loving your enemies is a profound challenge, yet it's a powerful way to embody Christ's teachings. When we choose love over resentment, we reflect God's grace and mercy. Remember, everyone is made in His image, deserving of kindness and compassion. We break down barriers and build bridges through love, creating a world that echoes Christ's peace and forgiveness. How should you live this out in obedience today?

But to you who are willing to listen, I say, love your enemies! Do good to those who hate you.
Luke 6:27

DO YOU BLAME OTHERS

Have you ever lost your keys? You looked in the usual places—the bedroom dresser, the kitchen counter, your pockets—but no keys. Our immediate response is, who can I blame? Spouses are always putting things up, so they must have put it somewhere and forgot. If not them, then it must have been a burglary… or it could have been one of your dogs. Why do we keep losing things? What's up with that? Why are we so quick to blame others? Thinking about this tendency reminds me of Adam. When God asked him to explain what happened that fateful day in the garden, he quickly pointed the finger at everyone but himself. "It was the woman You gave me." In other words, "Yes, I took a bite from the forbidden fruit, but it's mostly Your fault. You're the One who gave me Eve, and it was her idea." Adam couldn't have been more wrong. It wasn't Eve's idea at all. It was the serpent's—a.k.a. Satan. And it certainly wasn't God's fault. Adam freely chose to eat the forbidden fruit. How about you? Are you quick to blame others? It's one of those nasty tendencies we've all picked up from the first human being. Blaming others for our oversights or mistakes may seem safe and reasonable, but we know it's not.

The man replied, It was the woman You gave me who gave me the fruit,
and I ate it.
Genesis 3:12

February 5

WHEN LIFE IS OVER

What would you do if you had one week to live? Would you get in touch with some friends? Surround yourself with family? Travel? Go to the Beach? Knowing He had less than a week to live, Jesus responded differently than many of us would. His last week was tough. As the reality of Jesus' death sank into the hearts of His followers, so did despair—for their hopes died with Him. It was over. The man they believed in was going to die. Some days, we don't think we can keep going. The pressure is too much. Our world is crumbling around us. We have lost all hope. So why do we keep going? Because we know the rest of the story. Imagine if you had just one week to live. How would your priorities shift? In such a moment, the teachings of Christ urge us to focus on love, forgiveness, and service. This week, reflect on the relationships you cherish and the impact you've made. Seek reconciliation where there is discord and express gratitude for God's blessings. Each day, engage in acts that bring you closer to Him and His purpose for your life. By living with intentionality, you honor the time given and prepare your heart for eternity. What if tomorrow is your final day on Earth? What are you going to do today?

The angel said, Don't be alarmed. You are looking for Jesus of Nazareth, who was crucified. He isn't here! He is risen from the dead!
Mark 16:6

YOU'RE NOT FINISHED YET

It's easy to feel like giving up when things don't go as planned. Whether it's a job loss, a broken relationship, or a failed endeavor, these setbacks can make us question our purpose and worth. But as Christians, we have the promise that God is not done with us yet. Philippians 1:6 assures us that God, who started a good work within us, will continue His work until it is finally completed. This Scripture is a comforting reminder that our life's story is a work in progress. An intricate tapestry is woven, which may not be visible to us right now but is transparent to Him. Our journeys are marked by seasons of growth, learning, and transformation. Each trial we face is a stepping stone, refining us to become more like Christ. It's important to remember that God's timing is perfect, and even when we feel stuck or incomplete, He is faithfully working behind the scenes. Take heart in knowing that your current situation is not your final destination. God's plan for your life is unfolding in His perfect way. Trust in His process and allow Him to guide you through the unfinished chapters of your life. Stay hopeful and confident, for He is the author and finisher of your faith. Remember, with God by your side, it is not finished until He says it is finished.

Being confident of this, that he who began a good work in you will carry it on to completion until the day of Christ Jesus.
Philippians 1:6

THE DESIRE TO GET EVEN?

The desire to get even is often considered natural. However, the teachings of the Bible offer a different perspective. The urge to retaliate when wronged is a powerful emotion, but we are called to respond with grace and love. Our verse today urges us to resist the temptation to seek vengeance. Instead, it encourages us to act honorably, even when provoked. This isn't about being passive or ignoring injustice; it's about rising above pettiness and reflecting the love of Christ in our actions. When Jesus was wronged, He responded with forgiveness and compassion, not with anger. His ultimate sacrifice on the cross was the quintessential act of love, "Father, forgive them, for they do not know what they are doing" (Luke 23:34). Jesus' response to betrayal and hurt was not retaliation but redemption. When faced with situations where you feel compelled to get even, take a moment to reflect on how Jesus might respond. This week, identify one situation where you feel wronged. Instead of seeking retribution, choose to respond with kindness or understanding.

Do not repay anyone evil for evil. Be careful to do what is right in the eyes of everyone.
Romans 12:17

WHO ARE THEY KIDDING?

Do you love sports but are turned off by what seems to be an arrogant display of confidence exhibited by certain players? They are talented, but they believe their skills are entirely based on their abilities and hard work. Their success does not involve their coaches, teammates, or God-given talents. After helping his team win the Super Bowl a few years ago, a player declared in a post-game interview that he was the best player at his position in the world. From that day forward, he also suggested that opposing teams should send only their best players against him. His comments sparked a national discussion on the role of humility in sports. Maybe that is why we are attracted to famous athletes who give God credit for their abilities. What about followers of Jesus? Are we allowed to be confident, or is that somehow opposed to our calling to show humility? In 2 Corinthians, the apostle Paul makes it clear that we have reason to be confident, but it isn't based on our own merits at all. God has qualified us. He has given us our talents to bring glory to Him. Acknowledging our limitations, we open ourselves to His wisdom. We can be confident in our abilities as long as we recognize that God makes us exceptional at what we do.

It is not that we think we are qualified to do anything on our own. Our qualification comes from God.
2 Corinthians 3:5

February 9

THE PHONE IS FOR YOU

Our phones are constantly ringing, buzzing, and beeping. It's easy to get caught up, always ready to answer the next call or message. But amidst this noise, a call surpasses all others—God's call to you. Jeremiah 33:3 is a divine invitation—an open line to the Creator of the universe. God encourages us to call to Him, promising not only to answer but to reveal profound truths and insights beyond our understanding. This isn't just about asking for guidance when we're lost; it's about building an ongoing, dynamic relationship with God. Imagine a phone that rings purposefully, providing insights, peace, and direction beyond our superficial conversations. Unlike our devices, which can be a source of distraction or stress, God's call brings clarity and focus. It's a call to pause, listen, and engage with our faith on a deeper level. As Christians, we are encouraged to dial into this divine line, knowing God is always available and eager to converse with us. The challenge is prioritizing this call amidst the many others we receive daily. It's about intentionally setting aside time to seek God's wisdom, listen to His voice, and trust the answers He provides. Today, consider how you can make room to answer God's call. What can you do to ensure His voice is the One you hear?

Call to me and I will answer you and tell you great and unsearchable things you do not know.
Jeremiah 33:3

RUNNING LOW ON HOPE?

Hope is not something we gain on our own; it is gifted to us by God. He promises to fill us with joy and peace, which are the building blocks of hope. When we trust Him, we open ourselves to the power of the Holy Spirit, who works within us to renew our hope. Reflecting on God's faithfulness throughout Scripture reassures us that our circumstances are not beyond His control. Remember how He sustained the Israelites in the wilderness, provided for Elijah in times of drought, and raised Lazarus from the dead. These accounts demonstrate that God is aware of our struggles and actively working in our lives to bring about His good purposes. Remember that God's promises are steadfast whenever you feel your hope waning. By focusing on His Word and trusting in His plans, we allow His hope to overflow, guiding us through life's challenges. When life's burdens seem overwhelming, and hope feels distant, remember Psalm 42:11—"Why, my soul, are you downcast? Put your hope in God." By trusting in His promises, we can find renewed strength and peace, confidently moving forward with faith as our anchor.

May the God of hope fill you with all joy and peace as you trust in him,
so that you may overflow with hope by the power of the Holy Spirit.
Romans 15:13

February 11

LOOKING FOR A SHORTCUT?

What do you do if you need help getting from point A to point B? Google Maps. You have probably used it for years and would agree it is fantastic. Just key in your starting point, enter your ending point, and just like magic, you're there! There is one problem, however. It often takes us a long way to our destination because it doesn't factor in certain things. When the Lord intentionally takes us on a longer route, we can rest assured that He has a good reason. As the Israelites ex exited Egypt, "God did not lead them along the main road that runs through Philistine territory, even though that was the shortest route to the Promised Land." Instead, he chose to lead them on a different path because He knew the weaknesses of His people. Early battles would have discouraged the band of brick makers and construction workers—people with little fighting experience. Their faith needed to be expanded and strengthened. God prepared a perfect confidence builder by leading them to the edge of the Red Sea. Similarly, God has His reasons for the strange paths He sometimes leads us down. God is with us even when we take the long way home! Shortcuts in life often look appealing; however, we usually learn the lesson God has for us.

If the people are faced with a battle, they might change their minds
and return to Egypt.
Exodus 13:17

NEED A NEW CHURCH?

Within our church community, we find a unique sense of belonging and support that transcends daily challenges. Our church family is more than just a group of individuals who gather once a week. It's a network of believers united by faith, purpose, and love. Regularly coming together builds each other up and inspires one another to show love and perform good deeds. This community acts as a mirror, reflecting God's love and intentions for us. It serves as a reminder that we are not alone on this spiritual journey. Through shared worship, prayer, and mutual encouragement, your church family becomes a source of strength and guidance. Each interaction is an opportunity to grow in faith and character and be equipped to face the trials and joys of life. Remember, the church is not just a building but the people who fill it with their love and passion for Christ. Involving yourself in your church family can lead to spiritual growth and a deeper understanding of God's purpose for your life. Consider how you can contribute to this community through service, fellowship, or simply presence. Your church family is a divine gift that enriches your walk with God, offering connection and support.

And let us consider how we may spur one another on toward love and good deeds, not giving up meeting together, as some are in the habit of doing, but encouraging one another—and all the more as you see the Day approaching.
Hebrews 10:24-25

WANT TO GET TOGETHER?

We often connect virtually rather than face-to-face, so the call to gather physically as believers holds decisive significance. The unity found in the community is a gift from God, offering strength, comfort, and a shared purpose in Christ. The early church understood this well. They met regularly, sharing meals, prayers, and their faith journeys. This communal life wasn't just about socializing; it was about encouraging one another and growing together in their understanding and expressing the gospel. When we gather, we create space for God's presence to manifest. It becomes a time to share our burdens, celebrate victories, and seek guidance through collective wisdom and discernment. Community provides accountability and fosters spiritual growth, allowing us to live out our faith authentically. However, gathering isn't just a local church activity or confined to Sunday services. It's in Bible study groups, coffee shop conversations, and even shared service moments. Large or small gatherings bring believers together, creating a network of support and love. Today, let's challenge ourselves to prioritize these gatherings, recognizing their power and potential. Because when we come together in Jesus' name, we invite His presence and open ourselves to His work in our midst. It's time to get together.

Where two or three are gathered together in my name, there am I in the midst of them.
Matthew 18:20

WHAT IS YOUR "IT"?

Have you heard a sermon when the preacher reminds you that you can
have everything you desire if you ask God for it? And if you have yet to
receive it, you need to grow your faith. Health and wealth preachers
have been known to say: Whatever you ask of God, IT will be given to
you. What does the word IT refer to? When Jesus said, "Ask, and it will
be given you," what might we expect to receive? What would IT be if
you asked God for something today? This verse is misused and
misunderstood because, on the surface, it sounds carte blanche: You can
have whatever your heart desires; all you have to do is ask. We have all
prayed for things we have not received. Whether it's begging for a pony
at Christmas, asking for a raise at work, or for a scholarship to go to
college, we all know what it's like when we don't get what we asked for.
Some things may be small and trivial. However, some of you have
prayed for healing from cancer or food to feed our children. Sometimes
God answers: Yes — No — Not yet— or Yes, but not like that. In our
Scripture today, I don't believe Jesus means we can get whatever we
ask. If that were so, prayer would be like rubbing a genie bottle, and our
every wish would come true. God wants us to ask for things in line with
His will.

Ask and it will be given to you; seek and you will find.
Matthew 7:7

IT'S ALL ABOUT HIM

It can be easy to shift our focus from what matters most. The reminder is clear for us—it's all about Him, our Savior. Our lives, decisions, and everyday moments should reflect this truth. Jesus emphasizes our dependence on Him. He uses the metaphor of the vine and branches to illustrate the necessity of staying connected to His life-giving presence. Just as branches draw sustenance from the vine, we, too, must draw our spiritual nourishment from Christ. We are reminded of His grace and sacrifice when we focus on Him. This perspective encourages us to live lives that honor Him. It's easy to get caught up in the hustle and bustle of life, but when we pause and refocus, we realize that apart from Him, our efforts are in vain. Consider how you can make your daily actions reflect that it's all about Him. Whether through acts of kindness, words of encouragement, or moments of reflection and worship, align your heart with Him. True fulfillment lies in bearing the fruit of being deeply rooted in Christ. Make it your daily goal to remain in Him, knowing that with Him, your life will yield fruit and reflect His glory.

I am the vine; you are the branches. If you remain in me and I in you,
you will bear much fruit; apart from me you can do nothing.
John 15:5

February 16

IS BEING GOOD—ENOUGH?

We constantly measure success by achievements and accolades, we are often led to believe that being good is the ultimate goal. But as Christians, we are reminded that our worth is not defined by our actions alone but by the grace of God. Our Scripture clearly states that salvation is a gift from God, not something we can earn through good deeds. While striving to be good is commendable, it is crucial to understand that our relationship with God is built on faith and grace, not on a checklist of moral accomplishments. We often fall into the trap of comparing ourselves to others, gauging our worth on external standards. In doing so, we overlook the profound truth that God's love for us is unconditional. He sees beyond our shortcomings and embraces us as His children. Reflect on your own life and consider where you may be relying solely on being good enough to gain approval from God or others. Remember, our Heavenly Father calls us to live by faith, trusting His perfect plan. Challenge yourself today to focus less on outward appearances of goodness and more on cultivating a genuine and intimate relationship with God. Trust in His grace to guide you, knowing that you are more than enough in His eyes.

For it is by grace you have been saved, through faith—and this is not from yourselves, it is the gift of God—not by works, so that no one can boast.
Ephesians 2:8-9

WHO'S IN YOUR BOAT?

This little boat against this big storm, are you kidding me? We're going to sink. Maybe they should wake up Jesus to see if he can help! They did. Jesus spoke to the wind, and then the storm died, and it was eerily calm. Then, all they could hear was the gentle lapping of water against the hull of the old wooden boat. Once again, Jesus' voice breaks the silence: softly He spoke, "Where is your faith?" They couldn't bear looking at Him because they knew He was disappointed. They had doubted him. They forgot that he is Lord of heaven and Earth. They had seen Him raise a widow's son from the dead, heal a paralyzed man, and confuse religious leaders who intimidated everyone but Him. His loving acceptance of broken people had made their souls sing! His authority was undeniable! Yet they doubted him. Trusting Jesus while sitting on a lush grassy slope and listening intently to His words is easy. It's easy to have faith when people are hurting and being healed right before their eyes. It's easy to have faith when thousands are fed with just a few crumbs of food. But out there on the stormy lake, it seemed as if nothing was certain anymore. They remembered this day, and so will we. We should store it in our hearts so that we'll think of what we learned when the next storm comes.

Where is your faith?
Luke 8:25

KEEP TRYING

Life often presents challenges that test our faith and resilience. In these moments, it's easy to feel discouraged or think about giving up. However, we are called to persevere, trusting that God is with us every step of the way. The apostle Paul reminds us in Galatians 6:9, "Let us not become weary in doing good, for at the proper time we will reap a harvest if we do not give up." This verse encourages us to keep pressing forward, even when the road is tough. The promise of a harvest signifies that our efforts will be rewarded in due time, but only if we persist. Consider the story of Peter, one of Jesus' closest disciples, who experienced both triumphs and failures. After denying Jesus three times, Peter could have succumbed to guilt and given up on his calling. Instead, he chose to keep trying and became a foundational leader in the early church. His life illustrates that failure is not the end but an opportunity to learn, grow, and continue striving toward our divine purpose. When you feel like giving up, remember that God has equipped you with the strength and determination to overcome any obstacle. Keep trying. Hold onto your faith, seek encouragement from Scripture, and surround yourself with a supportive community. In doing so, you will draw closer to God and inspire others through your perseverance.

As the body without the spirit is dead, so faith without deeds is dead.
James 2:26

PLEASE, SKIP ME

There are times you may prefer if God would consider that you have learned enough from your trials and skip you with future opportunities for growth. While this is somewhat true, we welcome His counsel to make us more like Him. Why might God want to use a crisis in our lives? We naturally consider crises ominous, but God often does great things through these bad experiences. There are things that God teaches in a crisis that are much harder for us to learn at other times. For instance, in a crisis, we discover just how little control we have over our lives. Humbled, we begin to pray more often, sincerely, and deeply. We open our Bibles in search of the comfort we desire. We may also start to realize what matters most to us. Our trials often leave us more appreciative of people and less obsessed with our things. When we surrender to God, we discover a peace that lasts long after the crisis. What blessings has God brought you during a crisis in your life? God is waiting for your call. He is a great counselor. You're not in this alone. Pray that God will use your suffering to bring you closer to Him.

All kinds of trials ... have come so that the proven genuineness of your
faith ... may result in praise, glory and honor
when Jesus Christ is revealed.
1 Peter 1:6-7

LIFE CAN BE CRAZY

Sometimes, life is crazy. We look around and wonder why some people experience one hardship after another while others prosper. Why is it that so many have everything they need while others have less than nothing? Why is it that some people who care nothing about God live in luxury while millions of people dedicated to the Lord live in poverty and are persecuted? Our understanding of fairness is deeply rooted in God's word and His divine plan for us. Scripture suggests that life isn't always about fairness but about the unseen plan God has for each one of us. Consider Job, who was righteous and yet faced unimaginable suffering. His story teaches us that fairness is not always evident in our circumstances but in God's justice and sovereignty. Job eventually understood that his trials were part of a greater purpose, leading him to proclaim, "I know that you can do all things; no purpose of yours can be thwarted" (Job 42:2). While life may not always seem fair by human standards, we can take solace in knowing that God's plans are higher than ours. Let's hold onto the truth that, though we may not understand it all now, God is just, and His ways are perfect.

The race is not to the swift or the battle to the strong, nor does food come to the wise or wealth to the brilliant or favor to the learned; but time and chance happen to them all.
Ecclesiastes 9:11

February 21

WHEN YOU'RE NOT SURE

Life is filled with uncertainties, and even the most faithful believers can doubt or question the path ahead. During these moments of uncertainty, we are called to lean on our faith more than ever. The Bible reminds us in Proverbs 3:5- 6, "Trust in the Lord with all your heart and lean not on your own understanding; in all your ways submit to him, and he will make your paths straight." Uncertainty can arise from various facets of life—relationships, career decisions, health concerns, or even spiritual journeys. When we aren't sure, it can feel like we're standing at a crossroads, unsure which direction to take. However, this is precisely when our faith can be our guiding light. The scriptures encourage us to have faith and complete trust in God's plan and timing. Rather than relying solely on our limited human understanding, we are invited to submit our concerns and decisions to God. He promises to direct our paths, providing guidance and clarity when we need it the most. In those moments when we are unsure, it's essential to remember that God's wisdom far surpasses our own. When doubt clouds your path, His love and guidance steadfastly lead us through the uncertainties with grace and assurance.

For I know the plans I have for you, declares the Lord, plans to prosper you and not to harm you, plans to give you hope and a future.
Jeremiah 29:11

YOU WON'T BELIEVE THIS!

The story of Lazarus is one of the most profound accounts of Jesus' ministry, showcasing His power over life and death. In John 11, we learn that Lazarus, a close friend of Jesus, had died. When Jesus arrived at Lazarus' home in Bethany, He was met with grief from Lazarus' sisters, Mary and Martha. Despite the sorrow surrounding Him, Jesus assured them that Lazarus would rise again, declaring Himself as the resurrection and life. This miraculous event is a powerful reminder of Jesus' divine authority and His ability to bring life out of death. Through the raising of Lazarus, Jesus demonstrated His love and compassion and provided a glimpse of the eternal life promised to all believers. The story invites us to trust Christ, even when faced with insurmountable challenges. It encourages Christians to hold onto the hope of resurrection and eternal life, affirming that physical death is not the end for those who believe. The account of Lazarus challenges us to deepen our faith and trust in Jesus, recognizing Him as the source of eternal life. It is a testament to His compassion and the promise of resurrection for all who believe in Him.

Jesus said, I am the resurrection and the life. The One who believes in me will live, even though they die, and whoever lives by believing in me will never die. Do you believe this?
John 11:25-26

WHAT'S IN A NAME?

As part of a family, we represent that family. People who meet us will make assumptions about our parents, children, spouse, and siblings. If one is rude, self-centered, and vulgar, others may assume we all are just as unpleasant. If they met someone from our family who is kind and loving, they would reason that we are all like that. As children of God, we represent the family of God, whether we are aware of it or not. The world will judge our Father based on our words, behaviors, and attitudes. Jesus challenges us to let our light shine into the world's spiritual darkness. Our deeds, good or bad, beautiful or ugly, will reflect an image of the Father that others will see. If we are a Christian, we bear the name of Christ. We represent Jesus wherever we go. The Bible goes as far as to call us "Christ's ambassadors" to the world. Christ is making his appeal to the world through us. He sends us to share his transforming love with our neighbors, friends, relatives, coworkers—everyone we encounter on any given day. We carry the family name of Jesus wherever we go, whatever we do. If people only knew Jesus because of you, what would they think of Him?

Let your light shine before others, that they may see your good deeds
and glorify your Father in heaven.
Matthew 5:16

A SIMPLE WORD

To love as Jesus loves means to go beyond superficial gestures and engage in genuine care and compassion. It's about placing others' needs above our own, offering grace, forgiveness, and understanding in relationships. How do we practice this love in our daily lives? Start by seeking opportunities to serve those around you. Simple acts of kindness can speak volumes—a listening ear, a helping hand, or a word of encouragement can significantly impact another person. Through these acts, we become living testimonies of Christ's love. Consider also the power of empathy. Strive to understand others' perspectives and experiences. This empathy allows us to connect more deeply and show love in ways that resonate with their unique circumstances. Reflect on your interactions and relationships this week. Are there moments where you could have extended more love? Identify these instances and consider how to approach similar situations with a heart full of love and forgiveness next time. Loving others is not just an obligation but the essence of discipleship. By loving others deeply and authentically, we reflect Christ's love to the world, drawing people closer to Him.

A new command I give you: Love one another. As I have loved you, so you must love one another. By this everyone will know that you are my disciples, if you love one another.
John 13:34-35

February 25

LET IT GO

Forgiveness is a central part of Christian faith, yet it is often one of the most challenging to practice. We are reminded of this in Matthew 6:14-15, which says, "For if you forgive other people when they sin against you, your heavenly Father will also forgive you. But your Father will not forgive your sins if you do not forgive others." This Scripture highlights the reciprocal nature of forgiveness and its importance in our spiritual lives. Forgiving others does not mean condoning their actions or forgetting the hurt caused. Instead, it is about releasing the burden of resentment and anger that can weigh heavily on our hearts. By forgiving, we free ourselves from bitterness and allow love and peace to flourish. Consider Jesus' example on the cross when He said, "Father, forgive them, for they do not know what they are doing" (Luke 23:34). In His moment of most significant suffering, Jesus extended grace and compassion to those who wronged Him. This act of divine forgiveness serves as a powerful reminder of the potential for healing and reconciliation that forgiveness brings. We are called to reflect Christ's love and grace in our own lives by offering forgiveness to others. It may not always be easy, but it often requires humility and courage. Yet, through prayer and reflection, we can find the strength to forgive, knowing that by doing so, we are walking in obedience to God's will.

Love ... keeps no record of wrongs.
1 Corinthians 13:4-5

February 26

TIME TO DO WHAT'S RIGHT

Life often presents us with choices, some more challenging than others. In these moments, the right path might not always be apparent, but as Christians, we are called to act according to our understanding of God's will. The Scripture from James reminds us of the responsibility of knowing what is good. In today's fast-paced world, it's easy to get caught up in our routines, sometimes overlooking the opportunities to do what's right. We may know the good we ought to do, whether helping a neighbor, speaking a kind word, or standing up for truth, yet often we hesitate or delay. We think there will be a better time, or perhaps someone else will step in. However, the right time is now. God calls us to take that step, decide, and act upon the good we know. Each moment is an opportunity to reflect His love and righteousness in the world. By actively choosing to follow this path, we embody the teachings of Christ and become beacons of light in our communities. Reflect on your daily interactions and the choices you face. Ask yourself, Am I doing what I know is right? If you feel a nudge to act, don't ignore it. Trust that God has equipped you with the wisdom and courage to make a difference. Remember, doing what's right isn't merely about making big decisions; it's often found in small everyday acts.

Therefore, to him who knows to do good and does not do it,
to him it is sin.
James 4:17

YOU MAY BE SHOCKED

God is the ultimate guide in our lives. We can find clarity even amid emotional turmoil when we trust in God for His wisdom. Whether you're feeling lost or content, remember that God understands where you are and offers direction. Consider how you're feeling today. Are you anxious about a decision? Are you joyful over a recent blessing? Whatever your current state, acknowledge it without judgment. Then, bring these emotions to God, allowing His presence to provide insight and comfort. The Bible encourages us to turn to God with our whole hearts. In doing so, we align ourselves with His will, gaining strength and direction beyond our understanding. When emotions feel overwhelming, take a moment to breathe, reflect on God's word, and find solace in His unwavering love. Remember, feelings are fleeting, but God's love is eternal. How can you incorporate this truth into your daily life? Our understanding is often minimal; it doesn't compare with God's. Consider journaling your thoughts and rereading this Scripture when emotions cloud your judgment.

Trust in the Lord with all your heart and lean not on your own understanding; in all your ways submit to him, and he will make your paths straight.
Proverbs 3:5-6

February 28

YOUR PLAN, OR HIS?

It's easy to become caught up in our plans and ambitions. We often set goals and lay out step-by-step plans to achieve them, believing we have complete control over our lives. However, as Christians, we are reminded that God's plans for us are far greater than anything we could imagine. The passage from Proverbs encourages us to trust the Lord with all our hearts and not rely on our understanding. This can be challenging, especially when things go differently than planned. We may question why particular doors remain closed or why unexpected obstacles appear. Yet, in these moments of uncertainty, our faith is truly tested and refined. We acknowledge His sovereignty and wisdom when we submit our ways to God. This doesn't mean we abandon planning or stop striving for our goals; instead, we remain open to God's guidance and allow Him to direct our paths. By doing so, we align our lives with His divine purpose, which leads to a more fulfilling and meaningful life. Take a moment today to reflect on areas where you may need to rely more on your plans. Ask the Lord to reveal His plans for you and to give you the courage to follow His lead. Remember, God's blueprint is always aimed at our good, even if it differs from what we envisioned.

Trust in the Lord with all your heart and lean not on your own understanding; in all your ways submit to him, and he will make your paths straight.
Proverbs 3:5-6

ARE YOU RICH?

Money can often dictate the choices we make and the paths we follow. Yet, as Christians, we are called to view money not as an end but as a tool to fulfill God's purpose and serve others. Today's Scripture from Hebrews 13:5 reminds us of the importance of contentment and trust in God's provision. The love of money can easily lead us astray, causing us to prioritize wealth over our spiritual health and relationships. Today, let's reflect on your relationship with money. Are your financial decisions aligned with your faith and values? Do you trust God's sufficiency, or are you chasing after material security? Consider how money can serve your life in alignment with your Christian principles. Can it help provide for your family, support those in need, and contribute to church and community missions? Remember, money itself is not evil; the love of money and the pursuit of it at all costs can lead to spiritual imbalance. Take a moment today to evaluate your financial priorities. Seek guidance from the Lord to ensure you're not placing money above your faith. Reflect on how to use your resources to glorify God and bless others. Trust in His promise, and find peace knowing that true contentment doesn't lie in stuff.

Keep your lives free from the love of money and be content with what you have, because God has said, Never will I leave you; never will I forsake you.
Hebrews 13:5

WRITING YOUR STORY

In the grand scheme of things, each of us is a unique story being written every day. But who is the author of your life story? This central question is pivotal for Christians striving to live a life that reflects their faith and trust in God. Scripture reminds us that God is the ultimate author of our lives. In Hebrews 12:2, we are encouraged to look to Jesus, "the pioneer and perfecter of our faith." This verse highlights the belief that Jesus is not only our guide but also the one who is shaping and refining our faith narrative. Allowing God to write your story means surrendering to His plans and trusting His timing. It means acknowledging that the author knows the ending even when the plot thickens. Recognizing God's plans are for our good can give us peace amidst uncertainty. However, just as any good story faces conflicts and resolutions, our lives will also have moments of trial and triumph. By allowing God to steer our course, we invite Him into every chapter, ensuring that our story aligns with His purpose. Reflect today on who is holding the pen in your life and choose to place it in God's hands. Trust Him to write a story for His glory and our benefit. He is the perfect author, capable of turning even the most challenging chapters into tales of redemption.

For I know the plans I have for you, declares the Lord, plans to prosper you and not to harm you, plans to give you hope and a future.
Jeremiah 29:11

ALWAYS STAY ALERT

It's easy to become complacent in our faith. The routine of daily life can numb us to the spiritual battles waged around and within us. However, the Word of God calls us to be vigilant and aware of our surroundings and the spiritual realms influencing our lives. 1 Peter 5:8 is a stark reminder of the adversary we face—Satan, who is always on the lookout for an opportune moment to tempt and lead us astray. This verse doesn't just warn us; it equips us with the knowledge of how our enemy works. Like a lion, he prowls, waits, and watches for moments when we are least prepared. Being alert means more than just being awake; it means being spiritually attuned and ready to stand firm in our faith. We must guard our hearts and minds, filling them with Scripture and surrounding ourselves with a community of believers who can support and encourage us. The Holy Spirit guides and protects us, providing insight and discernment when we are open to His leading. In your daily walk, take a moment to pause and assess your spiritual readiness. Are you aware of the influences surrounding you? Are you grounded in truth and connected to God through prayer and study of His Word? By staying alert and sober-minded, we can resist the devil's schemes.

Be alert and of a sober mind. Your enemy, the devil, prowls around like a roaring lion, looking for someone to devour.
1 Peter 5:8

IS IT TRUE?

Discerning what is true from what is not can feel like navigating a puzzle. For us, the foundation of truth is found in Scripture. Consider how often we encounter claims, opinions, and beliefs daily. Social media, news outlets, and even our circles present perspectives that may or may not align with biblical truth. Ephesians 4:14 warns us against being swayed by every new teaching, urging us to grow in our understanding of Christ so we are not "blown here and there by every wind of teaching." Reflect on whether what you're hearing aligns with biblical principles. Philippians 4:8 encourages believers to focus on what is true, noble, correct, pure, lovely, admirable, excellent, and praiseworthy. When faced with a statement or belief, ask yourself if it meets these criteria. If not, turn to the Bible for guidance and clarity. Jesus emphasizes in John 8:31-32, "If you hold to my teaching, you are my disciples. Then you will know the truth, and the truth will set you free." To honestly know the truth is to immerse oneself in the teachings of Jesus. This freedom in truth leads to a life anchored in hope and certainty, regardless of the world's chaos. In your pursuit of truth, lean into Scripture, seek understanding through prayer, and remain steadfast in faith. By doing so, you will develop a discerning heart, able to identify what is true and live in accordance with God's will.

Sanctify them by the truth; your word is truth.
John 17:17

DON'T KEEP IT TO YOURSELF

Secrets often seem to rule the world, so it's crucial to remember the one truth we should never keep hidden—our faith in Jesus Christ. The Great Commission, as recorded in Matthew 28, reminds us of our calling to share the Good News with everyone, everywhere. It's not just a suggestion but a commandment for every believer. The message of salvation through Jesus is our most extraordinary gift. Imagine holding the key to eternal life and deciding to keep it locked away. Our faith is meant to be shared. When we tell others about Jesus, we're not just passing on information; we offer hope, peace, and a new life. Consider the early apostles who spread the Gospel far and wide despite persecution and great danger. They understood that the joy of knowing Christ was too significant to contain. We, too, should be motivated by love and gratitude to share what has changed our lives. Opportunities to witness are all around us—in conversations with friends, interactions with colleagues, or even casual chats with strangers. Let's not shy away from these moments. Instead, step out with courage and confidence, knowing that the Holy Spirit is with you, guiding your words and actions. Remember, your story might be the beacon of hope someone desperately needs.

Go therefore and make disciples of all nations, baptizing them in the name of the Father and of the Son and of the Holy Spirit.
Matthew 28:19

March 6

MAKE SOMEONE'S DAY

Taking a moment to brighten someone's day can seem like a small act, but it carries great significance in the eyes of God. The Bible reminds us of the impact of kindness and love through simple gestures. Our Scripture emphasizes prioritizing others, valuing their needs, and uplifting them through selfless actions. When we make a conscious effort to make someone's day better, we reflect the heart of Christ. Consider the power of a smile, a genuine compliment, or a listening ear in a moment of need. These actions, though small, create ripples of positivity and demonstrate the love we are called to share with our neighbors. Imagine the impact a simple act of kindness can have on someone who is struggling. It could be the nudge they need to feel valued and loved, reminding them that they are not alone. Today, pause and ask God to show you who might need encouragement. Whether it's a co-worker, a friend, or a stranger, your willingness to serve humbly can transform their day. Remember, our acts of kindness are not just about making someone smile; they're about living out our faith and creating a world that reflects God's love. By being intentional about serving others, we not only glorify God but also inspire others to pass on the love of Christ.

Do nothing out of selfish ambition or vain conceit. Rather, in humility, value others above yourselves.
Philippians 2:3

DO YOU HAVE ENOUGH?

We often find ourselves caught in the relentless pursuit of wealth, possessions, and status. It's easy to fall into the trap of believing that happiness and security lie in abundance. But as Christians, we must ask ourselves if this aligns with God's desires. In Luke 12:16-21, Jesus tells the parable of a rich man whose land yielded an abundant harvest. Instead of sharing his excess, he plans to build bigger barns to store all his grain and goods, saying, "I will say to my soul, Soul, you have ample goods laid up for many years; relax, eat, drink, be merry." But God calls him foolish, for that very night, his life is demanded of him, leaving his amassed wealth behind. This story challenges us to reconsider our priorities. Do we place our trust in material wealth or seek treasure in heaven where it truly lasts? God calls us to be rich toward Him, investing in acts of kindness, generosity, and love. These are the treasures that endure beyond this earthly life. The richness of life isn't measured by the size of our barns but by the fullness of our hearts. This week, reflect on what you truly value. Are you building bigger barns for yourself or seeking the kingdom of God? Shift your focus from accumulation to contribution, and discover the abundant life in giving.

What shall I do? I have no place to store my crops.
Luke 12:17

March 8

SALT OF THE EARTH

In the Sermon on the Mount, Jesus calls His followers the "salt of the earth." This metaphor invites us to reflect on the role we play in the world as Christians. Salt, in Jesus' time, was a highly valued commodity. It was used to enhance flavor and as a preservative to keep food from spoiling. In the same way, we are called to add flavor and preserve the goodness of God's creation through our lives. Being the salt of the earth means living a life that reflects the values and teachings of Christ. It challenges us to stand in contrast to the moral decay and spiritual apathy that can pervade our society. Just as a small pinch of salt can affect the taste of an entire dish, our influence—though it may seem small at times—can profoundly impact those around us. This passage also warns us about losing our saltiness. It prompts us to consider how we can stay true to our faith and mission. Are there areas in your life where you have become complacent? Jesus' words remind us that our faith must remain active, preserving the essence of His message in our daily interactions. Reflect today on how you can be the salt of the earth in your community.

You are the salt of the earth. But if the salt loses its saltiness, how can it be made salty again? It is no longer good for anything, except to be thrown out and trampled underfoot.
Matthew 5:13

EASIER SAID THAN DONE

Life often presents challenges that seem simpler in theory than practice, a concept perfectly encapsulated in the phrase easier said than done. This rings particularly true for Christians when striving to live according to biblical teachings. The Bible offers clear guidance on how to live a life that honors God, yet implementing these teachings daily requires more than just knowledge—it's about action and perseverance. Consider the call to love your neighbor as yourself. This command is straightforward, yet showing unconditional love, especially to those who may not reciprocate, can be incredibly challenging. Intellectually, we may acknowledge that God desires the best for us, but in moments of uncertainty and distress, maintaining unwavering trust can prove difficult. It requires a conscious decision to lean not on our understanding but on faith. Practical steps can help bridge the gap between knowing and doing. Start by setting small, achievable goals related to your spiritual growth. Surround yourself with a community that encourages accountability and spiritual support. Remember, God's grace is sufficient, and His power is made perfect in our weakness. While living out biblical principles is easier said than done, it is through God's strength that we can practice what we preach.

Do not merely listen to the word, and so deceive yourselves. Do what it says.
James 1:22

THE DESIRE FOR WISDOM

Information is everywhere, but true wisdom is scarce. Wisdom, as described in the Bible, is more than just knowledge or intelligence. It's the ability to make sound decisions and live a life that honors God. The book of Proverbs frequently emphasizes the value of seeking wisdom. It describes it as more precious than silver and gold, highlighting its incomparable value. Wisdom is a divine gift God gives to those who earnestly seek it. When we prioritize prayer and reflection and immerse ourselves in the Scriptures, we open ourselves to receive this profound gift. One key aspect of biblical wisdom is its rootedness in humility. To be wise is to acknowledge our limitations and to depend on God's guidance. We see this in the lives of biblical figures like King Solomon, who, when allowed to ask for anything, chose wisdom to govern God's people effectively. His story reminds us that true wisdom leads to personal growth and benefits those around us. Living wisely means aligning our actions and choices with God's will. It involves discernment, patience, and a heart willing to learn. We are called to be discerning in our daily lives, differentiating between what is temporary and what holds eternal value.

For the Lord gives wisdom; from his mouth come knowledge and understanding.
Proverbs 2:6

WE ARE ALL TEMPTED

Temptation is a universal struggle that we all face. Whether it's the allure of material wealth, the pull of unhealthy habits, or the challenge of maintaining spiritual discipline, temptation is an undeniable part of our lives. Yet, the Bible offers us guidance and strength to overcome these challenges. This powerful verse reassures us that we are not alone in our struggles. Temptation is a common human experience, yet God's faithfulness remains unwavering. He promises that the trials we face will not be more than we can handle, and He will provide us with a path to overcome them. This assurance reminds us that we have divine support in moments of weakness. When tempted, we must lean on our faith and seek God's guidance. Reflect on His word and trust He will equip you with the strength to resist. Remember, every temptation is an opportunity to reaffirm your faith and grow stronger spiritually. Take time today to meditate on this Scripture, and feel empowered knowing that God is walking alongside you, providing the support and strength to overcome any challenge. No temptation has overtaken you except what is expected of humanity. And God is faithful; he will not let you be tempted beyond what you can bear.

But when you are tempted, he will also provide a way out so that you can endure it.
1 Corinthians 10:13

March 12

GOD IS FAITHFUL

It can be easy to forget the faithfulness of God. Yet, the Scripture from
Deuteronomy reminds us that God is not distant or detached. Instead,
He is deeply involved in our lives, going before us and standing beside
us through every challenge. Consider the story of Abraham. Despite the
impossibility of having a child in his old age, he held onto God's
promise. In Genesis 21, we see the fulfillment of that promise with the
birth of Isaac, a testament to God's faithfulness even when
circumstances seemed impossible. In our lives, we may face
overwhelming situations—perhaps a complicated relationship, a career
uncertainty, or a personal struggle. During these times, it's crucial to
remember that God is with us, providing guidance and strength. When
we recognize God's presence and faithfulness, our response should be
one of trust and surrender. This means letting go of our fears and
worries, knowing He is in control and has a plan for our lives. Reflect
on how God's faithfulness has manifested in your own life. Think about
the moments you have felt His presence the most and the ways He has
provided for you. Hold onto those memories as a reminder that just as
God has been faithful in the past, He will continue to be faithful in the
future.

*The Lord himself goes before you and will be with you; he will never
leave you nor forsake you. Do not be afraid; do not be discouraged.*
Deuteronomy 31:8

ANGER CAN BE DANGEROUS

Anger is a powerful emotion that can lead us to regret decisions. While it's natural to feel angry, the Bible cautions us about the dangers of letting anger control our actions. In Ephesians 4, Paul advises believers to manage their anger wisely, highlighting the risks of allowing it to fester. Unchecked anger can disrupt relationships, damage our witness as Christians, and give the enemy a chance to influence our hearts and minds. Proverbs 29:11 reminds us, "Fools give full vent to their rage, but the wise bring calm in the end." Here, wisdom lies in the ability to pause, reflect, and choose our responses carefully rather than reacting impulsively. If you find anger bubbling up within you, take it as an opportunity to seek God's guidance. Ask Him to help you understand the root of your anger and give you the strength to respond with grace and patience. Remember, anger itself is not a sin but can lead to sinful actions if not handled with care. By leaning on God's wisdom and the Holy Spirit's guidance, we can transform anger into a chance for growth, understanding, and reconciliation. Strive to approach conflicts with love and a heart willing to forgive, reflecting Christ's peace to those around you.

In your anger, do not sin: Do not let the sun go down while you are still angry, and do not give the devil a foothold.
Ephesians 4:26-27

IS BEAUTY SKIN DEEP?

Beauty often gets measured by appearances—what the eye can see. But as Christians, we are prompted to look beyond the surface and understand the deeper essence of true beauty. This Scripture invites us to prioritize inner beauty, the kind that radiates from a heart aligned with God's will. Consider the life of Jesus. His earthly form was not described as remarkably beautiful by worldly standards, yet His actions and compassion drew many to Him. The purity of His heart, kindness, and unwavering love left a lasting impact, demonstrating that true beauty stems from within. In our interactions with others, we can practice seeing beyond the exterior. Engage with people's stories, understand their journeys, and appreciate the beauty of their spirit. Encourage others by affirming their inner qualities—like kindness, patience, and humility—over their outward appearances. Our challenge lies in cultivating a beauty that reflects Christ-like attributes. This means transforming our hearts and minds, allowing God to shape us from within. As we grow closer to Him, we naturally begin to reflect His grace and love in our lives. Remember, true beauty is not just what is seen but the light that shines from within, illuminating the world with God's love.

The Lord does not look at the things people look at. People look at the outward appearance, but the Lord looks at the heart.
1 Samuel 16:7

SHOULD YOU KEEP SINNING?

The question of sin is essential. This Scripture is a powerful reminder of the transformation that occurs when we accept Christ into our lives. The grace of God is a profound gift freely given to us through the sacrifice of Jesus. However, it is not a license to continue living in sin. Instead, it calls us to a higher standard—a life reflective of Christ's righteousness. The apostle Paul emphasizes that we have died to sin, meaning that our old ways no longer hold power over us. We are new creations through Christ, empowered to live in the freedom and victory He provides. Living a transformed life does not mean we will never stumble. The reality is that the struggle against sin is ongoing. But we are equipped with the Holy Spirit, who convicts and guides us toward holiness. Our response to His prompting should be one of repentance and a renewed commitment to follow Christ's example. Therefore, while grace abounds, we are called to strive for holiness, to turn away from sin, and to pursue a life that honors God. In this pursuit of righteousness, we find true freedom and fulfillment. Remember, grace is not only a covering for past sins but also an empowering force to live a life that reflects the love and holiness of our Savior.

What shall we say, then? Shall we go on sinning so that grace may increase? By no means! We are those who have died to sin; how can we live in it any longer?
Romans 6:1-2

THINGS ARE CRAZY

Unpredictability has become a constant. From global events to personal challenges, the uncertainties of life often leave us feeling anxious and overwhelmed. Yet, as Christians, we are called to find our steadfast anchor in God amidst these turbulent times. When the future seems uncertain, and our plans fall apart, relying on our limited understanding can be tempting. However, Proverbs reminds us to trust in the Lord wholeheartedly. This trust is not passive but an active submission to His will and guidance, acknowledging that His wisdom surpasses our own. In moments of unpredictability, seek God's presence. Spend time in His Word, allowing His promises to reassure you. Remember, He is the same yesterday, today, and forever. Our circumstances may change, but God's love and faithfulness remain constant. Consider how Jesus navigated His unpredictable path. Despite facing opposition and uncertainty, He consistently sought the Father's will. His life was a testament to unwavering trust and obedience, even unto death on the cross. Reflect on the advantages of trusting God amidst uncertainty. In these unpredictable times, trust Him, and He will guide you, making your paths straight.

Trust in the Lord with all your heart and lean not on your own understanding; in all your ways submit to him, and he will make your paths straight.
Proverbs 3:5-6

GOD IS WATCHING

Several highway drivers phoned the police, reporting a truck erratically swerving down the road and jerking from side to side. At about 6:30 a.m., the police spotted the vehicle and flashed their lights so that the truck could pull over. When the officer approached the vehicle, he found an eight-year-old boy at the wheel. The boy's father was passed out in the passenger seat. This father's reckless behavior put his son and others in immense danger. The boy's dad should have been the one person he could trust to keep him safe, yet this dad jeopardized his son. Many of us have had someone we trusted that left us exposed and unprotected. As a result, people wonder who will genuinely watch out for them. Who will never abandon them? The psalmist declares that there is only One who can always be trusted. God is the One who "will not let you stumble." He's the "One who watches over you" and "will not slumber" (Psalm 121:3). God's hand is always poised, ready to act. Each of us has felt the sting of betrayal. Each of us has borne the brunt of another's good intentions gone awry. What's more, we all have done the same to others. God is always attentive to our needs.

He who watches over Israel never slumbers or sleeps.
Psalm 121:4

ARE YOU DISCOURAGED?

Life often presents us with challenges that leave us feeling discouraged. This feeling can arise from unmet expectations, personal failures, or the weight of ongoing struggles. During these times, it is essential to remember that we are not alone in our discouragement; even the psalmist speaks of such moments. In Psalm 42, the writer asks his soul why it is so downcast, recognizing his despair. But instead of dwelling on his troubles, he deliberately turns his focus back to God, acknowledging God as his source of hope and salvation. This pivotal shift in perspective is essential for overcoming feelings of discouragement. It is within His presence that we find comfort and restoration. When we praise God despite our circumstances, we acknowledge His sovereignty and goodness, which helps lift our spirits. Consider reflecting on the ways God has been faithful in the past during your moments of discouragement. Surround yourself with Scripture and uplifting music that reminds you of His promises. Engage with a community of believers who can offer support and encouragement. Remember, discouragement is a temporary state, but God's faithfulness is eternal. By shifting our focus from our problems to His promises, we can experience His peace and renewed strength.

Why, my soul, are you downcast? Why so disturbed within me? Put your hope in God, for I will yet praise him, my Savior and my God.
Psalm 42:5

ARE YOU A TRUE FRIEND?

A true friend is steadfast, offering love and support through every season of life. It's a call to evaluate how we engage with those we consider friends. Do we stand by them in need or only appear when it's convenient? How do we show up for our friends? Are our interactions meaningful and filled with genuine concern, or are they superficial? It's essential to consider the depth of our relationships. Jesus modeled the ultimate friendship, laying down His life for us. While we may not be called to such extremes, we can follow His example by prioritizing our friends' well-being and bearing their burdens. True friendship requires vulnerability and honesty. It's being present, listening without the intent to reply, and celebrating others' successes without envy. It means offering a shoulder to cry on and a hand to help up. As Christians, friendship is not just a social connection but a spiritual partnership—supporting each other in faith, encouraging growth, and holding each other accountable. By striving to be a true friend, we reflect Christ's love and deepen our relationships, creating bonds that withstand the tests of time. Consider your friendships today. Are your friendships real or fake? How can you be a more trustworthy friend, reflecting the love and loyalty that God calls us to embody?

A friend loves at all times, and a brother is born for a time of adversity.
Proverbs 17:17

March 20

ARE YOU LISTENING?

It is easy to feel that no one is listening to God anymore. Yet, Proverbs 1:33 reminds us of the peace and security that comes from tuning our hearts to His voice. The challenge we face today as Christians is the silence around us and the internal clamor that drowns out God's whispers. We become so engrossed in our daily routines, smartphones, and social media that the divine guidance we seek often gets lost amid worldly chaos. Listening to God requires intentionality. It's about carving out quiet moments to reflect on His word and allowing it to speak to us. It means setting aside our agendas and desires to understand His will for our lives. We find clarity and direction that only He can provide in these quiet moments. Reflect on how you spend your time. Are the activities that fill your day drawing you closer to God or pulling you away? Consider setting aside time each day to sit quietly, read Scripture, and genuinely listen for His voice. Remember, God is always speaking; we need only to quiet ourselves enough to hear Him. By focusing on His word and seeking His guidance, we align ourselves with His purpose, entering into a life of peace and assurance, free from fear.

But whoever listens to me will live in safety and be at ease, without fear of harm.
Proverbs 1:33

March 21

THE TRUTH CAN HURT

We're often reminded that the truth is a powerful force. It can enlighten, liberate, and transform us. Yet, it's also important to acknowledge that hearing the truth can sometimes be uncomfortable or even painful. Consider the story of David and Nathan in 2 Samuel 12. Nathan, a prophet, approaches King David to confront him about Bathsheba. Nathan tells a parable that leads David to pronounce judgment on himself unknowingly. When Nathan reveals that David is the man in the story, the impact is immediate and profound. David is struck with the weight of his actions and their consequences. While it may sting at first, exposing our faults and shortcomings, it also offers growth and redemption opportunities. David's recognition and repentance lead him back into alignment with God's will. The truth, painful as it was, sets the stage for David's spiritual renewal. In our own lives, we must be open to receiving truths about ourselves—whether they come from Scripture, loved ones, or moments of introspection. Rather than shying away, we should seek understanding and transformation. Actual spiritual growth often follows painful realizations as we learn to align more closely with God's purpose. By embracing the truth, we allow ourselves to be refined and strengthened in faith.

And you shall know the truth, and the truth shall set you free.
John 8:32

March 22

ARE YOU CHEATING?

Cheating can take many forms—cutting corners at work, being dishonest in relationships, or even small acts of deception in daily interactions. The Bible consistently emphasizes the importance of integrity and honesty in our lives. Proverbs 11:1 clearly states that God detests dishonesty. This isn't just about literal scales; it's about the fairness and truthfulness God desires in every area of our lives. While society might sometimes reward cheating with short-term gains, the Bible reminds us that lasting favor is found in accuracy and honesty. Living with integrity aligns us with God's values and builds trust and respect in our communities. When we choose honesty, we reflect God's character to those around us, becoming His representatives in a world that often overlooks truth. Consider whether there are areas in your life where you might be tempted to cheat or deceive. What have been the consequences? It might offer temporary relief or reward, but the long-lasting effects of these choices can weigh heavily on our conscience and relationships. Challenge yourself to live with integrity. Seek daily opportunities to be honest and transparent, whether in small decisions or significant life choices. Remember, favor with God is worth far more than any ill-gotten gain.

The Lord detests dishonest scales, but accurate weights find favor with Him.
Proverbs 11:1

WHAT GETS YOU UPSET?

Life is full of moments that can upset and unsettle us. Whether it's a disagreement with a loved one, a stressful day at work, or unexpected news, these moments can leave us feeling emotionally overwhelmed. The Bible offers guidance on how to handle such situations with grace and serenity. When emotions run high, it's easy to respond impulsively. However, Philippians 4 reminds us to anchor our responses in faith rather than fear. Instead of letting anxiety take the lead, we are encouraged to turn to God, presenting our worries and frustrations to Him. This Scripture promises that God's peace—a peace that goes beyond human comprehension—can protect our hearts and minds. This peace isn't the absence of conflict or trouble but a sense of tranquility amidst the storm. It is found in trusting that God is in control and cares deeply about our struggles. By focusing on gratitude and leaning into God's presence, we reset our perspective, allowing His peace to fill us. The next time you find yourself upset, pause and breathe. Reflect on Philippians 4 and consider what you're grateful for, then offer your feelings to God.

Do not be anxious about anything, but in every situation, by prayer and petition, with thanksgiving, present your requests to God. And the peace of God, which transcends all understanding, will guard your hearts and your minds in Christ Jesus.
Philippians 4:6-7

GOD WILL PROTECT YOU

The promise of God's protection offers a profound sense of security and peace. The Scripture from Psalm 18 serves as a powerful reminder of God's unwavering presence and strength in our lives. David, the psalmist, uses vivid imagery to describe God as a rock, fortress, and deliverer, emphasizing His role as a steadfast protector against all adversities. Imagine being surrounded by towering walls that guard you against any external threat or standing atop a solid rock that the fiercest storms can't shake. This is the divine protection that God offers us. It's a promise extending beyond physical safety to emotional and spiritual protection. God's protection doesn't imply the absence of challenges or threats; instead, it assures us that we are not alone in facing them. He provides refuge and strength, enabling us to withstand adversity with confidence and faith. We can draw near to Him in moments of fear or doubt, trusting in His protective nature. Today, reflect on areas where you need God's protection. Invite Him into those situations, acknowledging His power and presence. Remember, His protection is not conditional but is offered freely to those who seek refuge in Him. Trust in His promise.

The Lord is my rock, my fortress and my deliverer; my God is my rock, in whom I take refuge, my shield and the horn of my salvation, my stronghold.
Psalm 18:2

STRESSED OUT?

Stress and busyness are constants in our lives. From work demands to family responsibilities, it's easy to feel overwhelmed and lose sight of what truly matters. Amidst this chaos, it is essential to remember the words of Jesus. These verses remind us of the rest and peace offered by Christ. When we feel overwhelmed, we are invited to bring our burdens to Him. Unlike the world's solutions that often add more to our plates, Jesus offers a yoke that is easy and a burden that is light. This isn't an invitation to escape responsibilities but a call to prioritize our relationship with Him. To find peace amidst stress, begin by setting aside time daily to connect with God. Even a few moments of quiet reflection can reset your mind and spirit. Meditate on His Word, allowing it to refresh and inspire you. Trust that God is in control, and lean on Him for strength and guidance. Remember, it's okay to pause and breathe. When life feels like a whirlwind, anchor yourself in the peace and rest that only Christ can provide. Doing so allows you to find serenity amidst the busyness and emerge with a renewed perspective and strength.

Come to me, all you who are weary and burdened, and I will give you rest. Take my yoke upon you and learn from me, for I am gentle and humble in heart, and you will find rest for your souls. For my yoke is easy,
and my burden is light.
Matthew 11:28-30

ARE THERE STILL MIRACLES?

It can be hard to see a way through when life tosses challenges. We might find ourselves in situations where nothing short of a miracle could change our circumstances. But as believers, we have access to the miraculous power of God. Jesus performs a miracle in this passage by raising Lazarus from the dead. It's a powerful reminder that human constraints do not limit God. This miracle was not just for Lazarus but for all those who witnessed it and those who read of it today so that they may believe it. When we need a miracle, let's remember that God's ability to act is not hindered by what seems impossible to us. His power is as real today as it was then. Our part is to remain steadfast in faith, trusting that He hears us and desires to work in our lives. In every situation, no matter how dire it seems, keep your faith anchored in the One who can do immeasurably more than we ask or imagine.

Then Jesus looked up and said, Father, thank you for hearing me. I knew that you always listen to me, but I said this to benefit the people standing here, that they may believe that you sent me. When he had said this, Jesus called in a loud voice, Lazarus, come out! The dead man came out, his hands and feet wrapped with strips of linen and a cloth around his face. Jesus said to them, Take off the grave clothes.
John 11:41-44

NEVER SATISFIED

Friendship is a cherished gift from God that requires nurturing and intentionality. The Bible calls us to examine the quality of our friendships and reflects on how we embody the essence of true friendship. In today's world, it's easy to find ourselves trapped in a cycle of wanting more. Whether it's material possessions, achievements, or status, there seems always to be a relentless pursuit for the next best thing. But what happens when the pursuit never ends, and satisfaction remains out of reach? The Bible encourages us to find contentment in godliness, a state often overshadowed by worldly desires. In his letter to Timothy, the apostle Paul emphasizes that true gain is found not in abundance but in contentment paired with godliness. This isn't a call to complacency or to ignore our goals and ambitions. Instead, it's an invitation to look deeper into our motivations and discover the value of what we already possess through Christ. Consider the story of King Solomon, who had unmatched wisdom, wealth, and power. Despite having everything, Solomon declared that "everything was meaningless, a chasing after the wind" (Ecclesiastes 2:11). He concludes that satisfaction comes from living a life in pursuit of God's righteousness rather than earthly gains. Reflect on areas in your life where you feel you need more.

But godliness with contentment is great gain.
1 Timothy 6:6

ARE YOU TIRED?

Are you whacking away at the same old problems in the same old way but achieving less each time? Or are you working harder and harder to achieve the same result as before? You may need to make some changes. This could mean taking some time off to sharpen your axe. How you do this is up to you and God, but we know one thing: God doesn't expect your life to be static or repetitive. If what you do now isn't working anymore, do something different or in a different way. Nobody watches the same film repeatedly to see if it has a different ending, so why do we try to solve our problems in the old ways that are no longer effective? We must learn when to take a rest. The strongest and most skilled woodsman knows when to take some time out to avoid getting tired and careless and feeling worn out. Remember that Jesus invites us to find rest in Him. Life's burdens are heavy, but His yoke is easy. Shift your struggles onto His shoulders, and allow His peace to refresh your soul today. Ecclesiastes 10:10 offers us some excellent advice for living in today's world. "Don't work harder, work smarter."

If the axe is dull and its edge unsharpened, more strength is needed, but skill will bring success.
Ecclesiastes 10:10

BEING AFRAID IS NORMAL?

Fear is a natural emotion that everyone experiences. Immediate threats or uncertainties about the future can trigger it. However, as Christians, we are called to respond to fear differently. The above Scripture from Isaiah reminds us that God is present with us in every situation. His promise is not just of presence but also of empowerment and support. When fear grips us, it often clouds our judgment and distorts reality. It makes us forget that we have a powerful ally in God. Isaiah 41:10 serves as a reassuring reminder that we are never alone. God's presence is a constant in our lives, giving us strength and courage. This verse encourages us to replace fear with faith, to look beyond our circumstances, and to focus on the divine assurance of God's support. Practically, overcoming fear involves a conscious shift in perspective— trusting God's promises over our intimidating situations. Share your fears with a trusted friend or mentor and seek their encouragement. By grounding ourselves in God's Word, we can confidently face fear, knowing that our God is always with us, ready to strengthen and uphold us. So do not fear, for I am with you.

Now the Jordan is at flood stage all during harvest. Yet as soon as the priests who carried the ark reached the Jordan and their feet touched the water's edge, the water from upstream stopped flowing.
Joshua 3:15

CALLING ON GOD?

These verses encapsulate the reassurance that God is always just a call away. Unlike the fleeting support we may receive from worldly sources, His presence is constant, and His support is unfailing. When we reach out to God honestly, we invite His divine intervention into our lives. Consider your current challenges. Are you reaching out to God as your first point of contact, or are you relying on temporary solutions? This Scripture encourages us to trust in God wholeheartedly, not just in times of crisis but daily. When we sincerely call upon Him, we open the door to His wisdom, guidance, and peace. This week, whenever faced with a difficulty or decision, pause and call upon God first. Invite His presence into your situation and watch how He transforms your heart and mind. Remember, God desires a relationship with us, and reaching out to Him strengthens that bond. In moments of need, ask yourself, Who am I going to call? And choose to call upon the Lord. His line is never busy, and His help is always on the way.

The Lord is near to all who call on Him, to all who call on Him in truth. He fulfills the desires of those who fear Him; He hears their cry and saves them.
Psalm 145:18-19

TIRED OF WAITING?

Waiting can feel like the ultimate test of patience. We often want instant solutions and immediate results. However, waiting on God is a recurring theme in the Bible, reminding us that His timing is perfect, even when it doesn't align with our own. The Scripture from Isaiah 40:31 paints a beautiful picture of renewal and strength for those who wait for the Lord. Waiting is not passive but an active stance of expectation, trust, and reliance on God's promises. When we wait on Him, we are not wasting time but investing it in our spiritual growth and developing a deeper relationship with Him. Consider Abraham, who waited years for the promise of a son, or Joseph, who endured years of trials before his dreams were realized. Their stories illustrate the truth that God's delays are not His denials. While we wait, God works diligently behind the scenes, preparing us. Waiting on God refines our character, teaching us patience, humility, and dependence. It is a period where our faith is tested but also strengthened. When we shift our focus from the waiting to the One we are waiting for, we find peace, knowing that His plans for us are good. Take heart and encourage yourself today that waiting on God is never in vain.

But those who wait on the Lord shall renew their strength; they shall mount up with wings like eagles, they shall run and not be weary, they shall walk and not faint.
Isaiah 40:31

April 1

IT'S TIME?

It's easy to feel overwhelmed. We face challenges at work, in relationships, and sometimes within ourselves. During these trying times, it's important to remember God's promise in Isaiah 41:10. This verse is a powerful reminder that we are never alone. God is with us, always ready to strengthen and support us. The assurance, "I am with you," is not just a comforting thought but a profound reality for Christians. It means that no matter what we face, we do so with the Creator of the universe by our side. His presence brings peace amidst chaos and courage in moments of fear. When we acknowledge God's presence, we can confidently confront our fears, knowing that our strength is not solely ours but comes from Him. This divine companionship encourages us to move forward despite uncertainties. It invites us to lean on God's unchanging character and promises. We are reminded to shift our focus from our limitations to His omnipotence. Throughout your day, take a moment to pause and reflect on God's promise to be with you. Allow His presence to fill you with peace and strength. Remember, His righteous right-hand holds you up, guiding you through every circumstance.

So do not fear, for I am with you; do not be dismayed, for I am your God. I will strengthen you and help you; I will uphold you with my righteous right hand.
Isaiah 41:10

STUFF IS IMPORTANT

In our quest for a comfortable life, becoming attached to material possessions is easy. We often equate success with the accumulation of things, believing that what we own defines our worth. Yet, the Bible provides a different perspective on the nature of possessions and actual value. Jesus reminds us in Matthew 6 that earthly treasures are fleeting. They can be destroyed by time or taken away by unexpected circumstances. The pursuit of material wealth can lead to anxiety and distraction from what truly matters. In this light, possessions should be tools to serve God's purpose rather than ends in themselves. Instead of amassing goods, Jesus encourages us to concentrate on treasures of eternal value. These are built on acts of love, kindness, and faithfulness that reflect God's Kingdom. Such treasures are imperishable and are safeguarded by the divine promises of heaven. Are they serving God's purpose, or have they become idols? By shifting our focus from the temporal to the eternal, we align ourselves with God's vision for our lives. May we use what we have to store up treasures forever.

Do not store up for yourselves treasures on earth, where moths and vermin destroy and where thieves break in and steal. But store up for yourselves treasures in heaven, where moths and vermin do not destroy, and where thieves do not break in and steal.
Matthew 6:19-20

PLEASE FORGIVE ME

A tiny little boy looked odd. His pockets were packed and overflowing with tiny baby frogs. While his family had been playing miniature golf, he had been picking up frogs and saving them. He was weighed down with the little green creatures. We sometimes save up past offenses until it becomes hard for us to move forward. Fortunately, we can unload these emotional weights when we forgive "from the heart" (Matthew 18:35). Peter asked Jesus, "Lord, how often should I forgive someone who sins against me?" Peter knew he might need to forgive the same person multiple times, so he suggested what seemed like an appropriate number—seven. Jesus said, "No, not seven times, but seventy times seven" (Matthew 18:22). Although some minor issues can be settled in the quietness of our hearts, more significant offenses require an honest conversation with the person at fault. If the guilty party listens and confesses their wrong, and we freely forgive them, our relationship can be salvaged. (Matthew 18:15) Jesus doesn't want us to endure the weight of grudges and past hurt. He wants us to enjoy the love that thrives when we forgive others. Instead of thinking about it, why not act?

How often should I forgive someone?
Matthew 18:21

IS MORE JUST MORE?

In pursuing more, we often equate wealth with accumulating material possessions or financial security. However, Christians are called to reassess what it means to be truly rich. Jesus's words in Matthew challenge us to shift our focus from earthly treasures to heavenly ones. What are these heavenly treasures? They are the fruits of a life lived in alignment with God's will—love, kindness, compassion, and faithfulness. These are the riches that cannot be quantified by earthly measures but have eternal value. Reflect on your own life. What are you investing in? Is it the latest gadgets, fashionable clothes, or an enviable lifestyle? While nothing is intrinsically wrong with enjoying God's blessings, the call is to ensure they do not consume our hearts. Consider your time, talents, and resources. Are they directed toward building up God's Kingdom, serving others, and deepening your relationship with Christ? It's in these pursuits that we find true richness. Richness, in God's eyes, is not about what we have but who we are becoming.

Do not store up for yourselves treasures on earth, where moths and vermin destroy, and where thieves break in and steal. But store up for yourselves treasures in heaven, where moths and vermin do not destroy, and where thieves do not break in and steal. For where your treasure is, there your heart will be also.
Matthew 6:19-21

April 5

YOU WERE CHOSEN

It's easy to feel lost in the crowd. Work, family, and countless responsibilities sometimes cloud our sense of purpose and belonging. Yet, the Bible reminds us that we are not just another face in the crowd; God chooses us. Being chosen means you have been picked for a unique purpose. Just as God selected Israel to be His special possession, He has called each of us to be a part of His royal priesthood. This isn't just a status; it's a mission. We are chosen to bring light into the darkness, to reflect His love and grace in our words and actions. Consider the implications of being chosen. It means your life has meaning beyond the immediate tasks and challenges. It means you have a role to play in God's grand design. Recognizing this can transform how you view yourself and your place in the world. Take a moment to meditate on the weight of this truth. Allow it to sink in and impact your daily interactions. What would it look like to live as God's special possession today? How can you declare His praises through your life? Remember, you are chosen—not because of your qualifications, but because of His grace and love. Step into this identity and carry it with confidence and humility.

But you are a chosen people, a royal priesthood, a holy nation, God's special possession, that you may declare the praises of him who called you out of darkness into his wonderful light.
1 Peter 2:9

KEEPING SCORE

Paul urges believers to release bitterness and anger, two emotions that often accompany grudges. The call to "be kind and compassionate" is coupled with the reminder of how God, in Christ, has forgiven us. This is a profound reminder that our call to forgive is not based on the merit of the other person but rather on the grace we have received. Consider how holding a grudge affects your heart and mind. Does it consume your thoughts or dictate your actions? Forgiveness doesn't mean forgetting or excusing harmful behavior; instead, it's a conscious decision to release resentment's hold over you. Reflect on how freeing it can be to allow God's grace to transform your heart, leading you to extend forgiveness and compassion to others. This week, identify someone you may be holding a grudge against. Spend time meditating on Ephesians 4:31-32, asking God to help you release bitterness and replace it with kindness and forgiveness. Remember, forgiveness is a gift you give yourself as much as it is to others, allowing you to move forward in peace and love.

Get rid of all bitterness, rage and anger, brawling and slander, along with every form of malice. Be kind and compassionate to one another, forgiving each other, just as in Christ, God forgave you.
Ephesians 4:31-32

YOU ARE ALWAYS TEACHING

What pleasant memories do you remember about growing up? Maybe you're reminded of a particular birthday party, a holiday, good times with a neighborhood friend, or even a special time you spent alone. As you're thinking about these things, how many of them include mealtimes? Eating together is often bonding time. Diplomats know it, and dating couples realize it. Regrettably, many families are so busy they are forgetting it. In many homes, when children have a birthday they can choose the day's menu or where the family would go to eat that night. Some of the decisions may be strange, but they always ate together. A great deal of teaching takes place at the family table. Parents teach children, and brothers and sisters teach each other, while Mom and Dad often listen. God's teaching calls for vital learning during the family's everyday activities. Talking at the table, walking around the block, doing homework, praying, and playing are all things a family needs to do together. Healthy, strong relationships are fostered by enjoying those together times. Find time to eat at least one regular meal with your family. Consider a new tradition of having friends around the table for Sunday lunch. This can be an unforgettable tradition.

Talk about them when you sit at home and when you walk along the road.
Deuteronomy 6:7

AVOIDING CONFLICT

Conflict is an inevitable part of life, stemming from misunderstandings, differing perspectives, and expectations. However, as Christians, we are called to pursue peace and resolve conflicts in a manner that reflects God's love and grace. In John 14:27, Jesus reminds us, "Peace I leave with you; my peace I give you." Avoiding conflict doesn't mean avoiding issues. Instead, it means approaching disagreements with a heart aligned with Christ's teachings. The Apostle Paul, in Romans 12:18, advises, "If it is possible, as far as it depends on you, live at peace with everyone." Here, Paul acknowledges that while we cannot control every situation, we can control our responses and seek harmony. Consider James 1:19, which encourages us to be "quick to listen, slow to speak, and slow to become angry." We open channels for understanding and healing by practicing active listening and empathy. Through these deliberate choices, we cultivate relationships rooted in respect and love. Being a peacemaker requires humility and patience. It's about honoring God's truth over personal pride. Therefore, when faced with potential conflicts, take a moment to pause and pray for wisdom. You become a beacon of God's peace by choosing gentleness over aggression and compassion over judgment.

Blessed are the peacemakers, for they will be called children of God.
Matthew 5:9

ENCOURAGE YOUR PASTOR

Pastors play a pivotal role in today's churches, shepherding congregations through life's ups and downs. Yet, amid their diligence, they can often feel overwhelmed or under appreciated. It's essential for us to lift up our pastors and encourage them. A simple word of gratitude can have a profound effect. Taking a moment to express thanks for their sermons, prayers, or guidance can remind them of the impact they're making. Consider writing a note or sending an email to articulate your appreciation. Another powerful way to encourage your pastor is through practical support. This can mean volunteering for church activities, helping organize events, or attending services. Your active participation is encouraging and demonstrates your commitment to the community they strive hard to nurture. Lastly, sharing Scripture or a devotional thought that has inspired you can be a source of encouragement. It reminds them of the fruits of their labor and that their teaching bears fruit in the spiritual growth of their congregation. Beyond mere words, your actions can breathe life into their ministry.

Now we ask you, brothers and sisters, to acknowledge those who work hard *among you, who care for you in the Lord and who admonish you. Hold them in the highest regard in love because of their work. Live in peace with each other.*
1 Thessalonians 5:12-13

THE SMALL THINGS

He wanted a new baseball glove very badly. He found the glove he wanted in a local sporting goods store and began to save up his money diligently. But when the day came for the purchase, he was $1.50 short because he needed to account for the sales tax. The store owner, who knew his family, told him he could take the glove. He wanted him, however, to bring him the $1.50 when he got the money. This request taught the boy the importance of little things. Flash forward a dozen years. As the same young man waited to purchase a newspaper from a coin-operated machine, the man buying a paper in front of him caught the spring-released door and held it open. He turned to him and offered him a free newspaper. He declined. In Luke 16, Jesus used a parable about a man who was more shrewd than honest. The man used his master's finances to ensure his own financial security. Jesus said, "If you are faithful in little things, you will be faithful in large ones. But you won't be honest with greater responsibilities if you are dishonest in little things." If we don't have integrity in the little temptations, we may not have a chance when the big ones come along. Someone is always watching.

If you are faithful in little things, you will be faithful in large ones. But you won't be honest with greater responsibilities if you are dishonest in little things.
Luke 16:10

WHAT MADE JESUS ANGRY?

Jesus, known for His compassion and love, rarely expressed anger. Yet, when He did, it was profoundly significant. In John 2, we see one of the few instances where Jesus acts angrily, revealing His deep concern for the sanctity of worship and the exploitation of people under religious pretenses. The temple, intended as a place of prayer and communion with God, had become a hub of commerce and greed. Merchants and money changers were exploiting worshippers, prioritizing profit over piety. Jesus' anger was not a mere emotional response but a righteous indignation against injustice and the distortion of worship. What can we learn from this? It reminds us that true worship cannot coexist with exploitation. Our churches and communities should be spaces of sincerity and service, not self-interest. It challenges us to examine our hearts. Are there areas where we prioritize profit or traditions over genuine faith and compassion? Are there tables that need overturning?

In the temple courts, he found people selling cattle, sheep, and doves, and others were sitting at tables exchanging money. So he made a whip out of cords and drove all from the temple courts, both sheep and cattle; he scattered the coins of the money changers and overturned their tables. To those who sold doves, he said, Get these out of here! Stop turning my Father's house into a market!
John 2:13-16

April 12

ARE YOU A HYPOCRITE?

Jesus calls out our tendency to judge others without first examining our faults. He uses the hyperbolic imagery of a plank and a speck to highlight the absurdity of focusing on the minor faults of others when we have significant issues to address. This Scripture challenges us to reflect inwardly, asking us to confront our shortcomings before critiquing others. It's a reminder that being a follower of Christ involves humility and self-awareness. Recognizing our hypocrisy is not about self-condemnation but about sincerity in our faith. Hypocrisy can distance us from truly experiencing God and building authentic relationships with others. It is easy to fall into the trap of self-righteousness, thinking that our sins are less significant than those of others. However, Jesus teaches us to be introspective and seek personal transformation to support and guide others genuinely. Today, reflect on areas where you may have been judgmental or hypocritical. Ask God to reveal the "planks" in your life today.

Why do you look at the speck of sawdust in your brother's eye and pay no attention to the plank in your own eye? How can you tell your brother, Let me take the speck out of your eye when there is a plank in your own eye? You hypocrite, first take the plank out of your own eye, and then you will see clearly to remove the speck from your brother's eye.
Matthew 7:3-5

LISTENING TO THE WORD

The Bible emphasizes the importance of listening to God, suggesting that it is through this practice that we find guidance and peace. This verse invites us to pause our hectic lives and focus on God's presence. In stillness, we can hear His whispers, guiding us through life's complex paths. How often do we truly stop to listen? With constant noise from social media, work demands, and daily responsibilities, finding time for quiet can seem elusive. Yet, listening to God doesn't always require complete silence; it's about attuning our hearts and minds to His presence throughout our day. One way to cultivate a listening ear is through meditation on Scripture. Start by selecting a verse that resonates with you—perhaps Psalm 119:105, "Your word is a lamp to my feet and a light to my path." Spend a few minutes each day reflecting on its meaning and asking God to reveal how it applies to your life. Another approach is to incorporate moments of gratitude and reflection into your routine. Consider setting aside a few minutes each morning or evening to thank God for His blessings and ask for His guidance. By consciously listening, you open your heart to the wisdom and love that God desires to share with you.

Be still, and know that I am God.
Psalm 46:10

ARE YOU PATIENT?

Patience is often regarded as a rare virtue. Yet, Scripture encourages us to cultivate patience as a fundamental aspect of our spiritual growth. Patience is more than just waiting; it is an active and hopeful anticipation of God's promises. Consider the story of Joseph, who was sold into slavery by his brothers and spent years in prison before rising to a position of power in Egypt. Joseph's patience was not passive resignation but trust in God's timing. Through the hardships and delays, Joseph remained steadfast in his faith, trusting that God had a plan. The Apostle Paul reminds us in Romans 8 that patience is intertwined with hope. When we are patient, we trust God's perfect timing and ultimate plan for our lives. Patience teaches us to surrender our desires and schedules, allowing God's will to unfold. Do you need help with impatience in your career, relationships, or personal goals? Reflect on the areas where impatience creeps in and ask yourself how these moments can be transformed into opportunities for growth. Patience builds character and produces perseverance, making us mature and complete. Remember, God works behind the scenes, aligning everything according to His purpose.

But if we hope for what we do not yet have, we wait for it patiently.
Romans 8:25

April 15

KEEPING YOUR PROMISES

In a world where commitments are often taken lightly, keeping a promise is a testament to one's character and faith. The Bible consistently underscores the importance of integrity and the power of spoken words. Numbers 30:2 reminds us that it should not be broken when we make a vow, especially to the Lord. Our words are not just mere sounds; they carry weight and significance. The act of keeping promises reflects God's nature. Throughout the Bible, God makes promises to His people and fulfills them, demonstrating unwavering faithfulness. As Christians, we are called to emulate this trait in our own lives. Whether it's a promise made to a friend, a family member, or a colleague, each commitment we make should be honored. It can be challenging to keep promises when circumstances change or challenges arise. However, maintaining our word fosters trust and strengthens relationships. It serves as a witness to others of our dedication to live by God's principles. Reflect on promises you've made recently. Have you neglected or forgotten anything? Remember, each promise kept is an opportunity to display the love and reliability of God to those around you. In your daily walk, strive to be a person of your word.

When a man makes a vow to the Lord or takes an oath to obligate himself by a pledge, he must not break his word but must do everything he said.
Numbers 30:2

LISTENING ONLY TO GOD

The ability to focus on the voice of God is a precious gift. Many voices vie for our attention—media, peers, and even our thoughts. But amidst the chaos, the voice of God remains constant and unwavering. Listening only to God requires intentionality and practice. Much like cultivating any relationship, it involves setting aside time daily to be in His presence. This could be through reading Scripture, quiet meditation, or simply sitting in silence, allowing His words to fill your heart and mind. The story of Samuel in the Bible is a powerful reminder of this practice. As a young boy, God called him, but he did not recognize His voice at first. Only when Eli instructed him to say, "Speak, Lord, for your servant is listening" (1 Samuel 3:9), Samuel began to discern God's voice. This moment changed the trajectory of his life and can serve as an inspiration for us all. As you go about your day, consider what it means to listen to God indeed. Are there areas in your life where other voices have taken precedence? Reflect on how you might create more space for God's voice. The more attuned we become to His guidance, the more peace, clarity, and purpose we'll find in our daily walk with Him. How can you tune out the world's noise and make space to hear God's voice more clearly in your life?

My sheep listen to my voice; I know them, and they follow me.
John 10:27

A DROWNING MAN

It is dangerous trying to save a drowning person. The natural reaction of the one going down, for possibly the last time, is to keep their head above water. To survive, they will grab hold of the rescuer and, in trying to get another breath of air, drown the person who is trying to help him. Too often, the person who is trying to save the person is drowned by the flailing, panicking drowner. A disgruntled, unhappy person is usually much like a drowning person. They are dissatisfied for whatever reason; they share their unrest and discontent with others. They are unloading their burden and anguish to others in hopes that the person can say something or change something to stop their dissatisfaction. However, their complaining or venting does much the same thing as the drowning man. He can take the listener down with them. Making yourself a listening post for complaining, gossip, or dissatisfaction can result in you having the same thoughts as the one floundering. Complaints and gossip can spread like an infectious disease. You may soon share the grumbler's frustrations and feelings. In the rush to respond, we often miss the heart of a conversation. Proverbs 18:13 reminds us that answering before truly listening can lead to misunderstanding.

To answer before listening—that is folly and shame.
Proverbs 18:13

MAKING A DECISION

Every day, we are faced with countless decisions. Some are small, like what to have for breakfast, while others have the potential to shape our entire lives. For Christians, decision-making is not just a matter of weighing pros and cons but involves discerning God's will and trusting His guidance. The verses from Proverbs remind us to trust wholeheartedly in the Lord rather than relying solely on our understanding. This doesn't mean disregarding our reasoning capabilities; instead, it calls us to align our thoughts with God's wisdom. When faced with a major decision, seek insight from the Bible. God's Word offers timeless wisdom and principles that can illuminate your path. Seek counsel from fellow believers who can provide a fresh faith-based perspective. Remember, God often speaks through His people. Lastly, take time for quiet reflection. In the stillness, listen for the gentle whisper of the Holy Spirit guiding your heart. Trust that God will straighten your way as you walk this path, even when the future seems uncertain. Decision-making can be daunting, but when we place our faith in God's wisdom, we can move forward confidently, knowing He is with us every step.

Trust in the Lord with all your heart and lean not on your own understanding; in all your ways submit to Him, and He will make your paths straight.
Proverbs 3:5-6

WORKING TO MUCH?

It's easy to get caught up in the hustle, constantly striving to do more and achieve more. Work can become an idol, consuming our time and energy until there's nothing left. But as Christians, we're called to find a balance, recognizing that rest is as important as hard work. God created the world in six days and rested on the seventh. This rhythm of work and rest is embedded in creation itself. When we neglect rest, we miss God's gift and the opportunity to renew our strength. Matthew 11:28 reminds us gently that Jesus invites us to come to Him for rest. This invitation is not just about physical rest but spiritual renewal. When we lay our burdens at His feet, we allow Him to refresh our souls and realign our priorities. Are you feeling overwhelmed by your workload? Take a moment to pause and reflect on the true purpose of your labor. Is it to glorify God and serve others, or has it become about personal gain? Remember, our identity is not found in our accomplishments but in being children of God. Consider setting aside time each week for Sabbath rest. Use this time to connect with God, family, and friends, engage in activities that bring you joy, and recharge. By honoring rest, you will find the strength to approach your work with renewed purpose and energy, keeping Christ at the center.

Come to me, all you who are weary and burdened, and I will give you rest.
Matthew 11:28

WHERE WAS GOD?

In times of uncertainty, many Christians ask, Where is God? This question is not new and is often echoed throughout the Bible. One of the most comforting scriptures that addresses this human experience is our Scripture today. This passage reminds us that God's presence is not confined to any single place or moment. Whether standing on a mountaintop or walking through the valleys of life, His Spirit is always with you. The assurance of God's omnipresence can provide solace and strength during life's trials. The disciples experienced this firsthand when they faced a storm on the sea. In Mark 4:37-39, Jesus was with them in the boat, sleeping, yet when they called upon Him, He calmed the storm, showing His power over nature and His presence in their distress. Remember that He is closer than we often realize when questioning where God is. He dwells in the ordinary moments of our day, in the comforting words of a friend or the gentle breeze that lifts our spirits. Trust that He walks with you through every season of life. In moments of doubt, it's natural to wonder, Where is God?

Where can I go from your Spirit? Where can I flee from your presence? If I go up to the heavens, you are there; if I make my bed in the depths, you are there. If I rise on the wings of the dawn, if I settle on the far side of the sea, even there your hand will guide me, your right hand will hold me fast.
Psalm 139:7-10

April 21

RUSH TO JUDGMENT

It's easy to make quick assumptions about others based on limited information. Rash judgments often stem from snap decisions made in haste, without understanding the full context of a person's actions or situation. These judgments can lead to misunderstandings, damaged relationships, and missed opportunities for compassion. Matthew 7 reminds us of the importance of withholding judgment and practicing empathy. Jesus encourages us to consider our own biases and imperfections before assessing others. By doing so, we create space for understanding and grace, mirroring the love and patience that God extends to us. Are we seeking to uplift others, or are we quick to criticize? Mindful of our thoughts and words can transform how we perceive and interact with those around us. In moments of doubt or misunderstanding, seek clarity and wisdom from the Holy Spirit. Approach situations with an open heart and a willingness to listen. By doing so, we fulfill Jesus' call to love our neighbors and embody the values of the Kingdom. Remember, we are all on a spiritual journey, growing and learning daily. Let's extend the same mercy and kindness God grants us.

Do not judge, or you too will be judged. For in the same way you judge others, you will be judged, and with the measure you use, it will be measured to you.
Matthew 7:1-2

THERE IS ONLY ONE WAY

It's easy to become overwhelmed by choices and opinions. Yet, as Christians, we hold onto the profound truth that there is only one way to eternal life: through Jesus Christ. This is not just a path we choose but a divine invitation into a relationship with God, facilitated by His love and grace. The Scripture in John 14:6 reminds us that Jesus is the singular path to God. He is not merely a guide or teacher; he embodies truth and life. This statement is central to our faith, offering clarity amidst confusion and assurance amidst doubt. Why is this important? In moments of uncertainty, when the world offers countless solutions to life's questions, we have a steadfast anchor in Christ. His life, death, and resurrection demonstrate the power of God's love and the fulfillment of His promises. This truth directs our lives, influencing how we interact with others and our decisions. Our challenge is to live out this truth daily. It calls us to align our actions with His teachings, ensuring that love, kindness, and integrity are evident in all we do. Doing so makes us living testimonies of His grace, drawing others towards Him. Reflect today on how you can embody this truth in your life. Trust in the way of Christ, knowing that through Him, we find our purpose and peace.

Jesus answered, I am the way and the truth and the life. No one comes to the Father except through me.
John 14:6

April 23

THE BEST IS YET TO COME

We often find ourselves caught in the present, overwhelmed by the daily grind or the challenges we face. It can be easy to lose sight of the future that God has planned for us. However, as Christians, we are reminded through Scripture that our current situation is not our final destination. The promise that the best is yet to come is not just a comforting thought but a reality rooted in God's Word. Jeremiah 29:11 assures us that God has plans for each of us—plans that are meant to bring prosperity, hope, and a promising future. This verse is a powerful reminder that God's intentions are always for our good. It redirects our focus from anxiety about the present to faith in a future that God has meticulously crafted. Whether you're navigating a career change, personal loss, or simply the uncertainties of daily life, remember that God sees beyond today's challenges. He is laying the groundwork for something extraordinary in your life. Our role is to trust His process, keeping our hearts and minds open to the good things He's preparing for us. Believing that the best is yet to come means walking by faith, even when the path isn't clear. It's about trusting God's promises will manifest in His time and way. Hold onto this truth in your walk with God.

For I know the plans I have for you, declares the Lord, plans to prosper you and not to harm you, plans to give you hope and a future.
Jeremiah 29:11

April 24

WELCOME TO THE WORLD

Welcome to the world to the newest citizen of the State of Texas. All cheeks, wrinkly skin, tiny fingernails, itty-bitty toes, loud cries, and funny faces. A perfect little nose and the most beautiful ears I've ever seen. She had a head full of hair and wore a much too-large diaper for her tiny six-pound frame. New babies are the sweetest, scariest, and most heart-consuming people. Our great God, who created majestic mountains, vast plains, endless oceans, and sweeping deserts… He planned the placement of each birthmark, carefully counted each hair on her head, and crafted just the right shade of brown for those sleepy eyes. These babies, created to perfection, arrive with nothing and need everything. I don't mean everything on the baby registry (well, stock up on diapers. They will need loads). No, it's the overwhelming love they need the most. Kiss their sweet cheeks, tickle their tiny toes, hold them close, and whisper God's blessing over their lives. Watch them sleep and smile as they wake. Laugh at their wiggles, speak their baby language, and have wordless conversations. In loving newborn babies, we are again allowed to love and be loved.

Before I formed you in the womb I knew you, before you were born I set you apart; I appointed you as a prophet to the nations.
Jeremiah 1:5

FINISHING STRONG

Finishing strong is more than just a motivational phrase; it's a call to remain steadfast in our faith and service to God until the end. The Apostle Paul serves as an excellent example of this resolve. Despite facing numerous challenges, from imprisonment to persecution, he remained committed to his mission and faith. His declaration in 2 Timothy 4:7 is a powerful testament to a life dedicated to God's calling. To finish strong, we must adopt a mindset of perseverance and resilience. Life is filled with trials and tribulations that can easily lead to discouragement. However, Christians are called to run our race with endurance, focusing on the eternal prize rather than temporary setbacks. Our journey is akin to an athlete's race. An athlete doesn't merely focus on the start but trains to endure and push through obstacles, keeping their eyes fixed on the finish line. Similarly, we are encouraged to lay aside every weight and sin that entangles us, looking unto Jesus, the author and finisher of our faith (Hebrews 12:1-2). Remember, finishing strong doesn't mean a life without failure or mistakes. It means getting up after each fall, learning from our experiences, and continuing to press forward with unwavering faith.

I have fought the good fight, I have finished the race,
I have kept the faith.
2 Timothy 4:7

April 26

THE UNEXPECTED

Unexpected journeys, little and big—life is full of them. A quick trip to the grocery store turns into a car accident, injuries, and several months of healing. A routine drive home from work turns into a breakdown on the highway and a lengthy wait for a tow truck. A call on the cell phone turns into the news that you are in for major repairs when you get home. We can usually negotiate the little unexpected journeys of life. However, extensive, unexpected journeys can turn our lives upside down. David wrote about such times in Psalm 23:4: "Even when I walk through the darkest valley, I will not be afraid, for You are close beside me. Your rod and Your staff protect and comfort me." We also go through times when we experience what David wrote about in Psalm 22:1, "My God, my God, why have You abandoned me? Why are You so far away when I groan for help?" Are you going through one of those significant, unexpected journeys of life? Is your faith like the one found in Psalm 23, or do you find yourself in Psalm 22? David's highs and lows recorded in the Psalms show us that during complex, unforeseen journeys of life, we will experience both moments of unquestionable faith and times of real pain.

Even when I walk through the darkest valley, I will not be afraid, for You are close beside me. Your rod and Your staff protect and comfort me.
Psalm 23:4

April 27

FACING SETBACKS

In life's journey, setbacks are inevitable. They can challenge our faith and resilience, but they also offer opportunities for growth and renewal. Scripture provides wisdom and comfort as we face such trials. Consider the words in this passage, which encourage us to find joy in trials, recognizing that they test our faith and build perseverance. Setbacks, though discouraging, are moments where faith can deepen, and character can develop. Reflect on Joseph's story in Genesis. Betrayed by his brothers and sold into slavery, Joseph faced numerous setbacks. Yet, through it all, he remained faithful to God. His story reminds us of God's sovereignty and purpose, even amidst challenges. When facing setbacks, it's natural to feel frustrated or defeated. However, these moments can be transformative. They teach us to rely more on God and less on our understanding. Romans 8:28 reassures us, "And we know that in all things God works for the good of those who love him, who have been called according to his purpose." Remember, setbacks are not the end of your story. With faith and perseverance, they become stepping stones toward a greater purpose.

Consider it pure joy, my brothers and sisters; whenever you face trials of many kinds, you know that the testing of your faith produces perseverance. Let perseverance finish its work so that you may be mature and complete, not lacking anything.
James 1:2-4

April 28

FRUSTRATIONS

In moments of frustration, it's easy to feel overwhelmed and lose sight of the bigger picture. But as Christians, we are called to find peace and reassurance in God's word, knowing that He is with us in every trial. Frustration often stems from unmet expectations or plans going awry, leading us to question our path and purpose. During these times, we must pause, breathe, and turn to God, who provides solace and clarity. Philippians 4:6-7 reminds us to approach God with our concerns, releasing our burdens into His capable hands. When we present our frustrations to God, we open the door to His peace, which surpasses all human understanding. This peace acts as a shield, guarding our hearts and minds against the chaos that frustration can bring. It allows us to refocus and realign our thoughts with His purpose, giving us the strength to persevere. Our Scripture encourages us to maintain a thankful heart, even amidst challenges. We can cultivate gratitude by shifting our focus from the source of our frustration to the blessings God provides. God's peace is not dependent on our circumstances.

Do not be anxious about anything, but in every situation, by prayer and petition, with thanksgiving, present your requests to God. And the peace of God, which transcends all understanding, will guard your hearts and your minds in Christ Jesus.
Philippians 4:6-7

WE TAKE IT FOR GRANTED

It's easy to overlook the blessings we receive every day. We often take for granted the simple things God provides, like the air we breathe, the food on our tables, or the warmth of a sunlit afternoon. These daily gifts may seem small, but they are constant reminders of God's unwavering love and generosity. The Bible tells us that every good and perfect gift is from above. This means that the blessings in our lives, whether as grand as a new opportunity or as humble as a quiet moment of peace, come from God. We Christians need to recognize and appreciate these blessings, not just during moments of prosperity but also when life becomes challenging. Taking time each day to reflect on the gifts we've received allows us to cultivate a heart of gratitude. When we acknowledge God's hand in the details of our lives, we begin to see His presence in everything. This awareness can transform our perspective and deepen our relationship with Him. Ask yourself today, what have I taken for granted? How can I show gratitude for the everyday blessings in my life? By consciously choosing to appreciate the gifts we've been given, we honor the Giver and strengthen our connection to Him. Let's take advantage of what we have to enjoy it; let's start today.

Every good and perfect gift is from above, coming down from the Father of the heavenly lights, who does not change like shifting shadows.
James 1:17

SHARING A BIT TOO MUCH

In our digital age, where sharing has become second nature, it's easy to forget the wisdom of restraint. Social media platforms encourage constant updates and unrestricted sharing, but as Christians, we're called to embody discernment and understanding in our interactions. The verse from Proverbs highlights the difference between impulsive expression and thoughtful reflection. It's not about stifling our feelings or hiding our true selves but about understanding the impact our words can have. Sharing every thought and emotion without consideration can lead to misunderstanding, conflict, and sometimes regret. Instead, let's focus on sharing with intention. Consider the motives behind your words. Are they meant to uplift, inform, or encourage? When we pause to reflect before speaking—or typing—we practice self-control and honor God in our communications. It's important to remember that some matters are best reserved for close friends or private conversations with God. Not everything needs to be aired publicly. Holding back and choosing words wisely can foster deeper connections and demonstrate respect for others' perspectives and feelings. Let's strive to be wise in our expressions, using our voices to empower and inspire rather than to vent and divide. In doing so, we align ourselves more closely with Christ.

A fool vents all his feelings, but a wise man holds them back.
Proverbs 29:11

SURROUNDED BY FRIENDS

In a world that often champions self-reliance and independence, it can be easy to overlook the profound importance of friendship and community in our spiritual lives. Yet, the Bible consistently highlights the significance of surrounding ourselves with fellow believers, encouraging us to gather in unity and strength. The verse from Matthew reminds us that Jesus is present when we come together, fostering an environment where the Holy Spirit can move and work among us. In this sacred gathering—whether in small groups or larger communities—we cultivate growth, accountability, and encouragement. These friendships are not merely social connections but spiritual lifelines supporting and nurturing our faith. Consider the friendships that have profoundly impacted your spiritual walk. Are there moments when a friend's prayer or counsel steered you back to God's path? Have you experienced the joy of sharing burdens and celebrating victories with those who understand your faith's core? These are the gifts of being surrounded by friends in faith. Reflect on how you engage with your spiritual community. Are there opportunities to deepen these relationships or extend an invitation to others? Remember, each interaction holds the potential to uplift and inspire.

For where two or three gather in my name, there am I with them.
Matthew 18:20

ARE YOU LONELY?

Loneliness is a feeling that can affect us profoundly, even when people surround us. Feeling isolated in a bustling world where meaningful connections sometimes seem out of reach is easy. However, Christians are reminded that we are never truly alone. God's presence is constant, and He walks with us even in our loneliest moments. Psalm 34 speaks to the heart of those who feel disconnected or isolated. It reassures us that the Lord is intimately near those who are brokenhearted. This closeness is not just a distant promise but a profound reality for those who seek Him. Consider the life of Jesus. He experienced deep loneliness, especially during His time in Gethsemane and on the cross. Yet, He remained steadfast, knowing the Father was with Him. His life exemplifies the strength found in divine companionship. When loneliness creeps in, take a moment to pause and remember God's promises. Reflect on His Word and allow it to fill the void that loneliness creates. Reach out to others, whether through a church community or a trusted friend and share your feelings. Sometimes, sharing can be the bridge to deeper connections both with God and others around you. Remember, God's love is vast, and His presence is real. He is the anchor for your soul, always there to comfort and guide you through the storms of life.

The Lord is close to the brokenhearted and saves those
who are crushed in spirit.
Psalm 34:18

WHEN LIFE'S NOT FAIR

Life often seems unfair. We witness the prosperity of those who disregard God's ways while those who strive to live righteously face hardship. It can be easy to feel disheartened, as if justice has taken a back seat. This age-old struggle is evident in Psalm 73, where Asaph grapples with the wicked's apparent success and his own envy. However, the psalm doesn't end with despair. Instead, it provides a profound insight into God's eternal perspective. In verses 16-17, the psalmist resolves his inner turmoil by entering God's sanctuary and gaining understanding. He realizes that while the wicked may flourish temporarily, their ultimate fate is far from desirable. This revelation shifts his focus from temporary, earthly circumstances to eternal truths. The key takeaway here is the importance of maintaining an eternal perspective. Our immediate experiences do not define God's justice or fairness. Instead, we are encouraged to trust His ultimate plan and justice, even when life feels unjust. In verse 26, the psalmist acknowledges, "My flesh and my heart may fail, but God is the strength of my heart and my portion forever ."When faced with life's inequities, how can you shift your focus from the unfairness around you to the eternal promises of God? Consider how this perspective might bring peace and strength amid adversity.

For I envied the arrogant when I saw the prosperity of the wicked.
Psalm 73:3

KEEPING A LOW PROFILE

Keeping a low profile can feel counter-cultural in a world that often glorifies attention and recognition. Yet, Jesus encourages us to live in humility, focusing on the substance of our actions rather than their visibility. When we perform acts of Christian love and service, it is tempting to seek validation from others. The accolade, the applause, or even a nod of approval can affirm our efforts, making us feel valued. However, the accurate measure of our actions lies not in human validation but in the quiet acknowledgment of our Father in heaven. Jesus reminds us that genuine acts of faith are often unseen and uncelebrated by the world. They are the moments when we serve, give, and love without an audience, trusting that God sees and treasures our sincerity. The challenge is to evaluate our motives. Are we acting from a heart of service and devotion, or does the lure of public admiration sway us? By keeping a low profile, we align our hearts with a higher purpose, finding joy in serving God rather than seeking the fleeting praise of people. Reflect on your daily actions and consider how to shift your focus from public recognition to private faithfulness. In what areas of your life can you practice humility and serve quietly, knowing that your reward is with God?

Be careful not to practice your righteousness in front of others to be seen by them. If you do, you will have no reward from your Father in heaven.
Matthew 6:1

I DON'T GET IT

Visiting a VA hospital is a most humbling experience. May God bless the men and women that have fought for our country. As I sat in the waiting room, I saw two women sit down. Young and attractive, one was downing a drink topped with a mountain of whipped cream. A designer purse sat at her feet like an obedient pet. The other, about the same age, gripped a metal walker as she moved to her seat. Thick plastic braces guarded her ankles. The nurse at the desk had to help her maneuver into her seat. As I looked at the two women, I wondered Why God seemed to allow some to suffer more than others. When Job lost his children, money, and health, his friends tried to explain why they thought it had occurred. They supposed it was payback for sin, but God said Job was "the finest man in all the earth" (Job 1:8).

Sin isn't always the source of suffering, yet when we're desperate for answers, we look for them everywhere. We ask questions such as Why? And, Is it God's will for me to suffer? Job fell into this trap when he demanded: "What have I done wrong?. . Why do you turn away from me? Why do you treat me as your enemy?" (Job 13:23-24) Ultimately, Job's questions were answered. Why do you think God allows some to suffer more than others?

Why do you turn away from me?
Job 13:24

ROAD RAGE

Millions take to the roads daily, each person with their own destination and deadlines. But what happens when the drive is smoother than we hoped? The frustration of being cut off or stuck in traffic can quickly ignite what's commonly known as road rage. Ecclesiastes 7:9 reminds us that anger can easily take residence within us if we allow it. This is particularly true when we're behind the wheel, where stress levels can rise quickly, and patience can wear thin. However, as Christians, we are called to a different standard of peace and self-control. Consider how Jesus handled anger in His time. Whether He faced doubters, accusers, or betrayers, He maintained His composure, addressing situations with calmness and wisdom. We are encouraged to emulate this behavior and allow it to direct our paths, even on the road. Next time you're driving, and someone cuts in front of you or roadworks delay you, take a deep breath and remember this Scripture. Use the moment to reflect on the peace Christ brings, even amidst chaos. Instead of reacting with anger, choose to respond with patience. In doing so, you'll find more peace in your journeys and inspire other drivers to do the same. May your travels reflect the serenity of a spirit anchored in Christ.

Do not be quickly provoked in your spirit, for anger resides
in the lap of fools.
Ecclesiastes 7:9

May 6

NO PROBLEM IS TOO BIG

Life is filled with challenges that can sometimes feel overwhelming. It's easy to wonder if our problems are too big or if we are too small to overcome them. However, the Bible reminds us that no problem is beyond God's ability to manage. In Jeremiah 29:11, God speaks directly to the Israelites who were facing exile—one of the biggest trials of their lives. Despite their grim circumstances, God assured them of His sovereign plan. He had not forgotten them, nor had He abandoned them. Instead, He had a purpose that promised hope and a future. We often encounter situations where we feel lost or helpless—maybe a daunting decision at work, a strained relationship, or a health issue looming over us. During these times, we must remember that God's wisdom surpasses ours. He sees the beginning and the end of every problem we face. God's promise in Jeremiah is not just for the Israelites; it extends to us today. We are invited to trust that He is working all things together for our good. When we anchor our faith in His promises, our perspective shifts. Our problems may not vanish overnight, but our burdens become lighter as we lean on His strength. Reflect on this truth as you move through your day. No matter how intimidating the problem is, no challenge is too large with God.

For I know the plans I have for you, declares the Lord, plans to prosper you and not to harm you, plans to give you hope and a future.
Jeremiah 29:11

OPEN UP TO YOUR FRIENDS

Our community is a vital aspect that significantly enhances our personal and spiritual growth. God designed us to live in fellowship with others, and one of the profound ways we experience this is through opening up to our friends. Sharing our struggles, joys, and vulnerabilities isn't just about laying bare our burdens; it's about connecting deeply with those around us and inviting them into our life's narrative. James 5:16 encourages us to confess our sins to each other, highlighting a crucial element of Christian friendship—transparency. Confession isn't about dwelling on our shortcomings but acknowledging them in a safe space where judgment is absent and love prevails. It is through such openness that healing begins. When we allow others to see us as we are, we empower them to intercede. Opening up isn't a one-way street. It builds trust and invites others to reciprocate. This transparency fosters an environment where faith can flourish, as each person is encouraged to count on the community for support. In being vulnerable, we become conduits of God's grace. Opening up to your friends invites God to work in and through your relationships.

Therefore, confess your sins to each other and pray for each other so that you may be healed. The prayer of a righteous person is powerful and effective.
James 5:16

SOME PEOPLE ARE SO HAPPY

Happiness sometimes seems elusive—often fleeting and hard to grasp in a world of challenges. Yet, we all know individuals who radiate joy regardless of their circumstances. What makes them different, and how can we cultivate that same joyful spirit? Proverbs 17:22 tells us that a cheerful heart acts as good medicine, implying that happiness is healing. Happiness isn't just an emotion; it's a choice and a heart reflection. Those who seem perpetually joyful have often learned to lean on their faith and trust in God's promises. Consider the Apostle Paul, who, while imprisoned, wrote letters filled with hope. His happiness wasn't dependent on his situation but deeply rooted in his relationship with Christ. It's a reminder that true happiness transcends earthly trials. To live with a cheerful heart, start each day by focusing on gratitude. What are you thankful for today? Make a habit of counting your blessings rather than your burdens. Remember, the joy of the Lord is your strength (Nehemiah 8:10). When we anchor our happiness in God's unwavering presence and love, we discover a joy that external circumstances cannot shake. Reflect on people in your life who exemplify this joyous spirit. Consider what you can learn from their outlook and how you might apply it.

A cheerful heart is good medicine, but a crushed spirit dries up the bones.
Proverbs 17:22

DISCIPLINING CHILDREN

Discipline, in a biblical context, is more than mere correction; it is an act of love and teaching. The Bible emphasizes the importance of disciplining children to guide them toward righteousness and wisdom. Proverbs 22:6 states, "Start children off on the way they should go, and even when they are old, they will not turn from it." Instilling discipline provides a foundation that supports a lifetime of peace and joy. However, discipline must be rooted in love and understanding, reflecting the nature of God's discipline towards us. Hebrews 12:11 reminds us, "No discipline seems pleasant at the time, but painful. Later on, however, it produces a harvest of righteousness and peace for those trained by it." This Scripture encourages us to view discipline as a necessary process that yields fruitful outcomes. It is crucial to balance correction with encouragement. Ephesians 6:4) advises, "Fathers, do not exasperate your children; instead, bring them up in the training and instruction of the Lord." We learn that discipline should not provoke or frustrate but build up and nurture. We must seek wisdom and patience in our approach. Reflect on how God disciplines with compassion. You can cultivate a household filled with peace and delight through consistent and loving discipline, honoring God in the process.

Discipline your children, and they will give you peace and bring you the delights you desire.
Proverbs 29:17

QUITE TIME

Finding moments of stillness can feel like a rare luxury. Yet, Scripture calls us to "be still" and recognize God's presence. Quiet time is a pause in activity and a sacred opportunity to connect deeply with Him. This verse from Psalms reminds us that stillness is a spiritual discipline, not an absence of action. It's about intentionally creating space in our day to focus on God's voice above all others. In these quiet moments, we allow our souls to rest and rejuvenate, realigning our thoughts and priorities with His will. Quiet time varies from person to person. For some, it involves reading Scripture and meditating on its meaning. For others, it might be journaling reflections or simply sitting silently, sensing God's presence. Regardless of how it's practiced, the goal remains to deepen our relationship with God and gain clarity and peace. Consider setting aside a specific time each day for this practice. It could be in the morning before the rush of the day begins or in the evening as a way to unwind. Protect this time fiercely, and approach it with an open heart and mind. In the stillness, we affirm that God is sovereign and exalted above all circumstances. We acknowledge His power and love, allowing them to transform our hearts and lives.

Be still, and know that I am God; I will be exalted among the nations; I will be exalted in the earth.
Psalm 46:10

PEOPLE ARE LISTENING

We often need to remember the power our words hold. The Bible constantly reminds us of the impact our speech can have on those around us. Words can inspire, heal, or hurt deeply. As followers of Christ, we are called to use our words wisely and graciously, acknowledging our influence over others. In James 1:19, we are instructed to be "quick to listen, slow to speak, and slow to become angry." This simple yet profound advice encourages us to pause before speaking. By first listening, we demonstrate respect and empathy, paving the way for meaningful conversations that can strengthen our relationships and witness. Think about the last conversation you had. Did you listen actively, or were you more focused on what you wanted to say next? When we truly listen, we give others our attention and create a space where they feel valued and heard. This approach not only aligns with the teachings of Christ but can also lead others to open their hearts to His message. Reflect on how you can embody this Scripture in your interactions today. How can you encourage and uplift those who listen to you? Choose your words with care and listen with intention. Remember, people listen to you. Make sure what they hear brings them hope and light.

Everyone should be quick to listen, slow to speak,
and slow to become angry.
James 1:19

ARE YOU CONTENT?

The story is about a king looking for satisfaction in life. His advisors told him to wear the shirt of a contented man for a day, and he would be cured of his discontent. His men searched the kingdom to find a contented man so they could bring his shirt to the king, but they returned empty-handed. The king was furious. In response, his men told the king, We found a contented man, but he does not own a shirt. We live in a world grasping for contentment. A pastor friend said contentment is not having all that you want. True contentment is wanting only what you have. The apostle Paul was a contented man, but it didn't come naturally to him. Paul said he had to learn to be content. Contentment is an intentional choice. There are two ways to get enough. One is to continue to accumulate more and more. The other is to desire less. Paul was in a Roman prison when he wrote, "I have learned how to be content . . . in every situation" (Philippians 4:11-12). His contentment didn't result from life's circumstances but from his commitment. Paul's secret to contentment was to find it "through Christ, who gives me strength" (Philippians 4:13).

I have learned how to be content with whatever I have. I know how to live on almost nothing or with everything.
Philippians 4:11-12

DO YOU HAVE A MENTOR?

Having a mentor can be invaluable. A mentor isn't just someone who guides you professionally; they're often a source of wisdom, encouragement, and spiritual growth. Reflecting on Proverbs 15:22, it becomes clear how important it is to seek counsel. This Scripture emphasizes the significance of having advisers in our lives to achieve success and avoid the pitfalls of navigating life's challenges alone. Jesus Himself modeled the mentorship relationship. Before His ascension, He invested time in His disciples, preparing them for the work ahead. Similarly, having a mentor allows us to learn from someone else's experiences, mistakes, and triumphs. They can help us see God's plan in our lives more clearly and guide us spiritually. Consider seeking someone who embodies the faith and qualities you aspire to develop. Your mentor doesn't have to be an expert in all areas but should be someone whose life reflects the love and wisdom of Christ. This relationship can be a powerful tool for growth, not just in knowledge but in character and faith. Reflect on your current circle of influence. Is there someone who encourages you to grow closer to God, challenges you to think deeply, and provides sound advice? If not, it's time to seek out that mentorship relationship.

Plans fail for lack of counsel, but with many advisers they succeed.
Proverbs 15:22

PLAYING YOUR PART

In a world that often celebrates individual accomplishments, it can be easy to forget the power of community. Yet, as Christians, we are reminded that we are part of a greater whole—the body of Christ. Each of us has unique gifts and roles to play, contributing to the larger mission of spreading love and faith. Consider the human body, where every organ and limb has a specific purpose. The heart pumps blood, the lungs breathe, and the brain processes information. Each part is essential; without one, the body wouldn't function as it should. Similarly, every believer has a distinct role within the church and the broader Christian community. Some are called to teach, others to serve, and some to lead. No role is more important than the other; each is necessary to complete the whole. Are there ways you can use them more effectively within your community? Remember, playing your part is not just about fulfilling a duty; it's about enriching the community's spiritual life as a whole. We contribute to something more significant than ourselves by stepping into our God-given roles. Take time today to consider how you can play your part in the body of Christ.

For just as each of us has one body with many members, and these members do not all have the same function, so in Christ we, though many, form one body, and each member belongs to all the others.
Romans 12:4-5

GOD KNOWS EVERYTHING

Technology seems to know more about us than we do, so it's comforting to remember that God's knowledge surpasses all. Psalm 139 portrays a divine narrative of God's omniscience — the idea that He knows everything about us, even before we speak or act. Consider this truth for a moment. Before we utter a word, God knows its form and intent. He understands our thoughts from afar, sees our actions before they unfold, and is intimately aware of every detail of our lives. This understanding is factual and profound, rooted in His love and care for us. Such knowledge should give us peace, which means we're never alone in our struggles or joys. Every concern we harbor, every triumph we celebrate, is known and cherished by Him. This also encourages us to live authentically, knowing that God sees beyond our facades and into the depths of our hearts. Reflect on your life today in light of God's perfect knowledge. Are there areas where you doubt His understanding or presence? Remember, He is fully aware of your needs and desires. You are known and loved by a God who comprehends every facet of your being. How does knowing that God understands every aspect of your life change how you approach challenges? Take a moment to ponder this question as you go about your day, trusting in His wisdom and insight.

Before a word is on my tongue, you, Lord, know it completely.
Psalm 139:4

A GLIMPSE OF JESUS

It can be easy to lose sight of what truly matters. We get caught up in our routines, responsibilities, and the world's noise. Yet, amidst all of this, Jesus invites us to pause and catch a glimpse of His presence in our lives. John 1:14 reminds us of the profound mystery and beauty of the Incarnation—the Word becoming flesh. It reminds us that Jesus isn't just a distant figure in history; He is God with us, living among us and revealing the Father's heart through every act of grace and truth. When we look at Jesus, we see the fullness of God's love. He embodies patience with the impatient, kindness to the unkind, and forgiveness to the unforgivable. In each encounter and every Word, Jesus reflects the glory of the Father—a glory marked by compassion, mercy, and justice. Today, take a moment to open your heart and allow yourself to see Jesus in your everyday experiences. Look for Him in the kindness of a stranger, in the beauty of creation, and even in moments of struggle. By seeking Him earnestly, we can catch glimpses of His divine nature and be transformed by His presence. May our eyes be opened to see Jesus more clearly and our hearts be willing to follow where He leads—full of grace and truth.

The Word became flesh and made his dwelling among us. We have seen his glory, the glory of the one and only Son, who came from the Father, full of grace and truth.
John 1:14

PRAYING FOR A MIRACLE

When all efforts seem futile in times of deep need, we often find ourselves fervently seeking a miracle. The Bible assures us that miracles are possible through faith and prayer. Mark 11:24 reminds us of the power of asking and believing. It encourages us to approach God with a heart full of faith, trusting that our prayers are heard. Consider the story of the woman with the issue of blood in the Gospel of Mark. After suffering for twelve years, she approached Jesus with the belief that touching His cloak would heal her. Her faith was acknowledged, and she was made whole. This narrative exemplifies the profound connection between faith, action, and divine intervention. Miracles are not merely acts of divine favor but are often responses to unwavering faith. They challenge us to transcend our doubts and align our desires with God's purpose. When praying for a miracle, reflect on the nature of your request and the strength of your belief. Are you prepared for the transformation that the miracle may bring? True faith involves openness to God's will, which may manifest differently than our expectations. Remember, miracles require us to hold on to hope and trust God's plan, even when the outcome is uncertain. With faith as your anchor, continue to seek divine intervention; God's power is limitless.

Therefore, I tell you, whatever you ask for in prayer, believe that you have received it, and it will be yours.
Mark 11:24

THE SECRET CODE

There is a secret code that is permeating our society, and it is terrific.
After the removal of the Ten Commandments, taking prayer out of our
schools, blacklisting the historical value of the Bible, and changing
Merry Christmas to Happy Holidays, we may be feeling, I am done.
Many of us are fed up with our faith being stripped out of public life.
America was formed by Christianity, and it will always be the
foundation of all we do. The secret code being spoken between
Christians is having a blessed day. You will realize that only some who
say it understand the true meaning; however, we do. Go into a store, and
often with a slight smile, an employee will say, have a blessed day. We
live in a country that prohibits Christianity, so we have to sneak around
to share our faith with others. Some dislike this saying so much that
they are going to a great extent to have it banned in businesses today.
When you say Have a blessed day, it's more than just a farewell—it's a
reminder to recognize God's presence in our daily lives. This simple
phrase encourages us and others to find joy in His blessings, to be
grateful for His grace, and to spread kindness and love wherever we go.

*I will also acknowledge whoever acknowledges me before others before
my Father in heaven. But whoever disowns me before others, I will
disown before my Father in heaven.*
Matthew 10:32-33

SAY IT LIKE IT IS

In our daily interactions, the phrase says it like it often carries a bold, no-nonsense connotation. For Christians, however, this directive takes on a deeper, more nuanced meaning. Ephesians 4:15 reminds us that truth must be coupled with love. It is not merely about being blunt or unfiltered but about communicating truth in a way that enlightens and uplifts. Truth spoken without love can wound and divide, while love without truth can mislead and enable. The balance of the two facilitates growth into Christ's likeness. This harmony allows us to encourage one another authentically and with grace. Consider your own conversations —does this balance mark them? When you communicate honestly with others, ensure that your words are rooted in love and aimed at building one another up. This approach aligns with Christ's teachings and fosters a community that thrives on mutual respect and understanding. Speaking truth in love is a powerful testament to our faith. It reflects the heart of Jesus, who was both truth and love personified. By embodying this principle, we fulfill our calling to be ambassadors of Christ, promoting unity and maturity in the body of believers. Today, as you engage with others, remember to say it like it is—with love.

Instead, speaking the truth in love, we will grow to become in every respect the mature body of him who is the head, that is, Christ.
Ephesians 4:15

DO YOU EVER HAVE DOUBTS?

It's natural to experience moments of doubt. Peter, one of Jesus' most devoted followers, faced his doubts one stormy night on the Sea of Galilee. When Jesus walked on water and called Peter to join Him, Peter initially stepped out in faith, demonstrating his trust in Jesus. However, as the wind howled and the waves roared, Peter's focus shifted from the Savior to the storm. Doubt crept in, and he began to sink. This passage reminds us that doubt often arises when we divert our attention from Christ and fixate on our circumstances. Life's challenges can be overwhelming, but Jesus reminds us that He is always near, ready to extend His hand to steady us. Our faith doesn't need to be perfect; it simply needs to turn us back to Him. When doubts assail us, we can find comfort knowing that even the early disciples struggled with them. It's essential to remember that doubts do not disqualify us from God's love or His plans for our lives. Instead, they can become growth opportunities, drawing us closer to Him. Consider how you can refocus your gaze from the storms to the Savior. In the moments when doubt feels overwhelming, hear Jesus' gentle reminder, "Why did you doubt?" Jesus's unwavering love and promise of peace remain constant.

Immediately, Jesus reached out his hand and caught him. You of little faith, he said, why did you doubt?
Matthew 14:31

ARE YOU TOLERANT

Tolerance is a virtue that can be challenging to practice, especially regarding matters of faith. In the Christian context, Romans 14 encourages us to accept fellow believers with different convictions. The Scripture doesn't ask us to compromise our beliefs but rather to refrain from passing judgment on others for theirs. Today's world is filled with diverse perspectives; sometimes, differences can lead to division within the church. It reminds us that everyone stands accountable not to each other but to God. Our role is not to judge but to support and love one another. Are you finding it difficult to accept a fellow believer's choices? Remember that tolerance involves understanding and grace. We are called to live harmoniously, respecting each other's journeys and trusting that God works in ways beyond our comprehension. Practicing tolerance, we reflect Christ's love and promote an environment where faith can flourish.

One person's faith allows them to eat anything, but another, whose faith is weak, eats only vegetables. The one who eats everything must not be treated with contempt by the one who does not, and the one who does not eat everything must not judge the one who does, for God has accepted them. Who are you to judge someone else's servant? To their own master, servants stand or fall. And they will stand, for the Lord can make them stand.
Romans 14:1-4

CARING FOR YOUR FAMILY

Family forms the bedrock of our earthly relationships, and we are called to nurture and care for these bonds deeply. Ephesians 6:1-4 provides foundational guidance on maintaining harmony within the family unit by highlighting mutual respect and godly upbringing as critical elements. In the hustle and bustle of everyday life, it's easy to neglect the needs of those closest to us. Yet, the Scripture reminds us that family deserves our time, patience, and dedication. Children are encouraged to honor their parents, not just in obedience, but in recognizing their efforts and sacrifices. This is the first commandment with an attached promise of well-being and longevity. Equally, parents, particularly fathers, are urged to nurture their children according to God's teachings. This means going beyond mere discipline to engage in loving instruction that is both meaningful and encouraging rather than frustrating or overbearing. By doing so, we plant seeds of faith. This Scripture challenges us to evaluate how we interact daily with family members.

Children, obey your parents in the Lord, for this is right. Honor your Father and Mother—the first commandment with a promise—so that it may go well with you and you may enjoy a long life on the earth. Fathers, do not exasperate your children; instead, bring them up in the training and instruction of the Lord.
Ephesians 6:1-4

GETTING EVEN

In our daily lives, we often encounter situations where our immediate reaction is to get even. Whether it's a coworker who takes credit for your ideas, a friend who gossips behind your back, or a stranger who cuts you off in traffic, the urge to repay the hurt can be compelling. Yet, we are called to a higher standard. The Apostle Paul, in his letter to the Romans, provides a counter-cultural approach to dealing with wrongs. Instead of seeking revenge, we are encouraged to "live at peace with everyone." This isn't about letting others walk over us but trusting God to handle justice. It's an invitation to rise above the cycle of retaliation and entrust our hurts to God, who promises to act on our behalf. Choosing not to get even doesn't mean we ignore injustice; it means we decide not to be consumed by it. Practicing forgiveness and understanding reflects the heart of Christ. Living according to these principles transforms our relationships and personal well-being. By letting go of the desire for revenge, we make space for healing, reconciliation, and peace that surpasses all understanding.

Do not repay anyone evil for evil. Be careful to do what is right in the eyes of everyone. As it depends on you, live at peace with everyone. Do not take revenge, my dear friends, but leave room for God's wrath, for it is written: It is mine to avenge; I will repay, says the Lord.
Romans 12:17-19

USING SOCIAL MEDIA

In today's digital age, social media has become integral to our lives, shaping how we communicate, share, and connect. For Christians, navigating this vast online landscape can sometimes be challenging. The Bible reminds us in Romans 12:2 not to conform to the world's patterns but to renew our minds continually. This is a powerful call to action for engaging with social media. Social media offers opportunities to spread positivity, share God's Word, and connect with others who share similar values. However, it also presents challenges, such as comparison, negativity, and distraction from our spiritual walk. By being intentional about our use of social media, we can ensure it aligns with our faith. Consider setting boundaries around your social media use that help you stay focused on what truly matters. Follow accounts that uplift your spirit and challenge you to grow in your faith. Be mindful of the content you consume and share, ensuring it reflects the love and grace of Christ. Remember that your identity is in Christ, not in likes or followers. Use social media as a tool to glorify Him and enrich your spiritual life, not as a replacement for real-life connections or spiritual disciplines.

Do not conform to the pattern of this world, but be transformed by renewing your mind. Then, you can test and approve God's will—his good, pleasing, and perfect will.
Romans 12:2

COUNTING ON HIS WORD

In the hustle and bustle of daily life, we often find ourselves seeking guidance and assurance. For Christians, the ultimate source of truth and direction is the Word of God. The Bible is not just an ancient text—it's a living document that speaks into our lives today, offering wisdom, comfort, and truth. The verse from 2 Timothy reminds us of the divine inspiration of Scripture. Every Word is "God-breathed," infused with His wisdom and authority. This makes the Bible a reliable foundation for our beliefs and actions. It is a tool for teaching what is true, helping us realize what is wrong in our lives, and guiding us onto the right path. When you turn to the Bible, you're tapping into a well of divine wisdom that has stood the test of time. In moments of uncertainty, it can be your compass, pointing you toward righteousness. It can reaffirm your faith and strengthen your resolve in times of doubt. Allow Scripture to be the lens through which you view the world. Engage with it daily, meditate on its teachings, and apply its principles. By doing so, you'll find that you can count on God's Word to guide you, correct you, and train you in righteousness. Trust in His Word, for it is steadfast and accurate, no matter your challenges.

All Scripture is God-breathed and is useful for teaching, rebuking, correcting, and training in righteousness.
2 Timothy 3:16

THAT'S JUST PERFECT

Suppose someone rudely swoops into that prime parking spot just ahead of you. You want to scream and throw things, but instead, you stop and say, Well, that's just perfect! Now I can get more exercise by walking farther. Such an approach can often help us stop whining about trivialities; however, some situations are far from perfect. Trying to be positive is not only tricky, but it is sometimes impossible. In a sense, the entire Bible is devoted to everything being imperfect on this earth. It's not supposed to be. Whole sections of Scripture tell of unspeakable deeds: murder, rape, cannibalism, betrayal and genocide. Earth's painful experiences are well documented. When we trust Jesus, we believe the one who put all of this in motion. He came to walk among us, offer the perfect sacrifice for our damage, and continue to inflict on His creation. He will restore everything to its proper order. Find strength in God's love and guidance when facing adversity. Jesus teaches compassion and forgiveness, empowering us to respond with grace rather than anger. Reflect on His example.

He made peace with everything in heaven and on earth by means of
Christ's blood on the cross.
Colossians 1:20

IF THERE IS NO TOMORROW

We often find ourselves engulfed in the daily grind, planning, and worrying about what tomorrow may bring. However, the Bible provides a liberating perspective—focus on today. Jesus' teaching encourages us to live in the present, trusting God with our future. Consider this thought-provoking question: What if there is no tomorrow? How would that change how you live today? The truth is tomorrow is never guaranteed; it is a gift. By living as if there is no tomorrow, we are encouraged to make the most of each moment, nurture relationships, and pursue our God-given purpose without delay. In Matthew 6, Jesus addresses the anxiety and stress of worrying about the future. He reminds us to trust in God's provision and sovereignty. This doesn't mean neglecting planning but surrendering control and placing our faith in His hands. Make today count by prioritizing what truly matters. Reach out to loved ones, express gratitude, and invest in your spiritual growth. By living with an eternal perspective, we can experience peace and fulfillment, knowing we are aligned with God's will. Reflect on shifting your focus from what if to what is. Doing so allows God's presence to guide your steps, providing peace in the moment.

Therefore, do not worry about tomorrow; tomorrow will worry about itself. Each day has enough trouble of its own.
Matthew 6:34

May 28

DO YOU LOVE CHILDREN?

Children hold a special place in Jesus' heart. The emphasis on their importance is evident throughout the Bible, with passages like Matthew 19:14 reminding us that they are integral to the kingdom of heaven. But what does this mean for us as Christians today? Loving children means valuing their innocence and openness. In a world often filled with cynicism and complexity, the purity of a child's faith is a beacon of hope and a reminder of the simplicity of Christ's love. Children approach the world with wide-eyed wonder, trusting those they love and eager to learn. Their faith is untainted by doubt or skepticism. By nurturing and guiding children in the ways of the Lord, we fulfill a divine responsibility. Teaching them about God's love and promises ensures that their faith's foundation is strong. Proverbs 22:6 says, "Start children off on the way they should go, and even when they are old, they will not turn from it." Loving children is about safeguarding their well-being, both spiritually and physically. We must stand as protectors, advocates, and role models, ensuring they grow up in environments that reflect God's love. We participate in God's grand design for humanity when we love children.

Jesus said, Let the little children come to me, and do not hinder them,
for the kingdom of heaven belongs to such as these.
Matthew 19:14

FEEDING THE HUNGRY

The United Nations Food and Agriculture Committee reports that 1.02 billion people (15 percent of the world population) went to bed hungry last night. Every day, 18,000 children under the age of 5 die from hunger-related causes in our world. This is the time of year when we begin to think about children getting out of school. Most of us will have food on the table tonight and in the morning. We seldom buy food for just one day, relying instead on quantities of stored provisions to make our next meal something we don't have to worry about. We only begin to worry about our next meal in times of economic downturn and job losses. Can you imagine being a parent trying to put a child to bed while they cry because they are hungry? As a loving Father, Jesus knows what children need; no request is too minute for Him to receive. He has equipped people like you and me with the resources, time, money, and desire to make sure His children don't go hungry. Hunger is a physical state and a spiritual call to act with compassion and generosity. As Christians, we are called to be the hands and feet of Christ, providing nourishment and hope to those in need.

Give us today the food we need.
Matthew 6:11

JESUS IS A ROCK

In our uncertain world, where change is often the only constant, it is comforting to know that we have a steadfast foundation to build our lives. The Bible repeatedly uses the metaphor of a rock to describe God's unchanging, reliable nature. Consider for a moment what a rock symbolizes. It is solid, unyielding, and enduring. It withstands the tests of time and the harshest elements. Similarly, God's presence in our lives provides us with a firm foundation. When everything else seems to shift around us, He remains our immovable Rock. When you face life's challenges, remember that God is your fortress. He is your shelter from the storms that come your way. In times of trouble, seek refuge in Him. He is your deliverer, ready to rescue you when the world's weight becomes too much to bear. Take a moment to reflect on the times God has been your Rock. Consider how He has provided stability and strength when you need it most. Trust in His unchanging nature and lean on Him to guide you through life's peaks and valleys. With God as your Rock, you can stand firm, regardless of what life throws your way.

The Lord is my Rock, my fortress and my deliverer; my God is my Rock, in whom I take refuge, my shield and the horn of my salvation. He is my stronghold, my refuge and my Savior—from violent people you save me.
2 Samuel 22:2-3

WHAT ARE FRIENDS FOR?

A few weeks after he left a high-profile job in a small town, people who had been his friends were now avoiding him as if he was contagious. It was as if the people he thought were his friends knew something terrible about him that he didn't know about himself. He had done nothing wrong, nor was he accused of doing anything wrong, but he just watched and heard his name paraded through the local rumor mills. We tend to condemn Job's friends for their incorrect representation of God and Job's situation. Indeed, they got things woefully wrong, but at least they came! Not only did they show up, but they wept with their friend just as we were instructed to do. Later, knowing they couldn't fix the situation, they merely sat with Job instead of talking or walking away. Before we condemn the poor comforters of Job, let's reflect on this: God sent the men to Job, and they were initially a comfort to him. He knew that they had wanted to help but went about it in the wrong way.

They sat on the ground with him for seven days and seven nights. No one said a word to Job, for they saw that his suffering was too great for words.
Job 2:13

June 1

DO YOU LOVE YOUR CHURCH?

Churches are different. Some have dramatically different service structures than yours. Each reveals the various facets of God's character. We must not confine God to one style of worship, as He created us with diverse personalities. There's a unity of Spirit in congregations, and if the Spirit is present in all, who's to say which is better?

John the Baptist and John the Apostle used contrasting words to appeal to different audiences. John the Baptist was straightforward and utilized strong terms in addressing the Pharisees. The apostle John exemplified the warmth of a doting father for his kids as he called his readers "my dear children" and "dear friends." (1 John 2:1,7) The Holy Spirit used both men to communicate God's heart and message. So, it's not surprising that churches practice a wide range of worship styles. Just because we love a particular style, it doesn't mean that other methods are wrong. We serve a God who gives us serene sunrises and occasional hurricanes. He provides the evening dew and the fury of a thunderstorm. He can't be defined, contained, limited, or constrained. The worship style blends into the background when it points to Jesus.

My dear children, I am writing this to you so that you will not sin.
1 John 2:1

June 2

FINISHING THE RACE

In our Christian walk, the concept of finishing strong is central. The Apostle Paul's words to Timothy resonate deeply when he speaks of fighting the good fight and finishing the race. It serves as a vivid reminder that our spiritual journey is not simply about how we start but how we persevere and complete the path God has set. The challenges we face in life can sometimes feel overwhelming. There are moments when the race appears too long and the hurdles too high. However, it is precisely in these moments that our faith is tested and strengthened. By holding fast to our faith, trusting in God's promises, and leaning on His strength, we find that we can overcome any obstacle. Finishing strong requires commitment, resilience, and a deep reliance on God's guidance. It means staying true to our beliefs even when the world offers more accessible paths. It involves continual growth in our relationship with Christ and an unwavering dedication to serving His purpose. Reflect on your race. Are there areas where you need to refocus and renew your commitment? Remember that God equips you with everything you need to finish strong. Seek His wisdom, draw on His strength, and know that He walks with you every step of the way. Keep pressing on. It is not just about finishing the race but finishing it strong.

I have fought the good fight, I have finished the race,
I have kept the faith.
2 Timothy 4:7

June 3

TRUSTING

Confusion is a common human experience. It's that unsettling feeling when circumstances are not aligned with our expectations or when choices seem overwhelming. Yet, as followers of Christ, we are invited to seek clarity in His Word and presence. Paul's letter to the Philippians offers a powerful reminder of how to handle confusion. When surrounded by uncertainty, we are encouraged not to be consumed by anxiety. Instead, we should bring our concerns to God with a heart full of gratitude. It's easy to forget that, even amidst confusion, there is always something to be thankful for. The promise attached to this practice is profound. By laying our confusion at God's feet, we open ourselves to His peace. This peace doesn't always provide the immediate answers we seek but offers reassurance in the waiting. Regularly setting aside time to reflect on the Word, listening for God's voice in silence, and maintaining an attitude of thankfulness. Remember, the goal isn't to avoid confusion and find peace and clarity. Trust that God holds your life in His hands.

Do not be anxious about anything, but in every situation, by prayer and petition, with thanksgiving, present your requests to God. And the peace of God, which transcends all understanding, will guard your hearts and minds in Christ Jesus.
Philippians 4:6-7

June 4

WHEN YOU ARE ANGRY

Anger is a natural emotion that we all experience. It signals that something is wrong; something isn't right with us. However, how we respond to anger can lead us closer to or further away from our faith. Ephesians 4 teaches us not to sin in our anger. This implies that feeling anger isn't wrong—but allowing it to lead us into harmful actions or words can be. Holding onto anger gives the devil a foothold, creating space for grudges, bitterness, and division. Instead of resolving conflicts, prolonged anger can build walls between us and those we care about. Paul's advice to not let the sun go down while we are still angry highlights the importance of resolving issues quickly. This doesn't mean every conflict will be instantly resolved, but it encourages us to seek peace actively and not allow anger to fester. To deal with anger effectively, consider the source of your frustration. Is it a result of unmet expectations, perceived injustice, or a misunderstanding? Reflecting on these can lead to healthier responses. Communicate openly with those involved, and remember that forgiveness is a powerful tool for mending broken relationships and restoring peace within your heart. In moments of anger, turn to Scripture to turn your anger into an opportunity for reconciliation.

In your anger, do not sin: Do not let the sun go down while you are still angry, and do not give the devil a foothold.
Ephesians 4:26-27

WHO DO YOU LOVE MOST?

We are often faced with decisions that reflect who or what we truly love. The world pulls us in many directions, each demanding time, devotion, and affection. However, Jesus reminds us of the importance of priorities. The greatest commandment calls us to love God with every fiber of our being—heart, soul, and mind. This love is not merely an emotion but a deliberate commitment to place Him above all else. It is a call to align our desires, choices, and actions with His will, ensuring He remains at the center of our lives. Following closely is the command to love our neighbors as ourselves. This requires us to extend grace, compassion, and understanding to those around us, reflecting the love that God has shown us. It challenges us to look beyond our preferences and comfort zones and act in ways that demonstrate genuine care and concern for others. Reflect on your daily life. Are there areas where you struggle to put God first? Do you find it difficult to love others as yourself? Take time to consider the influences that distract you from these commandments. Commit today to realign your heart. Ask God to help you show His love through your actions towards others.

Jesus replied: Love the Lord your God with all your heart and with all your soul and with all your mind. This is the first and greatest commandment. And the second is like it:
Love your neighbor as yourself.
Matthew 22:37-39

June 6

WHAT IS IMPORTANT?

The show is about people trading in their large homes for tiny houses. It is the rage now. In this episode, a lady downsized her 3-bedroom house and moved into a 384-square-foot tiny house. This transition liberated her from a monthly mortgage payment, and now she owns her own home and pays hardly anything each month in energy costs. Before moving in, she purged many of her most prized possessions. Old photos, love letters, and even her college letter jacket landed in the trash. She now allows herself no more than 300 belongings at once in her quest to continue living light. Her story may inspire you to consider how being attached to stuff can affect your spiritual life. Jesus met a rich man who wanted to know how to inherit eternal life. The man said he had obeyed God's commandments from childhood, but Jesus revealed a soft spot for this rule follower. "Jesus felt genuine love for him" (Mark 10:21). Despite the warmth of that moment, He delivered some hard truth: "There is still one thing you haven't done… Go and sell all your possessions and give the money to the poor, and you will have treasure in heaven. Then come, follow Me" (Mark 10:21). I wish this story had a fairytale ending, but it didn't. Jesus' challenge crushed the man. He would either choose Jesus or his stuff.

Go and sell all your possessions and give the money to people
experiencing poverty.
Mark 10:21

YOU ARE IN GOOD HANDS

There are no atheists in foxholes, as the old saying goes. Given that America's military is waging war with numerous terrorist groups, digging in for many situations throughout the world— it is an honor to be around the young men and women who have decided to make their life dream of serving our country. Visiting the United Air Force Academy in Colorado Springs should be on your bucket list. Four thousand, two hundred and thirty-seven of the brightest and most outstanding young people in the world are busy attending classes to prepare themselves to assume their role in the greatest military in the world. We should pray for these young warriors as these young men and women have many unique and pressing spiritual needs in their lives. They wrestle with an incredible mix of fear and worry, adrenaline spikes and emotional lows, physical hardship, and family problems. The Academy is an exquisite reflection of our nation. It should be no surprise that the military includes Christians of every denomination, Jews, Muslims, atheists, pagans, and, like the general population, a growing percentage of so-called nones. Pray for the confidence of these young people to find Jesus.

You will hear of wars and rumors of wars, but see that you are not alarmed. Such things must happen, but the end is still to come.
Matthew 24:6

June 8

A BIT FORGETFUL

Have you ever struggled to recall a Bible verse when you needed it most? In the hustle and bustle of daily life, it's easy to become forgetful. Sneakily, the worries of our world can push aside the spiritual truths we've held onto so dearly. This is where the beauty of the Holy Spirit shines through. Jesus promises us a Helper—the Holy Spirit—to guide, teach, and, importantly, remind us. It's not just about storing verses or sermons as fleeting memories but letting them become part of our heart's fabric through the Spirit's gentle whispers. The Holy Spirit's role is to illuminate our minds, especially when our understanding fails. When the Scripture seems distant or forgotten, the Spirit brings it back to life, revealing its truth and relevance. He is like a gentle tap on the shoulder, reminding us of God's comfort, guidance, and promises. Consider moments you've felt lost or unsure. How often did a verse, a hymn, or a biblical principle suddenly come to mind, bringing clarity or peace? That's the Spirit at work, doing what He does best—bringing to remembrance all that Jesus has taught. May we lean more upon the Spirit, trusting that even in our forgetfulness, He remains faithful.

But the Helper, the Holy Spirit, whom the Father will send in my name, he will teach you all things and bring to your remembrance all that I have said to you.
John 14:26

TO FORGIVE IS HARD

A fraternity on a college campus was caught on video singing a deeply offensive and racist song. Reaction by the university community was swift and stern. But what did Dr. Benjamin Hooks, the National President of the NAACP, who once attended the university, say from his office in Washington, D.C.? Stunningly, Dr. Hooks recommended that the offending students be forgiven. If you had seen the video or heard the appalling lyrics of the song, you likely understand just how radical his counsel was. When a news anchor pressed him as to why he didn't want retribution, Hooks replied, It is not smart to fight hate with hate. It is only logical to fight hate with love. In turn, those words point us directly to Jesus, of whom John said, "The light shines in the darkness, and the darkness can never extinguish it" (John 1:5). Throughout His ministry, Jesus taught His followers a radically peaceful set of principles. He lived it out to the end, confounding Pilate and embracing crucifixion when He could have defended Himself. When we experience hate, it's natural to hate in return. Jesus showed us the better, supernatural way—the way of His love. If someone has really hurt you? Jesus says, show them the love!

The light shines in the darkness, and the darkness can
never extinguish it.
John 1:5

IT NEVER GETS EASIER

Life is an endless series of challenges, each seeming as impossible as the last. In the face of adversity, the natural question is often: When will it get easier? But what if the answer lies not in the easing of our trials but in how we grow through them? James, in his letter to early Christians, offers a perspective that is both challenging and liberating. He suggests rejoicing in trials, for they serve a divine purpose. Our trials test our faith, and through this testing, perseverance is forged. This perseverance is not the end goal but a means to achieving spiritual maturity and completeness. Remember, it never gets more accessible because the purpose of these trials isn't to break us but to build us. Each challenge is an opportunity to deepen our faith and strengthen our reliance on God. The more we lean into Him, the more we understand that ease is not the goal; growth is. The real transformation happens not when life gets easier but when we become stronger through Christ. By viewing our challenges through this lens, we uncover a joy that transcends our circumstances, a joy rooted in the image of the One who faced the ultimate trial for us.

Consider it pure joy, my brothers and sisters, whenever you face trials of many kinds, because you know that the testing of your faith produces perseverance. Let perseverance finish its work so that you may be mature and complete, not lacking anything.
James 1:2-4

ANOTHER SLEEPLESS NIGHT?

Do you find yourself awake at night, burdened by worries and weighed down by life's uncertainties? Sleepless nights are not just a modern affliction; they have been a part of the human experience for centuries. Yet, the Bible offers timeless wisdom that speaks directly to this struggle. Psalm 4 reminds us of the peace and safety in God, a steadfast promise even in our most restless moments. The psalmist deeply trusts God's protection, allowing him to rest peacefully. This assurance comes from knowing that God is in control, watching over us through every trial and tribulation. When your mind races with concerns and your heart refuses to settle, remember that God invites you to cast all your anxieties on Him. He cares deeply for you and promises to be your refuge. Reflect on how you can experience God's peace in the quiet night hours. Consider what thoughts or concerns are keeping you from rest. Are they worried about the future or regrets about the past? Present them to God, who can transform your turmoil into tranquility. In the stillness, remind yourself that God's presence is with you, surrounding you with His comfort and love. Just as the psalmist lay down in peace, you, too, can find solace in the truth that God is your ultimate source of safety.

I will lie down and sleep in peace, for you alone, Lord, make me dwell in safety.
Psalm 4:8

June 12

WHY DID THAT HAPPEN?

In our walk with God, there are moments when we find ourselves puzzled by life's circumstances or the paths we're led to take. We all have times when we just don't get it. We question why certain things happen, why prayers seem unanswered, or why God's timing differs from ours. Isaiah 55 reminds us that God's perspective is infinitely greater than ours. It's easy to assume that our understanding of a situation should dictate how it unfolds. However, this Scripture encourages us to trust God's wisdom and sovereignty, even when we can't see the bigger picture. Consider the story of Joseph, who was sold into slavery by his brothers, imprisoned on false charges, and forgotten for years. Despite these trials, God was weaving a tapestry of redemption that would save many lives and elevate Joseph to a place of honor and leadership. At any point, Joseph might have said, I just don't get it. But through it all, he trusted God. Next time you're confused or uncertain, remember that God's ways are higher than yours. While you may not understand now, have faith that He will reveal His purpose in time, and it will be greater than anything you could imagine.

For my thoughts are not your thoughts, neither are your ways my ways, declares the Lord. As the heavens are higher than the earth, so are my ways higher than your ways and my thoughts than your thoughts.
Isaiah 55:8-9

June 13

YOUR WORD IS IMPORTANT

You have signed a few contracts in your life. You have probably also asked others to sign one as well. What we dislike most about contracts is their endless clauses, spelled out in complicated legal jargon. We've all known of opportunistic people with well-paid lawyers who find legal loopholes in most documents and cash in. So our contracts continue to get longer and longer. We signed contracts for one of our national men's conferences a few years ago. We received legal advice to have each speaker sign an agreement confirming their participation in the program. All of them did—except one. My Word is my promise, he emailed back, causing great consternation to some on our team. We, however, took him at his Word. Lee Corso kept his Word. A vow in Old Testament times was a promise made before God. The Pharisees, however, devised ingenious ways of slipping through the loopholes. For them, it all came down to the formula used when making your vow. A vow sworn by "the altar" wasn't binding, but one sworn by the gift on the altar was (Matthew 23:18-22). Jesus would have none of it. Whether you swear by the temple, the altar, heaven, or earth, it didn't matter since all of these were God's.

Just say a simple, Yes, I will, or No, I won't. Anything beyond this is
from the evil one.
Matthew 5:37

BELIEVING WHAT YOU SAY

The words we speak hold power not just over others but over ourselves. Proverbs 18:21 says, "The tongue has the power of life and death." This truth highlights the importance of aligning our words with our beliefs and believing in what we say. To truly embody this, we must first recognize that our declarations reflect what we hold in our hearts. It can be easy to fall into the habit of speaking without intention, but as believers, we are called to a higher standard of mindfulness. Are we expressing words that build up and give life, or do we find ourselves caught in negativity and doubt? Consider the story of Jesus calming the storm in Mark 4:39. With just a few words, He demonstrated unwavering faith and authority. "Quiet! Be still!" He commanded, and the winds and waves obeyed. This serves as a potent reminder that when our words are rooted in faith, they can bring peace and change the course of any situation. Reflect on your own life—are there areas where you need to align your speech with your faith? Begin by speaking words of hope, encouragement, and truth. Trust in the power of God's promises, and believe fully in the words you proclaim. Let's commit to being intentional with our language, ensuring that what we say aligns with the grace we've received through Christ.

Indeed, we have all received grace in place of grace already given.
John 1:16

June 15

YOUR GREATEST GIFT

I'm sure most of us remember the little bedtime prayer...Now I lay me down to sleep... And the dinner prayer...God is great, God is good; now we thank Him for our food. After a while, children just said them quickly and went to bed or began to eat. Sadly, for some adults, that is the depth of their prayer life. When we are in a crisis, we learn how to pray intensely. If we considered prayer engaging God, how intense would our prayer life be, how specific would our prayers be, and how often would we desire to be in prayer? One of the greatest gifts given to us is the gift of prayer. The Creator has provided a way for us to continue communion with Him. God desires to spend intimate, quality time with us. Have you ever stopped and thought how great that is? Think about a famous person you would love to hang out with...how would you feel if that person called and said, Hey, I want to spend as much time with you as possible. How would that make you feel? I am sure you would be elated and want to tell everyone! Well,...the Creator, God Almighty, the Lord Himself, wants to spend time with you—today!

And ye shall seek Me, and find Me, when ye shall search for Me with all your heart.
Jeremiah 29:13

June 16

HE'S GOT THIS!

It's easy to feel overwhelmed by the pressures and uncertainties surrounding us. We often question our decisions, worry about the future, and rely heavily on our understanding to solve problems. Yet, the Scripture from Proverbs 3 reminds us of a powerful truth that transcends our human limitations—God is in control. Trusting God requires a conscious decision to place our confidence in Him rather than our abilities. It means acknowledging that His wisdom surpasses ours and that, in His perfect timing, He will guide us through our challenges. This doesn't mean difficulties will disappear overnight, but it assures us that we are not alone in our struggles. God's plan for us is one of hope, and He promises to make our paths straight when we submit to His will. Reflect on your current situation and consider areas where you might rely too much on your strength. Are there burdens you're carrying that you need to release to God? He's got this. By yielding to Him, you're not giving up control; instead, you're entrusting your life to the One who knows you better than you know yourself. Allow His peace to fill your heart and guide your steps.

Trust in the Lord with all your heart and lean not on your understanding; in all your ways, submit to him, and he will make your paths straight.
Proverbs 3:5-6

WHAT JESUS WANTS MOST

It's easy to get lost in the demands of daily tasks. We often find ourselves prioritizing events that seem urgent but offer little lasting significance. Amidst this noise, what does Jesus truly desire from us? The passage from John 15 is a poignant reminder of Jesus' core message to his followers. He calls us to love one another as He loves us— selfless, sacrificial, and unconditional love. This command is a guideline and a direct reflection of Jesus' actions and character. Jesus' love is the epitome of commitment and sacrifice. He exemplified this love throughout His ministry, ultimately laying down His life for humanity. Through this act, He demonstrated that love is not merely a feeling but an action, a choice we make every day to put others before ourselves. By loving others as Jesus loves us, we fulfill His greatest desire. This form of love goes beyond mere acts of kindness; it's about genuinely caring for the well-being of others, advocating selflessness in our relationships, and fostering a community where compassion prevails. Reflect on your relationships and daily interactions. Are they guided by the love Jesus demonstrated? By choosing to love as Jesus commands, we align ourselves with His ultimate desire for our lives.

My command is this: Love each other as I have loved you. Greater love has no one than this: to lay down one's life for one's friends.
John 15:12-13

June 18

IF YOU HAVE TO ASK...

So often, we desire to live as close to the line of what is unacceptable to God as possible. To do this, we must have a list of do's & don'ts. We need to be willing to ask, is what I'm about to think...what I'm about to say...or what I'm about to do glorifying God? It would make our decisions concerning something being right or wrong much easier. A young man was upstairs getting dressed. His mother was downstairs in the living room talking with a friend. He yelled out, Is this shirt clean enough for me to wear? Without hesitation, she said no and went on talking. After a while, he came down, buttoning up another shirt. He asked, Mom, how did you know that shirt wasn't clean without looking at it? She said, If you had to ask, it wasn't. We often wonder whether a course of action is right or wrong. We're not quite sure, so since we don't know absolutely that it's terrible, we do it anyway. But if we think it may be wrong, we should leave it alone until we're sure it's right. The adage When in doubt, don't is often a good course to follow.

... and everything that does not come from faith is sin.
Romans 14:23

June 19

DO YOU BELIEVE THE BIBLE?

The Bible is often called the living Word of God, a divine guide meant
to direct our paths and shape our lives. Yet, a question arises that each
believer must confront personally and sincerely—do you genuinely
believe the Bible? Belief in the Bible encompasses accepting its
teachings, history, prophecies and promises as truth. It's about
recognizing it as the ultimate authority in our lives. Do we turn to these
pages for guidance when faced with challenges, doubts, and decisions?
Do we allow its wisdom to influence our actions and attitudes? Consider
this—when the Bible speaks of love, justice, mercy, and truth, do we
internalize these values? Are we letting the scriptures transform our
hearts and minds, becoming more Christ-like in our daily interactions?
Reflect on your own life and faith. Are there teachings or stories in the
Bible that you struggle to accept or understand? Acknowledging these
can be the first step towards a more profound understanding. Engaging
with the Bible isn't just an intellectual exercise; it's a spiritual journey.
Challenge yourself to read the Word consistently and meditate on its
meaning. Believing in the Bible means letting it become the foundation
on which you build your life. It requires trust even when they challenge
your preconceived notions.

All Scripture is God-breathed and is useful for teaching, rebuking,
correcting, and training in righteousness.
2 Timothy 3:16

June 20

CAN YOU HEAR ME NOW?

Do you remember the old cell phone commercial? Can you hear me now? In today's passage, God is concerned because no one is listening. You can almost feel the sadness in His heart as He speaks these words. He pleads with his people: Please listen to me! These words were directed toward Israel, but God wants all of his children to listen. Have you ever been involved in a conversation with someone who never gives you a chance to say a word? Frustrating. But sadly, this is what we so often do when we pray. We do all the talking and expect God to do all the listening! God wants us to talk to Him, and He promises to listen. The psalmist expressed it well: "For he has not despised or scorned the suffering of the afflicted one; he has not hidden his face from him but has listened to his cry for help" Psalm 22:24. God listens to us, and he wants us to listen to him. In our prayer time and throughout the day. Can you hear me now? Sometimes, we are guilty of spending our prayer time doing all the talking, never staying quiet long enough to listen to what God may say to us. In your prayer time today, commit yourself to listening. God may be saying to you, Can you hear me now?

My sheep listen to my voice; I know them, and they follow me.
John 10:27

SOME ADVICE IS NOT SOLID

Advice comes from countless sources—friends, family, social media, and even strangers on the internet. While some guidance can be uplifting and wise, it's crucial to recognize that not all advice is solid. Reflecting on 1 Corinthians 15:33, we are reminded of the profound influence that others can have on our character. The verse highlights the importance of discernment when choosing whose advice we heed. Just as a lousy company can steer us away from our values, misguided advice can lead us down paths that do not align with our faith. Consider the story of Rehoboam in 1 Kings 12. When faced with a significant decision as a new king, Rehoboam rejected the wise counsel of seasoned elders and instead followed the advice of younger, inexperienced peers. His choice led to division and weakened the kingdom. It emphasizes the necessity of seeking wisdom from those grounded in faith and possessing a track record of godliness and integrity. When faced with decisions—big or small—pause to evaluate the source of the advice you receive. Consult Scripture, seek counsel from trusted spiritual mentors, and pray for discernment. Doing so ensures that your decisions are anchored in truth and aligned with God's will. Remember, not all advice is created equal.

Do not be misled: Bad company corrupts good character.
1 Corinthians 15:33

TIME IS MOVING FAST

The sensation that time is slipping through our fingers is all too familiar. Days blend into weeks and weeks into months, leaving us to wonder where the time has gone. Ephesians 5 serves as a poignant reminder that our time is a precious commodity that should be spent with intention and wisdom. The Apostle Paul urges us to live wisely, recognizing that the world around us is fraught with challenges that can easily distract us from our spiritual walk. The call to make the most of every opportunity challenges us to consider how we are investing the time God has graciously given us. Are we prioritizing what truly matters—our relationship with God, family, and calling? It's easy to get caught up in the day-to-day demands and forget about the eternal perspective. Yet, each moment becomes significant when we focus on aligning our actions with God's will. Our days can reflect His glory through acts of kindness, spending quality time in the Word, or serving others. This week, take a moment to evaluate your schedule and commitments. Are there areas where you can be more intentional in your walk with Christ? Remember, time is a gift—use it wisely, for it is fleeting.

Be careful how you live—not as unwise but wise, making the most of every opportunity because the days are evil.
Ephesians 5:15-16

LETTING GO OF YOUR PAST

The past can often feel like a weight that we drag, hindering our progress and clouding our future. It's easy to dwell on past mistakes, regrets, and failures, allowing them to define who we are today. However, the Apostle Paul offers an inspiring perspective on handling our past. Paul, once a persecutor of Christians, had every reason to be haunted by his past actions. Yet, he chose a different path. In his letter to the Philippians, he encourages us to forget what lies behind and instead strain forward to what lies ahead. The key here is intentionality— actively choosing to release the past and focus on our divine calling. This doesn't mean that Paul forgot his past or didn't acknowledge it. Instead, he refused to allow it to control his present or determine his future. Paul could fully commit to his mission and destiny in Christ by letting go. We are invited to do the same. By trusting in God's grace and forgiveness, we can lay down yesterday's burdens and step into tomorrow's promises. Remember, your past does not define you; God's love does.

Brothers and sisters, I do not consider myself yet to have taken hold of it. But one thing I do: Forgetting what is behind and straining toward what is ahead, I press on toward the goal to win the prize for which God has called me heavenward in Christ Jesus.
Philippians 3:13-14

June 24

ENOUGH IS ENOUGH

Enough is Enough! Some people are trying hard to change our world, and many of the changes they are committed to should anger us. They intimidate us by suggesting we are not tolerant or insensitive, so we will stand silently by them as they change our world to one that makes them feel good. When will we begin to stand up for Jesus Christ and unashamedly declare His truth? When will we stop being afraid and intimidated and speak up regarding what we believe and know is true? When will we call out from the depths of our hearts, "As for me and my house, we will serve the Lord!" Who is trying to decide what is decent and what is not? Who is trying to determine when and where we can pray? Who is trying to make sure the Bible is omitted from all public events? Some people are trying to remold and remake society in their image instead of God's. Christians are called to embody Christ's love by extending understanding and patience towards others. Tolerance isn't about agreeing with everyone; it's about respecting differences and loving unconditionally. Practicing tolerance reflects God's grace and contributes to a more harmonious and compassionate world. It's time we said, enough is enough! How will you explain your silence when you stand in front of God?

And if it seems evil unto you to serve the Lord, choose you this day
whom ye will serve; ... but as for me and my house,
we will serve the Lord.
Joshua 24:15

BEING PREPARED?

Staying prepared is more vital than ever. The Bible offers us profound wisdom on the importance of readiness and vigilance in our spiritual lives. At midnight, the cry rang out: 'Here's the bridegroom! Come out to meet him!' Then, all the virgins woke up and trimmed their lamps. The foolish ones said to the wise, "Give us some of your oil; our lamps are going out." "No," they replied, "there may not be enough for you and us. Instead, go to those who sell oil and buy some for yourselves." But while they were going to buy the oil, the bridegroom arrived. The virgins who were ready went in with him to the wedding banquet, and the door was shut. Later, the others came. "Lord, Lord," they said, "open the door for us!" But he replied, "Truly I tell you, I don't know you. Therefore keep watch, because you do not know the day or the hour." This parable emphasizes the importance of spiritual preparedness. Just as the wise virgins kept their lamps ready, we must always be prepared for the return of Christ.

At that time, the kingdom of heaven will be like ten virgins who took their lamps and went out to meet the bridegroom. Five of them were foolish, and five were wise. The foolish ones took their lamps but did not take any oil with them. The wise ones, however, took oil in jars along with their lamps. The bridegroom was a long time in coming, and they all became drowsy and fell asleep.
Matthew 25:1-13

IT'S HARD TO BE TRUTHFUL

What's important is getting ahead, says one student. The better your grades, the better college you get into, the better you'll do in life. And if you learn to cut corners, you'll save time and energy. The better you do, that's what matters. It's not how moral you are in getting there. This quote is from an article about high school students cheating. Students think studying to get a grade is unfair, so they cheat. Others believe that music companies make too much money, so they download illegal songs. One writer said: For working stiffs, stealing office supplies and padding expenses feel like petty acts of revenge against a system in which rich people wangle their way out of their proper share of the tax burden, and corrupt CEOs get away with rap-on-the-knuckle fines. Some believe that convincing lying is associated with good social skills. It takes social skills to be able to control your words as well as what you say. Is convincing lying associated with good social skills? Study after study shows that lying is a way of life for many. The more people do it, the more it becomes accepted. The more people accept it, the more people do it.

The Lord detests lying lips, but he delights in men who are truthful.
Proverbs 12:22

THE LORDS PRAYER

Jesus teaches us to approach God with reverence, acknowledging His holiness and sovereignty. "Our Father in heaven, hallowed be your name" emphasizes our intimate relationship with the Creator while recognizing His sanctity. "Your kingdom come, your will be done" calls believers to align their desires with God's purpose, seeking His will above all. This surrender opens our hearts to His divine plan and ushers His kingdom into our lives and the world around us. The plea for "our daily bread" reminds us of our dependence on God's provision for our physical and spiritual needs. It encourages a daily reliance on God's sustenance and grace. Forgiveness takes center stage as we ask God to forgive our debts, just as we extend forgiveness to others. This reciprocal act reflects the grace we have received and are called to give. Lastly, we ask for protection from temptation and deliverance from evil, acknowledging our need for God's strength and guidance in overcoming trials. The Lord's Prayer is a guide for prayer and a blueprint for living a life that honors God.

This is how you should pray: Our Father in heaven, hallowed be your name, your kingdom come, you will be done, on earth as it is in heaven. Give us today our daily bread. And forgive us our debts, as we also have forgiven our debtors. And lead us not into temptation, but deliver us from the evil one.
Matthew 6:9-13

June 28

ARE YOU MOVING FORWARD?

The question of whether we are moving forward or remaining stagnant is crucial. The Apostle Paul, in his letter to the Philippians, provides a powerful perspective on living a life that continually seeks growth and progress in faith. An exemplary Christian figure, Paul admits he has yet to reach perfection. Yet, he emphasizes the importance of forgetting what lies behind and straining toward what lies ahead. This involves letting go of past failures, regrets, and even successes that might hinder our spiritual progress. Holding onto the past can prevent us from experiencing what God has prepared for us. Moving forward requires intentional effort and focus on the future. Paul's goal was clear—to win the prize of God's heavenly call in Christ Jesus. Are we deepening our relationship with God? Are we serving others more? Are you witnessing to those around you? What are you holding onto that might be keeping you from moving forward? How can you realign your focus toward the future God has for you? The Christian walk is a continuous journey, and every step is a step toward fulfilling His purpose.

Brothers and sisters, I do not consider myself yet to have taken hold of it. But one thing I do: Forgetting what is behind and straining toward what is ahead, I press on toward the goal to win the prize for which God has called me heavenward in Christ Jesus.
Philippians 3:13-14

UNHAPPY AT WORK?

Feeling unhappy at work is a struggle many face, but as Christians, we have a unique perspective that can transform our outlook. The Apostle Paul, writing to the Colossians, reminds us that our work should be done with enthusiasm and dedication, as though we are serving the Lord Himself. This shift in mindset can bring purpose and joy to even the most mundane tasks. Consider Joseph, who, despite being sold into slavery and later imprisoned, remained faithful and diligent in his work. His unwavering commitment and trust in God led to his eventual prominence in Egypt. Like Joseph, we can find fulfillment by viewing our work as an offering to God, knowing that He sees our efforts and rewards faithfulness. When work feels overwhelming or unfulfilling, take a moment to reflect on what God might be trying to teach you through your current circumstances. It's an opportunity to develop patience, humility, or perseverance. Seeing each day as part of God's larger plan, we can approach our work with renewed purpose. Remember, your true boss isn't your manager or CEO—God Himself values your commitment and integrity. By focusing on Him, you can find contentment and joy, no matter where you are employed. Seek to honor Him in all you do.

Whatever you do, work at it with all your heart, as working for the Lord, not for human masters.
Colossians 3:23

HAPPINESS IS A CHOICE

In a world filled with challenges and uncertainties, happiness might seem elusive or conditional. However, as Christians, we are reminded through Scripture that happiness—or rather joy—can be a deliberate choice. The Apostle Paul, despite facing trials and imprisonment, encourages us to "rejoice always." This isn't just a fleeting emotion tied to circumstances; it's a state of contentment and trust in God's sovereignty. Choosing happiness doesn't mean ignoring life's difficulties. Instead, it means anchoring our joy in the eternal promises of God rather than the temporary pleasures or pains of the world. When we intentionally focus on His faithfulness, love, and grace, we pave the way for happiness to flourish within us. Consider the daily decision to rejoice, no matter your situation. This is not about denying hardship but about acknowledging that our joy rests in something unshakeable—the love of Christ. Reflect on Psalm 118:24, "This is the day the Lord has made; we will rejoice and be glad in it." Notice the emphasis on choice —"we will rejoice." Today, take a moment to shift your focus from what might be lacking or challenging toward the abundance of God's love and blessings. By doing so, you invite genuine happiness into your life. Rejoice in the Lord, and find your strength in choosing happiness each day.

Rejoice in the Lord always. I will say it again: Rejoice!
Philippians 4:4

NO ONE LIKES A COMPLAINER

Complaining can often become second nature, a reflexive reaction to challenges or inconveniences. Yet, as believers, we are called to live differently. The Apostle Paul challenges us in Philippians to do everything without grumbling or arguing. This isn't just a command; it's a call to a higher standard of living that reflects our faith. Why is complaining such a big deal? On the surface, it might seem harmless. Still, it reveals a heart that does not fully trust God's provision and plan —complaining shifts our focus from gratitude and contentment to dissatisfaction and negativity. It closes our eyes to the blessings we already have and how God works in our lives. By consciously choosing to avoid complaints, we set ourselves apart in a world accustomed to airing grievances at every turn. Our attitude becomes a testimony, shining brightly against the darkness of discontent. It opens doors for us to demonstrate the hope and joy found in Christ, even amidst trials. This week, challenge yourself to pause before complaining. Instead, look for something to be thankful for in every situation. You'll not only glorify God but also experience a transformation in your own heart.

Do everything without grumbling or arguing, so that you may become blameless and pure, children of God without fault in a warped and crooked generation. Then you will shine among them l
ike stars in the sky.
Philippians 2:14-15

YOU DID GOOD

It is important to win. A famous coach said that Winning is not the main thing; it is the only thing. In today's scripture, Paul uses the analogy of a race and the need to continue until the race is won. It is the Lord who sets the perimeters of our race. He decides the course., He sets the length, and He determines how victory is obtained. Our race is not a race in the sense of classic athletic competition. We are all involved in this kind of race, and we cheer each other through. At times, we need to because our course has obstacles, and at times, we will need to give support as a friend is struggling through a difficult portion of their race. We are not in this race alone, yet we decide to continue. Cheating is silly in this race because the judge knows everything! We all want to hear Jesus say we did well and finished strong. We will only succeed if we try to run this race in our power. He gives us the ability to achieve victory. As we run our race, we are encouraged to stay the course. We each have a specific race to run. We are on a pilgrimage together. God has a plan for our lives with particular speed bumps, detours, and hurdles we will encounter.

Know ye not that they which run in a race run all, but one receiveth the prize? So run, that ye may obtain.
1 Corinthians 9:24

July 2

YOU DON'T HAVE TIME!

The phrase I don't have time is often used as a reason for neglecting our spiritual lives. Yet, the Bible reminds us in Ephesians 5:15-16 that time is a precious commodity, and we are called to use it wisely. The apostle Paul urges us to live intentionally, making the most of every opportunity, because time is fleeting. Consider your day-to-day activities. How often do you catch up on tasks that seem urgent but aren't truly important? It's easy to fall into the trap of busyness, but this can leave little room for spiritual growth and reflection. Instead, we are encouraged to prioritize what genuinely matters—our relationship with God and our impact on those around us. Take a moment to assess your daily schedule. Are you dedicating time to dig into the Word, to reflect on its teachings, and to apply them to your life? Could there be pockets of time you could reclaim—a few minutes in the morning, during lunch, or before bed—to connect with God? Remember, it's not about the quantity of time you spend with God but the quality. Even brief, focused moments in His presence can transform your day and perspective. Choose to live wisely, crafting a life that reflects God's love and wisdom in each encounter and decision.

Be very careful, then, how you live—not as unwise but as wise, making the most of every opportunity, because the days are evil.
Ephesians 5:15-16

IF YOU HAD $1,000,000?

In the movie Indecent Proposal, a newly married young couple is approached by a billionaire with an offer. The offer was this: the billionaire would give the couple a million dollars in exchange for one night alone with the new bride. One night of romance for one million dollars. The temptation of such a large sum of money was too much. People are willing to do strange things for money. The reality show Fear Factor has people eat cockroaches, cheese filled with maggots, and raw half ostrich eggs just for money. Our verse today is perhaps one of the most misquoted texts in the Bible, and it has been used to degrade many wealthy people. It's not money that is the root of all evil; it's the love of money. The love of money and devotion to getting more and more money is the root of all kinds of evil. Paul says that the drive to get rich is a source of all types of evil behavior, leading to many griefs. Money is such an integral part of our lives that we can't ignore it. What would you do for a million dollars?

Those who want to get rich fall into temptation and traps, into foolish and harmful desires that plunge people into ruin and destruction. For the love of money is the root of all kinds of evil. Some people, eager for money, have wandered from the faith and pierced themselves with many griefs.
1 Timothy 6:9-10

July 4

MAKING A DIFFERENCE

It can be easy to feel like our efforts to make a difference are insignificant. Yet, as Christians, we are called to be the salt and light of the earth. James 1:22 reminds us that it's not enough to absorb God's Word; we must act on it. This verse challenges us to move beyond passive listening to active doing. Consider how Jesus lived His life. He made a profound impact through acts of compassion, healing, and teaching. He saw the potential in others and empowered them to transform their lives. We are called to follow His example, using our unique gifts and opportunities to serve and uplift those around us. Making a difference can sometimes require grand gestures. It can begin with small, intentional actions. Offering a listening ear, volunteering your time, or sharing an encouraging word can all have a more significant ripple effect than you might imagine. Remember, each act of kindness reflects God's love for those who might not yet know Him. Reflect on the areas where you can be more intentional about living out your faith. How can I be an agent of change in my community? When we take action, we open doors for God to work through us, impacting the world. Step out in faith today, knowing that your actions, aligned with God's Word, can make a difference.

Do not merely listen to the Word, and so deceive yourselves.
Do what it says.
James 1:22

DEALING WITH TEMPTATION

Temptation is an experience shared by all, yet it often feels isolating. The Apostle Paul, in writing to the Corinthians, reminds us that our struggles with temptation are not unique. This universal aspect of the human experience can provide comfort, knowing that others have faced —and overcome—similar challenges. God's faithfulness is at the heart of this verse. He promises not to allow us to face temptations beyond our ability to withstand. What a reassuring thought that God is actively involved in our spiritual battles, ensuring we are equipped to prevail. Furthermore, God promises a way out, though it might not always be the most obvious path. It requires us to stay vigilant and discerning, seeking His guidance through the Word and the Holy Spirit. Temptation often disguises itself as something enticing, but by focusing on God's faithfulness, we can recognize it for what it truly is—a distraction from His best for us. When facing temptation, remember that God has already prepared an escape route. This transforms the battle with temptation from mere resistance to a strategic retreat towards God's provision. Seek His wisdom and trust in His faithfulness to guide you out of every trial.

No temptation has overtaken you except what is expected of mankind. And God is faithful; he will not let you be tempted beyond what you can bear. But when you are tempted, he will also provide a way out so that you can endure it.
1 Corinthians 10:13

DEALING WITH HATE

Hate, a powerful emotion, can easily take root in our hearts if not addressed. Christians need to remember that hate is not of God. It consumes, divides, and erodes the love and peace we are called to uphold. In today's world, where divisiveness seems prevalent, how can we respond in a way that reflects our faith and values? The key lies in Jesus' teachings. In Matthew 5, Jesus gives us a radical instruction — to love our enemies. This command might feel impossible, especially when faced with opposition or persecution. However, it is a calling to rise above the human tendency for retaliation. Instead of harboring ill will, Jesus encourages us to embody the love of God, which is unconditional and unending. Loving our enemies doesn't mean condoning wrong actions or ignoring injustice. It means choosing a path of compassion and forgiveness, which can ultimately lead to healing and reconciliation. When we pray for those who oppose us, we open our hearts to God's transforming power, allowing His peace to reign within us. By living out this command, we align ourselves with God's will and become a testament to His love in the world. Let's strive to break the cycle of hate by reflecting Christ's love in all our interactions. In doing so, we can be agents of change.

But I tell you, love your enemies and pray for those who persecute you,
that you may be children of your Father in heaven.
Matthew 5:44-45

COMPARING YOURSELF

It's all too easy to fall into the trap of comparison. Whether through social media, workplace achievements, or personal accomplishments, there's always a temptation to measure our worth against others. However, as Christians, we are called to a different standard. The Apostle Paul addressed this issue with the Corinthians, cautioning them against comparing themselves with others. He pointed out that such comparisons are not wise, as they often lead to misunderstanding our actual value and purpose in God's eyes. Comparison can foster feelings of inadequacy, jealousy, and pride, pulling us away from the unique path God has set for us. Instead of focusing on others, we should focus on Christ and His purpose for our lives. Each of us is uniquely crafted for specific tasks and roles within the body of Christ. Celebrate your individual gifts instead of striving to match someone else's achievements. Reflect on how God has equipped you for your unique purpose, and seek His guidance in honing your strengths for His glory. Life is about becoming more like Christ, not like another person. Abandon the need to compare yourself to others and focus on becoming the person God created you to be.

For we dare not classify, compare ourselves with some who commend themselves. When they measure themselves by themselves and compare themselves with themselves, they are not wise.
2 Corinthians 10:12

YOUR SINS ARE FORGIVEN

The hope embedded in Christianity is the promise of forgiveness. The verse from 1 John reminds us of this fundamental truth — that our sins are washed away through confession. This assurance of forgiveness isn't based on our efforts or merits but on God's unwavering faithfulness and justice. Daily, we often carry burdens of guilt and regret over past actions. These feelings can weigh heavily on our hearts, making us feel unworthy of God's love. However, the central message here is liberating. By acknowledging our wrongs and committing them to God, we open ourselves to His grace and cleansing power. Forgiveness in Christianity is not just a divine act; it's a call to transformation. Once forgiven, we are invited to walk in newness, leaving behind the chains that once held us. This ongoing transformation requires a conscious choice to live aligned with God's will. Remember, forgiveness is a gift freely given. God's grace is sufficient, no matter how big or small the transgression. Reflect today on the areas where you need forgiveness and how you can extend this grace to others. Meditate on areas in your life that need confession and forgiveness. Trust in God's promise to cleanse and renew you.

If we confess our sins, he is faithful and will forgive us our sins and purify us from all unrighteousness.
1 John 1:9

July 9

THE TEN SUGGESTIONS

Commandments are commands, not suggestions. They are to be written on our hearts and revealed in our walk. Ted Koppel, ABC's original Night-line host for decades, addressed the graduating class at Duke University. If he never says anything else right, he said a mouthful to those students that day: In place of truth, we have discovered facts; for moral absolutes, we have substituted moral ambiguity. We now communicate with everyone and say absolutely nothing. He said that what Moses brought down from Mount Sinai was not the Ten Suggestions. They are commandments. The sheer brilliance of the Ten Commandments is that they codify acceptable human behavior in a handful of words, not just for then or now, but for all time. Mr. Koppel got it just right! The law of God is perfect, and while it is true, we have all broken His law, and no one is perfect...it does not change that His law is perfect. Does that mean that now we have a Savior, we discard the Commandments of God? I don't think so. It is a tragedy that The Ten Commandments have been removed from the walls of public institutions today. But more importantly, they should be taught in our homes.

...but whose delight is in the law of the Lord, and who meditates on his law day and night.
Psalm 1:2

A PERSON OF INTEGRITY

Today, deception and shortcuts often lead to success; the call to live as a person of integrity stands out as a beacon of truth and authenticity. Integrity is more than just honesty; it is a steadfast adherence to a moral code, even when no one is watching. Regardless of the circumstances, it is about consistency in our actions, words, and beliefs. Proverbs 11:3 highlights the guiding power of integrity. When we live with integrity, we allow God's truth to direct our paths. This commitment to truthfulness and moral uprightness becomes a compass in decision-making, helping us steer clear of deceit and its consequences. The verse contrasts this with the fate of the unfaithful, ultimately undone by their duplicity. Their lack of consistency leads to destruction because their lives are built on unstable ground. For Christians, integrity is rooted in our relationship with God. It reflects His nature within us and shines as a testimony to those around us. Living with integrity means acknowledging that our actions speak louder than words and that every choice can reinforce or undermine our witness as believers. In your daily walk, consider the areas where integrity might be challenged. Are there places in your life where you've compromised?

The integrity of the upright guides them, but the unfaithful are destroyed
by their duplicity.
Proverbs 11:3

HAVING FEW FRIENDS

Your number of friends is often seen as a measure of your popularity or success; it's essential to remember the wisdom found in the Bible. Proverbs 18:24 reminds us that the quantity of friends is not as important as their quality. Having a small circle of authentic, reliable friends can be more fulfilling and supportive than being surrounded by many acquaintances. True friends stand by you in times of trouble, offering guidance, encouragement, and love. They are like family, providing the support and strength you need to face life's challenges. The Bible speaks of such friendships in the story of David and Jonathan. Despite their obstacles, their friendship was marked by loyalty and sacrifice. Jonathan stood by David, even when it meant defying his father, King Saul. Reflect on your friendships today. Do mutual support and reliability mark them? Are you investing time and effort into those relationships that truly matter? Jesus laid down his life for us, his friends, demonstrating the most incredible love one can have. Like Him, strive to be a friend who sticks closer than a brother, nurturing relationships with those who build you up in faith and character. Remember, having a few trustworthy friends who uplift and encourage you in your Christian walk is far more valuable than having many who do not.

One who has unreliable friends soon comes to ruin, but there is a friend who sticks closer than a brother.
Proverbs 18:24

RESPONDING VS. REACTING

The urge to react instantaneously is a constant challenge. Reacting often seems natural, whether a heated conversation or an unexpected event. However, as Christians, we are called to respond thoughtfully rather than react impulsively. James 1:19-20 offers a timeless wisdom that calls us "quick to listen, slow to speak and slow to become angry." This approach calms our spirit and aligns us with the righteousness God desires for us. Responding—not just reacting—requires intentionality and patience, qualities cultivated through our relationship with Christ. Reacting can be driven by emotion and may lead to regretful actions or words. It is often a knee-jerk impulse, lacking reflection. In contrast, responding involves a conscious choice to pause, reflect, and consider our actions in light of Christ's teachings. By responding, we create space for the Holy Spirit to guide our words and deeds toward wisdom and grace. Today, how can I be more like Jesus in my interactions? The next time emotions rise, take a moment to breathe, listen, and seek God's guidance. You can foster peace and understanding by choosing to respond rather than react.

My dear brothers and sisters, take note of this: Everyone should be quick to listen, slow to speak and slow to become angry, because human anger does not produce the righteousness that God desires.
James 1:19-20

HAPPILY MARRIED

Marriage is a union that requires dedication, patience, and love. Within the Christian faith, these qualities form the foundation of a harmonious partnership. Ephesians 4:2 provides a powerful reminder of how these virtues can manifest in our marriages. The call to be humble and gentle with one another is an invitation to put aside personal pride and selfish desires. Instead, we are encouraged to approach our spouse with understanding and kindness. Humility allows us to see our partner not as someone to be controlled or changed but as an equal partner in the marriage covenant. Practicing gentleness creates a safe space for our spouse to express their thoughts and emotions, fostering deeper trust and connection. Patience, too, is essential in navigating the daily challenges that married couples face. Through patience, we learn to bear with one another in love, as Paul instructs. This means being willing to forgive shortcomings and to wait for growth, both in ourselves and in our partners. Furthermore, love is the foundation upon which a happy marriage is built. According to 1 Corinthians 13, love is patient, kind, and selfless. By embodying these aspects of love, we strengthen the bond we share with our spouse, ensuring that our marriage can withstand trials and flourish in times of joy.

Be completely humble and gentle; be patient, bearing with one another in love.
Ephesians 4:2

CREATING A SPIRITUAL FIRE

It's easy for that initial spark of enthusiasm for our faith to dwindle over time. But just as a fire requires fuel and attention to keep burning brightly, so does our spiritual life. Paul's exhortation in Romans encourages us to maintain our zeal and enthusiasm, urging us to cultivate our relationship with God actively. The Word of God is the most nourishing fuel for our spiritual fire. Daily reading and meditating on scripture can rekindle our passion and remind us of God's truths. Through His Word, we are reminded of His promises, love, and purpose for our lives. Engaging with fellow believers provides the encouragement and accountability needed to sustain our spiritual zeal. Attending church, joining a small group, or participating in Bible studies are excellent ways to stay connected and inspired. Our collective fire burns brighter when we surround ourselves with others who share our faith. Serving others in the name of Christ is a powerful way to keep our spiritual fire alive. Whether volunteering at a local charity, helping a neighbor in need, or simply extending kindness to a stranger, acts of service bring the love of Christ into the world and invigorate our spirit. By feeding on God's Word, engaging in community, and serving with passion, we can keep the flame of our faith burning brightly.

Never lack zeal, but keep your spiritual fervor, serving the Lord.
Romans 12:11

July 15

ARE YOU A FIXER UPPER?

How wonderful it is that God is a God of restoration. We have all wandered away from God, and the world has left us broken, dirty, and in need of some serious help. A wonderful Christian couple has a television show called Fixer Upper...their names are Chip & Jo Gaines. The tagline for their show is...We take the worst house in the best neighborhood and turn it into our client's dream home. They take their clients through neighborhoods and find homes that have been neglected, abused, outdated, or worn out. They begin the restoration process, which takes a couple of months, but by the end of the hour-long show, the clients have a lovely dream home that is even more wonderful than they could imagine. It is a great show to watch; the Gaines family have significant interaction and are not ashamed of their faith. As incredible as the Gaines' ability and giftedness are, as amazing as it is to see what they can do with old homes needing restoration, God does so much more with us when He restores us. He can take the worst of sinners and transform them into the best of saints. God never does a patch job; he always does a complete restoration inside and out. His work is so excellent that we are not even the person we were when He was finished.

And I will restore to you the years that the locust hath eaten.
Joel 2:25

July 16

LISTENING TO YOUR COACH

God is our ultimate coach, guiding us through challenges and celebrating our triumphs. Like any sports coach, His role is to direct, correct, and encourage us. But to truly benefit from His coaching, we must be willing to listen. Listening is more than just hearing. It requires intentional focus and the readiness to act upon what you hear. Athletes are trained to tune out distractions to respond to their coach's instructions amid the game's noise. Similarly, as Christians, we need to quiet our hearts and minds to listen for God's voice amidst the clamor of everyday life. God speaks to us in various ways—through His Word, the Holy Spirit, and circumstances or other people. By developing an attentive spirit, we become more receptive to His guidance. We align ourselves with His will and purpose when we follow His lead. Just like following a coach's strategy can lead a team to victory, listening to God can lead us to spiritual success. Every instruction from God is given with our best interest in mind, aimed at refining us and leading us toward a life that glorifies Him. Next time you face a decision or dilemma, pause and seek understanding from the ultimate Coach who knows you intimately and desires to guide your steps. In doing so, you'll find yourself better equipped to play the game of life.

My sheep listen to my voice; I know them, and they follow me.
John 10:27

DOES GOD LOVE FOOTBALL?

What does Jesus have to do with sports? This question often leads to others like, Does God care who wins a game? or How does praying help an athlete during a game? These questions were also at the forefront during Tebow Mania when Tim was at the height of pop culture because of his incredible athletic accomplishments but chose to use his platform to express his faith and love for Jesus Christ. The sight of Tim Tebow on one knee praying before, during, and after games became a phenomenon. NBA superstar Stephen Curry writes bible verses on his shoes before games and points up after every made shot. Stephen's new signature shoe, the CURRY ONE by Under Armour, features his favorite verse, "I Can Do All Things Through Christ..." Philippians 4:13, within the actual shoe design. Then and now, the question of what Jesus has to do with sports continues to arise. When we think of all the issues the world is facing, do you believe God cares about who wins an athletic competition? There are usually Christian players on both teams, so did the losing team's players not pray as hard as the winning team? While I don't believe Jesus cares who wins or loses games, God can use the players to bring Glory to His name.

And whatever you do, whether in Word or deed, do it all in the name of the Lord Jesus, giving thanks to God the Father through Him.
Colossians 3:17

DO YOU BELIEVE THE BIBLE?

When we consider the question, Is the Bible true? We are engaging with the very foundation of our faith as Christians. This passage affirms the divine origin of the Bible, suggesting that its teachings are not merely human ideas but are inspired by God Himself. Various archaeological discoveries and historical research have affirmed the Bible's historical accounts. For instance, the Dead Sea Scrolls, found in the mid-20th century, include some of the oldest known manuscripts of the Hebrew Bible and confirm the accuracy of the text we have today. The Bible contains numerous prophecies, many of which have been fulfilled precisely. For example, the prophecies concerning the birth, life, death, and resurrection of Jesus Christ were written hundreds of years before His birth. Beyond historical and prophetic evidence, many Christians find confirmation of the Bible's truth in their personal experiences. The Scriptures act as a living document, offering guidance, comfort, and profound wisdom in their lives. Through historical evidence, prophetic fulfillment, and personal experience, many find that the Bible holds the truth that transforms lives.

All Scripture is God-breathed and is useful for teaching, rebuking, correcting and training in righteousness, so that the servant of God may be thoroughly equipped for every good work.
2 Timothy 3:16-17

THE SIMPLE THINGS

The admired legendary college basketball coach John Wooden was a great man. When visiting him in his small apartment in California for four hours, the stories came one after the other. After that, It was terrific. His answer was surprising when asked about the most valuable advice he'd ever given his players. Put your socks on correctly. Over time, Coach Wooden noticed that his players weren't smoothing out the wrinkles around their toes and heels, which caused painful blisters. He also made sure his players laced up their sneakers correctly and wore the right size of shoes and socks. Why was this the most important of all the advice he gave his players? This was important because he couldn't coach a team with blisters while they sat on the bench. And so it is with God. If we don't listen to His instructions on the small things in life, we will remain on the sidelines, unable to make a difference in the big moments in the game of life. Jesus himself modeled a life focused on simplicity. He often spent time with those who had little, taught in parables that spoke to the everyday person and found significance in acts as humble as washing feet. His life was a testament to the power of simplicity and its profound impact on our hearts and lives.

Whoever can be trusted with very little can also be trusted with much.
Luke 16:10

ARE YOU READY?

Go. Set. Ready. You'll always need more time to be prepared. You'll never be ready to get married. You'll never be ready to have kids. You'll always need more time to be prepared to start a business, return to school, or move to the mission field. You'll always need more time to prepare financially, emotionally, or spiritually. You'll always need more faith, more cash, and more courage. And if you are looking for an excuse, you will always find one. We have never been and will never be ready for what God calls us to do. And that's OK. God doesn't pick those who are ready; He qualifies those who are not. The author of Hebrews writes that Abraham didn't know the final destination, but it didn't keep him from taking the first step in the journey. What's the first or next step you need to take in your journey? If you take the first step, God will reveal the second step. The problem is that most of us want the twenty-five-year plan before we're willing to step out in faith. God doesn't operate that way; He gives us just enough information, grace, and strength. So we will live in daily dependence on Him. We'll never be ready. Sometimes, we need to go for it. Go. Set. Ready.

By faith, Abraham obeyed and went when called to go to a place he would later receive as his inheritance, even though he did not know where he was going.
Hebrew s 11:8

JUST BE QUIET

The noise around us can be overwhelming. From the constant buzz of notifications to the demands of daily life, it's easy to feel lost in the chaos. However, as Christians, we're called to seek moments of silence and solitude to reconnect with God. The verse from Psalm 46 is a powerful reminder of the peace that comes from resting in God's presence. "Be still" is a call to physical stillness and an invitation to quiet our hearts and minds. It's about surrendering our worries and trusting in the sovereignty of God. In the Bible, many instances highlight the importance of silence. Elijah heard God's gentle whisper not in the wind or earthquake, but in the stillness. Jesus, too, often withdrew to solitary places to pray and listen to His Father. These examples remind us that silence is not the absence of activity but the presence of God. Challenge yourself this week to carve out moments of quiet. Begin with a few minutes each day, finding a space free from distractions. Reflect on God's promises and presence in your life during these moments. Allow the silence to renew your spirit and deepen your faith. In the stillness, you might find that God's voice becomes more apparent, His guidance more evident, and His love more profound. Remember, it's in the quiet that we come to know Him.

Be still, and know that I am God; I will be exalted among the nations
and exalted in the earth.
Psalm 46:10

WHERE ARE YOU HEADED?

Do you remember Alice in Wonderland? When Alice came upon the Cheshire Cat sitting in the tree, she needed some help, so she stopped for some advice. Which way should I go from here? Well, that depends significantly on where you want to go, said the cat. I don't much care where I end up going, said Alice. Then it doesn't matter which way you go, said the cat. As long as I get somewhere, Alice added as an explanation. Oh, you're sure to do that, said the cat, if you only walk long enough. Often, we feel like Alice. We stand at a fork in the road, unsure which way to go. The cat's response offers a profound and troubling truth: If we don't know where we are going, any road will do. And if we keep going in no particular direction, we're sure to get somewhere, but we shouldn't be surprised if it's not the place we desire. Where are you headed? You may be thinking, That's simple-my purpose is survival. My head touches the pillow each night, and I'm just thankful I made it through another day. Do you need direction? You may not be sure which way to go, but based on your calendar, you may just need to stop, pray, and ponder.

For we are God's handiwork, created in Christ Jesus to do good works,
which God prepared in advance for us to do.
Ephesians 2:10

DO YOU TRY TO BLEND IN?

Have you tried blending in with the crowd, just like everyone else? In our daily lives, we often face pressure to conform to societal norms and standards, sacrificing our unique God-given identities. But as followers of Christ, we are called to something greater. In Romans 12:2, the Apostle Paul urges believers not to conform to the world's ways. Instead, we are encouraged to transform and renew our minds. This transformation is not about outward appearances or actions but about an internal change that aligns us with God's will. It's about understanding and living out God's purpose while being a testament to His love and grace. Reflecting on this scripture, consider where you may be tempted to conform rather than stand out as a beacon of faith. The challenge is to live authentically as Christians, allowing the Holy Spirit to guide and shape our thoughts and actions. By doing so, we fulfill our divine calling and inspire others to seek the same transformation. Today, it's easy to follow the patterns laid out by society. However, our true fulfillment and purpose come from aligning our lives with God's perfect will. Let's strive to renew our minds daily.

Do not conform to the pattern of this world, but be transformed by renewing your mind. Then you will be able to test and approve what God's will is—his good, pleasing and perfect will.
Romans 12:2

YOU ARE ONE OF A KIND

In a world that often measures value by comparison, it's vital to remember that the Creator uniquely crafts you. The Apostle Paul reminds us in Ephesians 2:10 that we are God's handiwork. This isn't just a casual observation; it's a profound declaration of your intrinsic worth and purpose. Imagine a master artist carefully sculpting each detail of a masterpiece. That's what God has done with you. Every quirk, talent, and trait was intentionally designed. You weren't an afterthought or a random assembly of traits but a deliberate creation with a specific purpose in mind. The fact that we are created in Christ Jesus means our identity is rooted in Him. Societal standards or fleeting trends do not dictate it. Your purpose is intertwined with His plans, intricately woven into the fabric of God's grand design. God has already paved the way for those good works you were created to do. They are tailor-made for you, aligning with your unique gifts and abilities. You are the only one with your precise combination of experiences and attributes. Your life has a distinct impact that only you can make. Celebrate your one-of-a-kind nature today, and step confidently into the path set before you, knowing that you are loved, valued, and purposed by God.

For we are God's handiwork, created in Christ Jesus to do good works,
which God prepared in advance for us to do.
Ephesians 2:10

WHAT CHILDREN NEED

Children are precious gifts from God, entrusted to us with the responsibility of nurturing their physical and spiritual growth. But what do children genuinely need as they develop into the individuals God intends them to be? First and foremost, children need love. This love is not merely a feeling but an active choice to care for them, provide stability, and show them that they are valued family and community members. Love gives them the courage to explore the world and the assurance that they have a safe place to return to. Second, children need guidance. Proverbs 22:6 reminds us of setting them on the right path. This involves instilling values such as honesty, kindness, and faith. When we model these virtues ourselves, children learn by example, understanding the importance of living a life that honors God. Third, children need to hear about the love of Jesus. Sharing Bible stories and truths creates a foundation for their faith, enabling them to grow into adults who know and trust God's promises. Lastly, children need encouragement. Life's challenges can be daunting, especially for young hearts and minds. Encouragement helps them build resilience and confidence, knowing God's love and purpose for them is unwavering.

Start children off on the way they should go, and even when they are old they will not turn from it.
Proverbs 22:6

ARE YOU BEING CALLED?

In the Gospels, Jesus calls His disciples with a simple yet profound invitation—"Come, follow me." This call is not just for the twelve who walked the dusty roads of Galilee with Him but extends to each of us today. The essence of this calling is relational, a beckoning to walk with Christ and to trust in His guidance. For many Christians, being "called" can feel elusive, as if it is reserved for those entering ministry or mission work. However, each of us has a distinct calling that fits within the tapestry of God's greater plan. It is not always about leaving everything behind but aligning our lives with His purpose wherever we are planted. The call to follow Jesus may lead us into unexpected paths or require us to step outside our comfort zones. It may involve using your skills and talents in ways that glorify God and serve others. Listen to the gentle nudges and the open doors. These could indicate that God is drawing you towards something new or significant. Reflect on where God is leading you. Are there areas where you tug to step out in faith? Consider how you can align your daily actions with His will. Remember, being called by God is a journey, not a destination. It's about faithful steps, day by day, in response to His loving invitation to follow.

Come, follow me, Jesus said, and I will send you out to fish for people.
Matthew 4:19

July 27

TAKING CARE OF YOURSELF

It's easy to neglect self-care, often prioritizing the needs of others over our own. Yet, as Christians, we're reminded that our bodies are temples of the Holy Spirit. This profound truth imparts the responsibility to care for ourselves physically, mentally, and spiritually. Self-care is not an act of selfishness but a form of stewardship. By caring for our health, we honor God, who created us in His image and dwells within us. When we maintain our well-being, we are better equipped to serve others, fulfilling our roles within the body of Christ with vitality and vigor. Consider practical ways to nurture yourself. This could mean setting aside time for rest, engaging in regular physical activity, or nourishing your body with wholesome foods. Similarly, nurturing your spiritual health is vital. Spend time in God's Word, fellowship with other believers, and cultivate a prayerful spirit. Reflect on how you currently take care of yourself. Are there areas that need attention? Remember, honoring God with your body is a daily commitment. By prioritizing self-care, you enhance your own life and enrich the lives of those around you, shining as a testimony of God's love and grace. Do you not know that your bodies are temples of the Holy Spirit, who is in you, whom you have received from God? You are not your own; you were bought at a price.

Therefore, honor God with your bodies.
1 Corinthians 6:19-20

SHEDDING INNOCENT BLOOD

The concept of shedding innocent blood is a serious matter in the Christian faith. It's an act explicitly condemned in the Scriptures as something the Lord hates. Innocence implies purity and freedom from sin or wrongdoing, making the act of taking such a life not only morally wrong but deeply despicable in the eyes of God. Proverbs 6 lists "hands that shed innocent blood" among the things detestable to the Lord. This scripture points to the value God places on life and the sanctity of each individual. From a Christian perspective, we are called to be stewards of life, protectors of the innocent, and voices for those who cannot speak for themselves. In society today, this principle can extend to various forms of violence and injustice that harm the innocent. From a Christian ethical standpoint, it's crucial to reflect on how our direct and indirect actions can contribute to such shedding of blood. This might involve standing against systems perpetuating injustice or being vigilant in our personal lives to ensure we advocate for peace and justice.

There are six things the Lord hates, seven that are detestable to him: haughty eyes, a lying tongue, hands that shed innocent blood, a heart that devises wicked schemes, feet that are quick to rush into evil, a false witness who pours out lies and a person who stirs up conflict in the community.
Proverbs 6:16-19

ARE YOU FAKING IT?

A new missionary went to Venezuela for the first time. He needed help understanding their language. He visited a local church, but having arrived late, the church was packed. The only pew left was on the front row. And so as not to make a fool of himself, he decided to pick someone out of the crowd to imitate. He chose to follow the man sitting next to him. The man clapped his hands as they sang, and the missionary clapped. When the man stood up to pray, the missionary stood up also. When the man sat down, he sat down. He just sat there and tried to look like that man in the front pew. He perceived that the preacher was giving announcements and people clapped, so he looked to see if the man was clapping. He was, and so he applauded, too. Then he saw the man next to him stand up. So he stood up also. Suddenly, a hush fell over the entire congregation. After the service, the preacher stood at the door, shaking the hands of those leaving. When the missionary greeted the preacher, the preacher said: I take it you don't speak Spanish. The missionary replied: No, I don't. It's that obvious? Well, yes, said the preacher. I announced that the Rodriguez family had a baby boy and asked the proud father to stand up. The church may be filled with many people who are faking it.

Live such good lives among the pagans that, though they accuse you of
doing wrong, they may see your good deeds and glorify God.
1 Peter 1:21

July 30

ARE YOU EASY TO LIKE?

In our new and old relationships, it's often worth reflecting on the question, Am I easy to like? While this may sound simple, its implications are profound. It goes beyond mere likability and dives into the essence of Christian love and fellowship. Proverbs 17:17 reminds us of the importance of being there for others through thick and thin. Being easy to like isn't about seeking approval or popularity; it's about embodying a spirit of genuine love and support. It's about being the kind of person who is reliable and uplifting, someone who others find comfort in during times of trouble. Consider your daily interactions. Are you patient and understanding, or quick to judge and criticize? How you react to others' successes and failures can either draw them closer or push them away. Kindness, patience, and empathy are critical to developing friendships and strengthening community bonds. Jesus showed us the ultimate example of love, caring deeply for those often shunned in society. By following His example, we become more accessible to like and reflect His love to the world around us. Next time you interact with others, pause and ask yourself, Am I embodying the love of Christ? Your actions and attitude can be a testament to your faith.

A friend loves at all times, and a brother is born for a time of adversity.
Proverbs 17:17

July 31

I CAN DO IT MYSELF

In a world that often glorifies self-reliance and independence, it is easy to fall into the trap of thinking, I can do it myself. We pride ourselves on our ability to handle challenges and solve problems alone. While independence is valuable, it's essential to remember that true strength comes not from our abilities but from our relationship with Christ. Philippians 4:13 reminds us that our confidence and capability are rooted in Christ's power working through us. This verse, often quoted for its empowering message, reinforces the idea that while we may have the skills and determination, God's strength ultimately enables us to overcome obstacles. Reflect on times when you've felt overwhelmed by life's demands. Did you pause to seek God's guidance or push through on your own? The beauty of our faith lies in the assurance that we don't have to carry burdens alone. God is always ready to guide, support, and empower us to do what seems difficult or even impossible. Consider the areas where you might need to rely more heavily on your strength. Remember, admitting we need help is not a sign of weakness but wisdom. Invite God into your daily activities and decisions, trusting His strength will carry you through whatever challenges you face.

I can do all this through him, who gives me strength.
Philippians 4:13

I WILL NOT BE AFRAID

He rolled up his sleeve and looked away. The shot was going to hurt, and he knew it. He also knew, however, that he didn't want the flu, so he tried to act like a big boy. He thought if my grandchildren could do this, so could I. There's an emotional ailment that can also be quite catchy. Fear. Moses advised his military leaders to take a pre-battle poll of the troops and ask, "Is anyone here afraid or worried?" (Deuteronomy 20:8). Soldiers who admitted their anxiety were discharged before they could scare off anyone else. The commanders wanted to prevent the panic of a few from hurting the entire army. When we advertise and live out our fear, it can spread to others. Parents pass phobias on to their children. Friends infect their friends with superstitions. Employees alarm their co-workers when the fate of the company is in question. Fortunately, there's a way to stop the spread of panic. Moses prescribed this message for fearful soldiers: "Do not be afraid as you go out to fight your enemies today! Do not lose heart or panic or tremble before them!" (Deuteronomy 20:3) In other words, Be brave. Stand tall. Don't back down.

Then the officers shall add, Is anyone afraid or fainthearted? Let him go home so that his fellow soldiers will not become disheartened, too.
Deuteronomy 20:8

August 2

GIVE IT AWAY

The act of giving stands as a profound expression of faith. Jesus' words remind us that the true essence of life lies not in what we hold on to but in what we give away. Through giving, we experience the fullness of joy and the richness of life that God intends for us. Consider the story of the widow's offering in Mark 12. Despite having so little, she gave all she had. Her action was not just about the money but a powerful demonstration of trust and devotion. When we give, we acknowledge God as the ultimate provider. This act liberates us from the shackles of materialism and opens our hearts to experience God's abundant blessings. Giving does not necessarily mean financial gifts. It encompasses our time, talents, and love. Each day presents countless opportunities to give—to lend a listening ear, offer a word of encouragement, or share our skills with those in need. Every small act of kindness reflects God's love and can have a ripple effect, touching lives beyond our immediate reach. Reflect on what you can give away today. Is it your time, resources, or perhaps a forgiving heart? Ask God to reveal opportunities to share His love with others. Remember, in giving, we are truly blessed.

In everything I did, I showed you that by this kind of hard work, we must help the weak, remembering the words the Lord Jesus himself said: It is more blessed to give than to receive.
Acts 20:35

August 3

FEELING PRESSURE

Standing firm in our faith can feel daunting. The pressure to conform isn't just a modern-day challenge; it's one even the early Christians faced. In his letter to the Romans, Paul reminds us of a profound truth—our identity is rooted in Christ, not the world. The world promotes trends and ideals that often clash with our Christian beliefs. These societal pressures can lead us to question our values, sometimes tempting us to compromise on what we know is right. However, Paul encourages a different path of transformation through the renewal of our minds. This transformation doesn't happen overnight; it requires intentional effort and reliance on God's Word. We allow God to reshape our thoughts, attitudes, and behaviors when we immerse ourselves in Scripture. This alignment with His will empowers us to discern what is truly good and pleasing, ensuring our lives reflect His purpose. We're called not to blend into the cultural norm but to stand out as beacons of hope and truth. By focusing on the eternal rather than the temporal, we find peace and confidence in who God has created us to be in moments when the pressure to fit in mounts; remember that our true identity is found in Christ.

Do not conform to the pattern of this world, but be transformed by the renewing of your mind. Then you will be able to test and approve what God's will is—his good, pleasing and perfect will.
Romans 12:2

August 4

THE NAME OF THE LORD

The Lord's name should be used in reverence. Using the Lord's name in vain goes beyond profanity and casual mention—it encompasses any use that strips it of its holiness or diminishes its significance. We live in a world where language is often casual, and expressions can become empty gestures. This Scripture invites Christians to reflect on how we speak of God and ensure that our words honor Him. Misusing the Lord's name can occur in moments of anger or even in jest, where the weight of His name becomes trivialized. Consider your daily conversations and interactions. Are there instances where the name of the Lord is used without due respect? How can you be more intentional in your speech to honor Him? This reflection isn't just about avoiding the wrong words; it's about cultivating a heart that reveres God in every aspect of life. Make a conscious effort to speak God's name with reverence. Whether in prayer, discussion, or thought, ensure it reflects your love and respect for Him. Demonstrate respect for God's name in your community. Your example can encourage others to treat His name with the same reverence. Regularly examine your heart and motivations. Are they aligned with honoring God through your words and actions?

You shall not misuse the name of the Lord your God, for the Lord will not hold anyone guiltless who misuses his name.
Exodus 20:7

August 5

GRUMBLING

Grumbling is a typical human response to discomfort, dissatisfaction, or inconvenience. The Apostle Paul, in his letter to the Philippians, encourages believers to do "everything without grumbling or arguing." This directive is about avoiding complaints and cultivating a spirit of gratitude and contentment. When we choose not to grumble, we trust God's sovereignty and plan for our lives. It becomes a powerful testimony of our faith, allowing us to shine like stars in the sky amidst a world prone to negativity and discord. Grumbling affects our inner peace and can hinder our witness to others. By choosing gratitude over grumbling, we open our hearts to joy and position ourselves as beacons of light. Consider for a moment the Israelites in the wilderness, who, despite witnessing God's miracles, frequently grumbled against Him. Their dissatisfaction led to prolonged wanderings. Likewise, we risk missing out on God's blessings when we focus on our grievances. Today, reflect on areas in your life where grumbling has taken root. Ask yourself how you can replace those complaints with gratitude.

Do everything without grumbling or arguing, so that you may become blameless and pure, children of God without fault in a warped and crooked generation. Then you will shine among them like stars in the sky.
Philippians 2:14-15

A HIGHER STANDARD

Living by a higher standard can seem challenging. Yet, as Christians, we are called to rise above the ordinary and reflect the character of God in our daily lives. The Apostle Peter reminds us that our calling to holiness is not merely a suggestion but a divine expectation. It is a call to align our behavior and thoughts with the purity and love that defines God's nature. Living a holy life isn't about perfection but about intention. It's about making choices that honor God in our relationships, work, or personal habits. Each decision is an opportunity to reflect His light in the world. This might mean choosing kindness over retaliation, honesty over deceit, or selflessness over self-interest. Remember, the pursuit of holiness is a journey, not a destination. Sometimes, we falter, but God's grace is sufficient to lift us back up. By keeping our eyes on Jesus, the author and perfecter of our faith, we can strive towards the higher standard He has set for us. Take a moment today to reflect on areas of your life where you can embody a higher standard. Ask yourself how you can better represent the holiness of Christ in your actions and attitudes. Through this intentionality, we become not only followers of Christ but also bearers of His love and truth.

But just as he who called you is holy, so be holy in all you do; for it is written, Be holy, because I am holy.
1 Peter 1:15-16

WHAT'S YOUR PROBLEM?

Life, as we know it, is filled with many challenges and setbacks. Everyone faces problems that sometimes seem impossible, from minor inconveniences to monumental hurdles. But what if these problems are not merely obstacles but opportunities in disguise? In the book of James, we are encouraged to view our trials as a source of joy. This is not a call for superficial cheerfulness but a deeper understanding of the purpose behind our struggles. Problems test our faith in profound ways. They stretch the muscles of our spirit, making us more robust and resilient. Our natural inclination might be to shy away from difficulties, but Scripture reminds us that through these trials, perseverance is born. This perseverance molds our character, fortifying us against future challenges. For us, the question is, What's your problem? It isn't meant to trivialize our difficulties but to invite us to look beyond them. It encourages us to discern God's hand at work, even in adversity. The very problems we wish away might be the ones that lead us closer to God. Next time you encounter a challenge, pause and reflect. Ask yourself how this trial can shape your faith and draw you nearer to God.

Consider it pure joy, my brothers and sisters, whenever you face trials of
many kinds because you know that testing
your faith produces perseverance.
James 1:2-3

IS IT WORTH IT?

Lou Gehrig may not have died from Lou Gehrig's disease after all. The Hall of Fame pro baseball player is the namesake for Amyotrophic Lateral Sclerosis (ALS), a debilitating neurological disease that slowly paralyzes its victims and ultimately leads to death. Recent research has revealed that Gehrig may not have had ALS but instead exhibited similar symptoms due to the many concussions he encountered in his long career. Gehrig was the legendary Iron Man who played in 2,130 consecutive baseball games. He started one game only hours after two pitches hit him in one inning. It has been recorded that he had a bump on his head so large that he wore Babe Ruth's much larger cap. We praise Gehrig for his resolve to play through pain, but his commitment to not let his team down may have led to the disease that killed him. This question nags at the young teacher grading papers deep into the night. This question haunts the dreams of the traveling businessman. He's making more money than expected, but he's never home. You owe it to God, yourself, and those who love you to ask the big question: Who are you working for?

There was a man all alone; he had neither son nor brother. His toil had no end, yet his eyes were not content with his wealth. For whom am I toiling, he asked, and why am I depriving myself of enjoyment? This, too, is meaningless—a miserable business!
Ecclesiastes 4:8

WHY ME?

Life often presents us with insurmountable challenges, leaving us questioning, Why me? In these moments, it's vital to remember that such trials do not reflect our worth or a punishment from God. Instead, they are opportunities for growth and deepening our faith in Him. The Book of James offers profound insight into the purpose behind our hardships. It encourages us to perceive trials not as obstacles but as catalysts for developing perseverance. This perseverance is not just about enduring difficulties; it's about strengthening our faith and character. When faced with adversity, it's natural to feel overwhelmed and ask why we must endure such pain. During these times, turning to Scripture can provide solace and understanding. The Bible reassures us that our struggles are temporary and that God walks alongside us through every storm. Reflecting on the lives of biblical figures like Job, who faced immense suffering yet remained steadfast in his faith, reminds us that questioning Why me? It is part of our human experience. The next time you find yourself amid a trial, remember that it shapes you into a more resilient and faithful disciple of Christ.

Consider it pure joy, my brothers and sisters, whenever you face trials of many kinds because you know that the testing of your faith produces perseverance.
James 1:2-3

August 10

HOW BRIEF IS LIFE?

The Butterfly Garden at the Memphis Zoo is an outdoor cage with thousands of colorful-winged beauties. As you step in, they land on you. Most of us are not a big fan of anything that resembles an insect—especially when it's the size of our hand. Our instinct is often to flick it away, but we are warned not to touch the butterflies because of their fragile nature. Our life, like butterflies, is delicate. David said, "At best, each of us is but a breath" (Psalm 39:5). Thinking about our mortality can be depressing, but it is essential to remember that our lives are fleeting. Accepting our mortality keeps us humble. James told a story about a man who was heading off on a year-long business trip. Before departing, he bragged about the money he would earn. James challenged them: "You're here a little while, then you're gone. What you ought to say is, If the Lord wants us to, we will live and do this or that" (James 4:14-15). God signs off on everything in our lives—from our plans to our last breath. Humility and thankfulness are appropriate responses to a God who knows we are like "a traveler passing through this life" (Psalm 39:12).

You have made my days a mere handbreadth; the span of my years is as
nothing before you. Everyone is but a breath, even
those who seem secure.
Psalm 39:5

DOING WHAT IS RIGHT

The call to do what is right remains a constant beacon for Christians. The Scripture from Micah 6:8 delivers a timeless message that encapsulates God's desire for His people—to act justly, love mercy, and walk humbly with Him. Acting justly means living with integrity and fairness in all our dealings, whether in business, relationships, or everyday interactions. It's about standing up for what is right, even when it's not popular or easy. It means making choices that reflect God's justice, ensuring we are fair and compassionate. Mercy is a profound expression of God's character, and loving it requires us to extend grace and forgiveness to others as God has done for us. It's about showing kindness to the undeserving, offering forgiveness, and being patient. This path of mercy transforms our hearts and aligns us with the ultimate example of Jesus Christ. Walking humbly with God involves acknowledging our dependence on Him and submitting our will to His greater plan. It's about being teachable, recognizing that we don't have all the answers, and seeking His guidance. Humility allows us to grow spiritually, understanding that everything we have is a gift from God. In choosing to live by these principles, we reflect God's kingdom here on Earth.

To act justly to, love mercy, and to walk humbly with your God.
Micah 6:8

EXPECT GOD TO ANSWER

Oklahoma was in a severe drought, so a church decided to have a prayer meeting and ask the Lord to send rain. On that Sunday afternoon, the people started to gather to pray; when the church was packed, the Pastor got up to speak and said something that startled the group. He said, This service is over. You were to come here to pray for rain, but I don't see one umbrella! In Acts 12. there was a great prayer meeting. James and Peter were put in prison for preaching about Jesus. James was killed, and they planned to kill Peter as well. The believers met in a home and began to pray. The Lord answered their prayer, and Peter was miraculously set free from prison. Peter went to the house where they were praying, but when they saw him at the door, they didn't believe. They were praying for his release but still didn't believe it. They were praying, but they were praying with little expectation of an answer. Today, as we pray…we should pray with expectation and faith that God can and will answer our prayers. We should pray believing God loves us and He will act in response to our prayers of faith. Many of our prayers are vague, so if God were to answer them, would we know?

Therefore, I tell you, whatever you ask for in prayer, believe that you have received it, and it will be yours.
Mark 11:24

PUTTING IT TOGETHER

One activity you may not enjoy is putting together complicated puzzles. It may result from our need for more patience and the tedious process. However, once completed, the process can remind us of life and how God sees it. Only God sees the finished picture, while we get to see at least one or two pieces of the picture. With only a piece of the picture, it is easier to tell what the whole picture is. Only when all the pieces are put together do we see the end. In life, God always sees the whole...it is complete to Him. We live in the mystery of life, but one day, all the pieces will be put together for us, and then we will see it and understand. Until then, we must trust the One who has already seen the entire picture. Throughout the pages of His Word, we see His hidden hand working in mysterious ways. God is in the shadows, arranging things, moving things we cannot see. God is working in our life, but we can't see Him. Sometimes, everything we thought we had nailed down comes loose, and the devil pulls nails as fast as possible. Life is not a problem to be solved; it is a mystery to be lived. Sometimes, we must back off and watch for the hidden hand of God. Just because you cannot see Him working doesn't mean He is not.

He had James, the brother of John, put to death with the sword. When he saw that this met with approval among the Jews, he proceeded to seize Peter also.
Acts 12:2-3

August 14

TAKING THE BACK SEAT

Getting caught up in the race for personal success and recognition is easy. We are often encouraged to be assertive, push our limits, and strive for the best in all we do. While ambition has its place, as Christians, we are called to a higher standard that values humility over self-promotion. The Apostle Paul, in his letter to the Philippians, reminds us of this crucial principle. In Philippians 2:3-4, he urges believers to act out of humility, prioritizing the needs and interests of others above our own. This is not about neglecting self-care or dismissing our needs but about fostering a spirit of selflessness and service. Taking the back seat can be challenging, especially when society often rewards those who are front and center. However, true greatness in the kingdom of God is measured not by how high we climb but by how willingly we serve. Jesus embodied this by washing his disciples' feet, illustrating that leadership and humility go hand in hand. Today, consider one way to practice taking the back seat in your life. It might be allowing someone else to take credit, offering your time to help a colleague, or simply being more attentive to the needs around you. By doing so, you reflect the character of Christ, inspiring others through love.

Do nothing out of selfish ambition or vain conceit. Rather, in humility value others above yourselves, not looking to your own interests but each of you to the interests of the others.
Philippians 2:3-4

YOUR LIFELINE WITH GOD

It's easy to become disconnected from the very source that sustains us. John 15:5 beautifully captures the essence of our relationship with God —as vital as a vine to its branches. Just as a branch cannot survive if severed from the vine, our spiritual growth and well-being hinge on our connection with God. This Scripture emphasizes the importance of remaining in Jesus, highlighting that true fruitfulness stems from this divine union. Without it, our efforts lose meaning, and our spiritual lives can wither. When we draw our strength and guidance from Him, we align ourselves with His purpose and bear fruits that reflect His love and grace. Consider your daily routines and choices. How do they reflect your connection with God? Are they drawing you closer to Him, or do they pull you away? Cultivating practices in this relationship is crucial — studying the Word, meditating on His promises, or worshipping in spirit and truth is vital. Take heart in knowing that you are empowered to overcome challenges and flourish in every season of life with God as your lifeline. Remember, the strength and vitality of a branch lie in its connection to the vine. Similarly, your spiritual vitality springs from staying connected to Christ, your eternal vine.

I am the vine; you are the branches. If you remain in me and I in you, you will bear much fruit; apart from me you can do nothing.
John 15:5

August 16

TAKING A BREAK

Rest and taking a break can feel foreign amidst our busy schedules and endless to-do lists. Yet, as Christians, we are regularly reminded about the importance of rest, not just for our physical well-being but for our spiritual health. Jesus's invitation in Matthew 11 is not just an offer of physical rest but a deeper, spiritual refuge. He invites those who are weary to find solace in Him, promising rest for the soul. It's a call to pause from life's burdens and recharge under His gentle guidance. Taking a break doesn't mean abandoning responsibilities or becoming idle. Instead, it's about finding balance and making intentional time for God. In these moments of rest, we can reflect, renew our strength, and realign our priorities with His will. The Bible offers numerous examples of the importance of rest. After creating the world, God Himself rested on the seventh day, establishing a pattern for us to follow. The Sabbath was designed as a time to stop working and focus on worship and reflection. Incorporating rest into our lives can take many forms. It might be a quiet walk, reading a favorite devotional, or simply sitting silently, meditating on God's Word. In moments of rest, we are reminded of our reliance on God rather than our strength.

Come to me, all you who are weary and burdened,
and I will give you rest.
Matthew 11:28

August 17

THANKS, I NEEDED THAT!

Many years ago, there was a commercial on television advertising men's aftershaves. The commercial had men half asleep being slapped on the face with the aftershave to wake them up. After being jolted awake by the slap of aftershave, each man would say, Thanks, I needed that! Sometimes, we all need something to wake us up and jolt us back into awareness that we have been asleep far too long. Those who have served in our country's military know that falling asleep while on duty is a grave offense. For that to happen causes many to be placed in danger, even to the point of losing their lives. Jesus told us to redeem the day...He said, "Work while it is yet day, for the night comes when no one can work." Some of us have fallen spiritually asleep in our apathy and our busy attitudes to be concerned with people's souls. We have made our religious organization the main thing, rather than remembering there are precious souls all around us for whom Christ died. We must ask the Holy Spirit to wake us up and help us see the world like the Lord does. We need to live each day as the precious gift that it is. It's time to wake up! If this were your last day on Earth, how would you spend it?

And that, knowing the time, that now it is high time to awake out of sleep: for now is our salvation nearer than when we believed.
Romans 13:11

August 18

TOMORROW NEVER COMES

It's easy to fall into believing that tomorrow is guaranteed. We plan for the future, setting goals and ambitions, often neglecting the present moment where life truly unfolds. However, Scripture repeatedly reminds us of the fleeting nature of life and the importance of living in the now. Proverbs 27:1 cautions against boasting about tomorrow, highlighting the uncertainty of what lies ahead. While it's wise to prepare and make prudent plans, this verse encourages us to avoid presuming the future as if it were a certainty. Tomorrow may never come; thus, our focus should be on the present, where we can actively engage with God's purpose. Living fully in the present requires trusting God with our future. It calls us to surrender our worries and anxieties about what is to come, resting in the assurance that God is already there. In Matthew 6:34, Jesus tells us, "Therefore do not worry about tomorrow, for tomorrow will worry about itself. Each day has enough trouble of its own." We are reminded that God's grace is available today, offering comfort and strength for our challenges. By focusing on today, we experience His presence, cultivate gratitude, and build relationships that reflect His love. Take a moment to reflect on how you can live fully in the present, trusting that God holds tomorrow.

Do not boast about tomorrow, for you do not know
what a day may bring.
Proverbs 27:1

STRONGER EVERYDAY

As believers, we hold onto the promise found in Philippians 4:13 that through Christ, we have the strength to face any obstacle that comes our way. Every day offers us a new opportunity to strengthen our faith and trust in God. It's easy to feel weak when confronted with difficulties, but it's important to remember that our strength does not come solely from our abilities. Instead, it is derived from our relationship with God and His unwavering support. Consider the steadfast mountain that stands through raging storms and harsh winds. It doesn't crumble because its foundation is solid. Similarly, our spiritual foundation is built on God's love and power. By seeking His guidance and relying on His strength, we become like that mountain—unshakeable, resilient, and stronger day by day. To become stronger every day, we need to nourish our spiritual lives. This means immersing ourselves in Scripture, surrounding ourselves with fellow believers, and continually seeking God's presence in prayer and meditation. Remember, each small step you take in faith builds upon the last. Trust that God is with you, granting you strength for today and courage for tomorrow. With Christ as your source of strength, you can face each day with confidence and boldness, knowing you are growing stronger daily in Him.

I can do all this through him, who gives me strength.
Philippians 4:13

PARENTING

Parenting is a divine assignment infused with both joy and challenge.
Sometimes, you may face disappointment with your children's choices.
It's a universal experience, no matter how diligently you've raised them
according to biblical principles. However, this does not mean all hope is
lost or that your efforts have been in vain. God entrusts us with children,
giving us the responsibility to guide them according to His ways.
Proverbs 22:6 is a reminder of this duty. It's a call to instill godly values
in your children's hearts and minds, nurturing their faith and character.
Yet, even with such guidance, children may stray. They are, after all,
individuals endowed with free will. The Bible is filled with stories of
godly men and women whose children chose paths contrary to their
teachings. It is essential to remember that God understands these trials
and remains with you through them. When confronted with
disappointment, reflect on God's patience and enduring love toward us
despite our imperfections. This understanding can help us extend grace
and forgiveness to our children, encouraging them with love rather than
judgment. While it's natural to feel disheartened sometimes, remember
that God does not forget the seeds of faith you've planted.

Train up a child in the way he should go, and when he is old, he will not
depart from it.
Proverbs 22:6

CAN ONLY GOD OPEN DOORS?

Do you want to know the will of God in your life? How much time do you spend reading the Bible? Do you think God believes you want to know His will when you don't spend even 15 minutes a day reading the one book God has written to show us His will, reveal His will to us, and unfold His will to us? We must surrender our will to His, read His Word, meditate upon it, share it, and study it. When we bow to His will and read His will, we will begin to know His will. Commit to reading God's Word at least 15 minutes a day for 30 days. When the month is over, reevaluate what you have learned and ask God to help you be obedient to daily Bible reading from this day forward. Are you doing the will of God that He has already given you? God's Word is filled with His will for every one of us. If we are not actively doing what He has revealed in His Word, how can we expect that He will show us more? Some of us believe in the open-door approach to finding God's will. We wait until a door opens, assume it is God who is opening it, and then go through it believing this to be God's will. The only problem is that it is not only God who opens doors.

If ye abide in Me, and My words abide in you, ye shall ask what ye will, and it shall be done unto you.
John 15:7

HAVE YOU BEEN THERE?

Facing trouble is an inevitable part of life. Have you considered how these trials might serve a greater purpose? The Apostle James urges us to view our challenges with a strangely counterintuitive perspective— joy. This doesn't mean we delight in suffering; instead, we rejoice in the growth that trials produce. Life's difficulties can often feel overwhelming. Whether financial strain, health issues, or relational conflicts, each problem seems like an insurmountable mountain. But remember, mountains are where climbers strengthen their skills, where faith is tested and refined. James reminds us that these trials test our faith, producing perseverance. Perseverance is not just a passive endurance but an active steadfastness. It equips us to handle future challenges with greater strength and wisdom. It's like building spiritual muscles through resistance training; each trial strengthens our endurance. Consider the heroes of faith throughout Scripture—Joseph, David, Esther—all faced immense difficulties. Yet, through perseverance, they fulfilled God's plans in powerful ways. Trust that He is using your experiences to refine and prepare you for what lies ahead.

Consider it pure joy, my brothers and sisters, whenever you face trials of many kinds, because you know that the testing of your faith produces perseverance.
James 1:2-3

WHEN ONE DOOR CLOSES

Every opportunity is not from the Lord. We have heard it, or we have said it yourself: I will wait and see what door opens, and that's where I will go. This sounds more like chance than faith. Just because a door opens does not mean it is from the Lord. We are to walk by faith, not by sight and not by chance. The Bible tells us to test every opportunity to see if it is from God. Why do you suppose the Scripture would give such instruction? Because there is more than one voice out there. More than one voice is trying to speak into your life. More than one voice is trying to control you. Every opportunity is not from God, so we need Biblical discernment to determine who the voice is and if it is there from the Lord. It is the same with the doors that open to us. We need biblical discernment to determine if the door is opened by Jesus or by someone else. Jesus said in the Gospel of John that He "is the Door." We must do everything through Him to go through the right doors. Discernment is not a feeling; it is based on the Word of God and on having the lines of communication open with Jesus. He is ready to guide you and me in all things and through all things. Before you go through any door, ensure it is the door the Lord is leading you through.

I am the door: by Me if any man enter in, he shall be saved.
John 10:9

August 24

YOUR COMFORT ZONE

We often find ourselves nestled in the comfort of our routines, where familiarity breeds a sense of safety and predictability. Yet, the Bible reminds us that God calls us beyond these boundaries. Our comfort zone, while reassuring, can sometimes hold us back from experiencing the abundance God has planned for us. Consider Peter, who stepped out of the boat and walked on water towards Jesus. Only when he stepped out of his comfort zone did he witness a miracle firsthand. Similarly, God challenges us to step out in faith, trusting He can do "immeasurably more" than we can envision. When you remain in your comfort zone, you rely on your strength. But when you step out, you lean on God's power. In these moments of stretching, you grow, your faith deepens, and you witness God's blessings in unexpected ways. Reflect on areas where God might be calling you to step out. It could be reaching out to someone in need, taking on a new role in ministry, or trusting Him with an uncertain future. Challenge yourself today to identify one way you can step out in faith. Trust that as you do, God's power will work within you, accomplishing more than you could have imagined. Take that step, knowing He is with you every moment.

Now to him who is able to do immeasurably more than all we ask or imagine, according to his power that is at work within us.
Ephesians 3:20

GIVE IT TO HIM

Life often feels like a balancing act. We juggle responsibilities, relationships, and sometimes the unexpected challenges that come our way. It's easy to become overwhelmed under the weight of anxiety and stress. Yet, in these moments, Scripture offers us a profound invitation that encourages us to step into an entirely new way of living, to give our burdens to God. 1 Peter 5:7 is a gentle reminder of God's care for us. It doesn't suggest that we won't encounter difficulties or that life will be free from stress. Instead, it offers a solution—a divine exchange where we can hand over what troubles us. The verse invites us to cast, literally throw, our anxieties onto God. Why should we do this? Because He cares deeply about our well-being. This is more than a fleeting concern; it's an enduring commitment. God's care is constant and personal. He knows each worry and fear that tugs at our hearts, and He wants us to trust Him. Imagine what it would look like to release your anxieties to God. To no longer carry the weight but to live in the freedom His care provides. It's a daily decision, one that requires faith and surrender. Today, take a moment to identify what's weighing you down. As you reflect, envision giving each of those burdens to Him.

Cast thy burden upon the Lord, and He shall sustain thee: He shall never suffer the righteous to be moved.
Psalm 55:22

August 26

IT'S TIME FOR A SALE

WOW! Probably not what you wanted to hear first thing on this beautiful morning! What is the most valuable thing in your life? Some would say their family—spouse, children, or parents. Others would list career, education, or material possessions. Those struggling with sickness would say that health tops the list. Jesus illustrated this same question with a parable (Matthew 13:44-46),

Our relationship with Jesus is of great value, and we ought to be prepared to give everything we have to possess it. We have nothing of value that we can offer to God. We can't buy our way into Heaven; our salvation is a gift from God. We can only have the treasure above if we give up our treasures here. The rich young ruler in Luke 18:17-24 wasn't prepared to sell all his earthly possessions to have treasure in Heaven. So he went away very sad. The young ruler knew the significant risks he took in liquidating all his assets. He was right in assessing what is truly valuable. Missionary Jim Elliot confidently said He is no fool who gives what he cannot keep gaining what he cannot lose. Jesus is saying: "Sell all your possessions . . . . Then come, follow Me" (Luke 18:22). He promises you "treasure in heaven" and "a rich and satisfying life" on Earth (John 10:10).

Sell all your possessions...and you will have treasure in Heaven. Then come, follow Me.
Luke 18:22

NEED A CHURCH HOME?

Finding a church home provides a spiritual anchor. It's a place where we can gather, grow, and support one another in their faith journeys. The concept of a church home extends beyond mere attendance; it involves actively participating in a community that fosters love, encouragement, and accountability. Hebrews 10:24-25 reminds us of the importance of communal worship. We can spur one another toward love and good deeds by meeting together. This isn't just about gathering for the sake of it; it's about building relationships that strengthen our faith and inspire us to live out Christ's teachings. Is the church a place where you feel welcomed and valued? Do you leave each service feeling spiritually enriched and motivated to live out your faith in daily life? A church home is not simply a building; it's a community of believers who share the purpose of glorifying God and reaching out to others. Reflect on how you can contribute to your church community. Whether it's through volunteering, joining a small group, or simply being present to support others, your involvement is vital.

Let us consider how we may spur one another on toward love and good deeds, not giving up meeting together, as some are in the habit of doing, but encouraging one another—and all the more as you see the day approaching.
Hebrews 10:24-25

August 28

BEING THANKFUL

It can be easy to focus on the challenges we face and overlook the big and small blessings that fill our days. The Apostle Paul, in his letter to the Thessalonians, reminds us of the importance of thankfulness. This gratitude isn't confined to moments of joy and abundance but extends to every circumstance we encounter. Being thankful is more than a polite gesture or a fleeting moment of appreciation; it's a posture of the heart. When we express gratitude, we shift our focus from what's lacking in our lives to the abundance of God's blessings. This perspective honors God and transforms our outlook, instilling peace and joy regardless of our situation. Consider the story of Jesus healing the ten lepers (Luke 17:11-19). Only one, a Samaritan, returned to express his thanks. In doing so, he received physical healing and a more profound spiritual blessing. This narrative underscores the power of gratitude — it opens doors to more incredible blessings and deeper communion with God. Take a moment today to reflect on your life. What are you thankful for? Make a list, starting with the seemingly small things, and watch how this gratitude can change your heart's focus. By cultivating a habit of thankfulness, we align ourselves with God's will and invite Him into every aspect of our lives.

Give thanks in all circumstances, for this is God's will for
you in Christ Jesus.
1 Thessalonians 5:18

August 29

TIME TO SHAKE THINGS UP

Change can be both exciting and intimidating. It often requires us to step out of our comfort zones and challenge the familiar routines we have grown accustomed to. Isaiah 43:19 reminds us that God is constantly at work, creating new paths and opportunities, even in the most barren circumstances. When God calls us to shake things up, it's an invitation to trust in His plan, even when it seems unclear. Just as He promised to make a way in the wilderness and streams in the wasteland, He assures us of His presence and guidance as we venture into uncharted territories. For Christians, this means being open to the movement of the Holy Spirit, allowing Him to guide us into new experiences, ministries, or callings. It might mean stepping into a role at church, reaching out to someone in need, or simply being open to God's voice in our daily lives. But how can we prepare ourselves for these changes? Start by seeking God through His Word, as with this devotional. Listen for His guidance through Scripture, and be willing to act upon it. Reflect on your current situation and ask yourself if there are areas that God is nudging you to alter or improve. It's time to shake things up and witness the new things God is doing in your life.

See, I am doing a new thing! Now it springs up; do you not perceive it? I am making a way in the wilderness and streams in the wasteland.
Isaiah 43:19

THE MOST IMPORTANT JOB

We often measure success by our job titles, salaries, and achievements. Yet, the Bible invites us to reevaluate what truly matters. Philippians 2:3-4 reminds us that our most important job isn't tied to our career but to how we serve others in love and humility. The Apostle Paul, who penned these words, exemplified this throughout his life. Despite his accolades and opportunities, he prioritized serving others and sharing Christ's love. He saw value not in personal gain but in lifting others. In reflecting on these verses, consider how you can embody this spirit of service in your daily interactions. Whether in your workplace, family, or community, look for ways to place others' needs above yours. This doesn't mean neglecting yourself but discovering the joy and fulfillment of genuine care for others. Think about your current roles and responsibilities. How might they shift if you approached them with service as your highest priority? By valuing others above ourselves, we align with God's heart and unlock a more profound sense of purpose. In recognizing that our most important job is to love and serve others, we fulfill God's command and become a testament to His grace and love in action.

Do nothing out of selfish ambition or vain conceit. Rather, in humility value others above yourselves, not looking to your own interests but each of you to the interests of the others.
Philippians 2:3-4

August 31

SITTING ON THE FENCE

To the Christian, there is one thing that the Lord cannot condone. It is the one thing that would cause Him to "spew them out of His mouth!" He said He cannot tolerate lukewarm Christians or a lukewarm church. Today, it is a virtue to be called moderate or tolerant. It is good to be mild in some things, but not when we are called to follow Jesus. The first and greatest commandment, according to Jesus, is to "love the Lord your God with all your heart, mind, and soul." There is nothing moderate about that! He gave His all for us and calls us to do the same. When we think of the story of the rich young ruler who came to Christ and asked, "What must I do to inherit eternal life?" Jesus said, "There is just one thing you lack, go and sell all you have and come follow Me." We may think that Jesus was unfair to this young man. The truth is, what Jesus required of him, He expects of us. The Lord knows if there is anything in our lives that is keeping us from following Him completely. Some things in moderation are good, but moderation is a sin when it comes to spiritual warfare. When it comes to believing the Bible, moderation is a sin. When it comes to loving Jesus, moderation is a sin!

I eagerly expect and hope that I will in no way be ashamed, but will have sufficient courage so that now as always Christ will be exalted in my body, whether by life or by death.
Philippians 1:20

September 1

STICK TO THE PLAN

It can be easy to veer off course, especially when faced with uncertainty or challenges. However, as believers, we can find comfort and guidance in sticking to God's plan, trusting that His ways are higher than our own. Consider the imagery of a well-charted course laid out by a skilled navigator. While we may have our plans and desires, Scripture reminds us that God is the ultimate navigator of our lives. The verse from Proverbs highlights that while we make our plans, God directs our steps, ensuring that we reach the destination He has prepared for us. Jeremiah reassures us that God's plans are filled with hope and a future. Even when life feels chaotic, we have the assurance that God's plan is designed for our good and His glory. We may not always understand or agree with our paths, but we can trust the One who sees the bigger picture. In our walk with Christ, trusting and adhering to God's plan is crucial, even when the path seems unclear. Jeremiah 29:11 reminds us that God has plans to prosper us, not to harm us, and to give us hope and a future. Lean on His wisdom and remain steadfast in faith, knowing His timing is perfect. This week, reflect on areas where you might resist God's leading due to your plans. Surrender to Him, and ask for the courage to stick to His plan.

Humans plan their course in their hearts, but the Lord
establishes their steps.
Proverbs 16:9

September 2

HIS PLAN-NOT YOURS

In our walk of faith, we often chart our paths, mapping out plans that align with our dreams and aspirations. Yet, how frequently do those plans diverge from the path God has intended for us? Consider the story of Joseph. Dreaming of greatness, he never imagined his brothers would sell him into slavery. Nor could he have foreseen the years spent in an Egyptian prison. Despite these setbacks, Joseph ultimately rose to power, fulfilling a divine purpose far beyond anything he could have planned. When our plans clash with God's, the discomfort can be profound. We might feel lost, frustrated, or even abandoned. It's crucial to remember that God's vantage point transcends our own. He sees the broader picture, understanding how today's detours lead to tomorrow's destinations. God's promises offer reassurance. Jeremiah 29:11 reminds us that even when we cannot comprehend the why behind our circumstances, we are assured of His unwavering commitment to our well-being. His plans are crafted out of love, aimed at providing us with hope and a future enriched by His presence. When your path seems uncertain, know that God's plan is firmly rooted in your best interest. Trusting in Him might require surrender but will lead to growth and peace.

For I know the plans I have for you, declares the Lord, plans to prosper you and not to harm you, plans to give you hope and a future.
Jeremiah 29:11

IS HEAVEN REAL?

Many Christians wonder about the reality of heaven and what it means for their faith. The Bible speaks directly to this in John 14, where Jesus provides us with comforting assurance about the existence of heaven. In this verse, Jesus tells His disciples, and by extension all believers, that He is preparing a place for them in His Father's house. This promise offers a glimpse into the eternal home awaiting those who follow Him. The concept of heaven is woven throughout Scripture, affirming its existence and significance. In Revelation 21, we read about the new heaven and earth, where God will dwell with His people, wiping away every tear and eradicating suffering. This vision of heaven is a future hope and an encouragement to live a life faithful to Christ today. Heaven is described as a place of indescribable beauty, peace, and joy— qualities that resonate deeply within us. Yet, understanding heaven goes beyond its physical description. It represents an eternal relationship with God, free from pain and sin. As Christians, the promise of heaven should inspire us to deepen our relationship with God, knowing that our eternal future is secure in Him. Heaven is real, not just as a destination, but as a motivation for living a life that reflects the love and grace of Jesus Christ.

In My Father's house are many rooms; if it were not so, I would have told you. I am going there to prepare a place for you.
John 14:2

September 4

WHAT WILL YOU GIVE JESUS?

We are often reminded of the immense gift we received through Jesus Christ—His love, sacrifice, and grace. This divine gift compels us to reflect on what we can offer in return. But what can we truly give to Jesus that reflects our gratitude and love? The answer lies in intentional giving from our hearts. It's not about material wealth or grand gestures; it's about devotion, kindness, and living in a way that honors Him. Our gifts can take many forms—time spent in prayer and worship, acts of service to those in need, or even sharing our faith with others. Consider the story of the widow's offering in Mark 12:41-44. Her gift was small compared to others, but Jesus valued it more because it came from her heart. This teaches us that the quality of our giving is not measured by its size but by its sincerity. In this season of reflection, ask yourself, What will I give to Jesus? Maybe it's dedicating more time to studying His word, volunteering in your community, or simply being present and supportive to family and friends. Remember, whatever you decide to give, do so cheerfully and with a loving heart. Your genuine offerings hold great value in the eyes of the Lord, reflecting your commitment to follow Him and spread His love to the world.

Each of you should give what you have decided in your heart to give, not reluctantly or under compulsion, for God loves a cheerful giver.
2 Corinthians 9:7

September 5

WHO DO YOU HANG WITH?

The people we surround ourselves with profoundly influence our thoughts, decisions, and actions. It's a simple truth yet deeply impactful in our daily lives. The Bible reminds us through 1 Corinthians 15:33 that the company we keep can either build us up or lead us astray. Consider the moments when you've felt encouraged, motivated, or even challenged to grow. Those were times spent with individuals who inspired you to be your best self. On the flip side, recall instances where you may have strayed from your values. Often, these moments involve being influenced by negative or misguided company. The Apostle Paul's warning is clear—don't be deceived. It's easier than we think to underestimate the impact others have on us. Choosing friends who share similar values and encourage us to grow spiritually is essential. This doesn't mean avoiding all who think differently but being mindful of who we allow into our inner circle. Take a moment to reflect on your relationships. Are they nurturing your walk with God or hindering it? Seek out those who uplift your spirit and walk alongside you in faith. Engage with a community that encourages growth, both personally and spiritually. Evaluate your circle today. Are you surrounded by people who help you grow in faith and character?

Do not be misled: Bad company corrupts good character.
1 Corinthians 15:33

September 6

GET UP AND PRAY

It's easy to become spiritually complacent, like the disciples who succumbed to slumber in the Garden of Gethsemane. Jesus's call to "Get up and pray" is a powerful reminder of prayer's vital role in our spiritual well-being. Prayer is not merely a ritual but a dynamic lifeline connecting us to God. In moments of temptation and trials, prayer becomes an essential tool that fortifies our spirit and provides divine guidance. Through prayer, we find strength beyond our human limitations, trusting in God's wisdom and timing. Consider how Jesus, knowing the immense trial He was about to face, chose to spend His final hours in fervent prayer. His example teaches us that turning to God in earnest prayer in times of uncertainty can equip us with the resilience and peace needed to confront whatever lies ahead. Today, reflect on your own prayer life. Are there areas where you have become spiritually drowsy? Challenge yourself to rise above the comfort of routine and engage in heartfelt conversations with God. Allow His presence to empower you to stand firm in faith, resisting the temptations of this world. Prayer is our invitation to bring our burdens and our blessings before God. Experience the profound transformation that comes when we prioritize communion with our Creator.

Why are you sleeping? he asked them. Get up and pray so that you will not fall into temptation.
Luke 22:46

A NAME ABOVE ALL NAMES

Names often signify respect, identity, and authority. The name holds power, whether a family name or a title earned through hard work. In Philippians 2:9-11, we are reminded of the unparalleled significance of the name of Jesus. This passage emphasizes that God has given Jesus the highest honor, exalting His name above all others. For Christians, recognizing Jesus as having a name above all names is an acknowledgment of His divine status and an invitation to live under His Lordship. The Scripture assures us that, eventually, all creation will recognize His authority. It's a profound reminder of the sovereignty of Christ, urging us to align our lives with His teachings and commands. Living with the consciousness that the name of Jesus holds ultimate power can transform our daily walk. It encourages us to confidently approach life's challenges, knowing that we serve a Master who has overcome the world. It inspires us to worship more passionately, live humbly, and serve more selflessly. Consider today how the name of Jesus impacts your life.

Therefore, God exalted him to the highest place and gave him the name that is above every name, that in the name of Jesus, every knee should bow, in heaven and on earth and under the world, and every tongue acknowledge that Jesus Christ is Lord, to the glory of God the Father.
Philippians 2:9-11

September 8

DON'T WORRY; HE'S GOT THIS

It's easy to feel overwhelmed and uncertain about the future. Whether it's personal challenges, work pressures, or global uncertainties, we often question whether we're making the right decisions or heading in the right direction. During these times, it's crucial to remember the comforting truth—He's got this. Proverbs 3:5-6 reminds us to trust wholeheartedly in the Lord. It's an invitation to shift our focus from our limited understanding and place our confidence in God's infinite wisdom. Trusting God means acknowledging that He sees the bigger picture. He knows what lies ahead, even when we cannot see it ourselves. Submitting to God's guidance requires a conscious decision to prioritize His will over our desires. It means seeking His direction through His Word and aligning our actions with His teachings. When we do, He promises to make our paths straight. This doesn't mean life will be without challenges, but it assures us that we have a steady guide to lead us through. Today, take a moment to reflect on areas where you need to release control. Are there aspects of your life where you rely too much on your understanding? Remember, you are not alone. God is in control, and He has a plan for you.

Trust in the Lord with all your heart and lean not on your own understanding; in all your ways submit to him, and he will make your paths straight.
Proverbs 3:5-6

A SEASON FOR EVERYTHING

We often find ourselves at the mercy of time's unwavering rhythm. Seasons change, circumstances shift, and the pace of life ebbs and flows like the tides. The Scripture from Ecclesiastes reminds us of this natural order—a time for every purpose and activity under heaven. Consider the seasons of nature. Spring brings renewal, summer offers growth, autumn harvests, and winter rests. Each season, with its unique characteristics, serves a distinct purpose in the cycle of life. Similarly, our lives experience seasons that shape, challenge, and refine us. In moments of joy, we flourish like summer's bloom, basking in the warmth of God's blessings. During trials, we may feel the chill of winter, yet those are the times when we draw closer to Him, finding strength in His presence. Autumn's harvest symbolizes the times when the fruits of our labor and faith are realized. And in spring, we are renewed, encouraged by fresh opportunities and beginnings. Understanding the season you're in can bring clarity and peace. It's essential to recognize that each phase, whether tumultuous or peaceful, is part of God's plan. We allow ourselves to align with His purpose by trusting in His timing. Reflect on your current season. What lessons is God teaching you? How can you grow and thrive within this time?

There is a time for everything and a season for every activity under the heavens.
Ecclesiastes 3:1

JUST ANOTHER DAY

September 11 is a date imprint on our national consciousness and will never fade. But today is September 10, and that is the day that also stands out. That day may be the last day of an era. That day, we were all doing life with no idea what the next day would have for us. September 10, 2001, was a perfect late-summer day, like the infamous day that would follow. New Yorkers went about their business, absorbed by the daily trials and rewards of life in the city. The baseball pennant races were on, important enough to make the front pages of the tabloids. Since that day, much of our life has changed. But on September 10–we could not have known what the future held. That's what stays with us about this day; it even haunts us–the complete uncertainty of tomorrow. If we knew what would happen tomorrow, we may decide to stay in bed. We don't see the future. We are, however, given knowledge that is far more significant than the ability to see the future. We know, with the utmost certainty, that whatever the next day may bring, God is with us today, tomorrow, and forever. Jesus' love and protection are the ones we can count on. What a difference a day can bring.

And surely I am with you always, to the very end of the age.
Matthew 28:20

SEPTEMBER 11

This date will be engraved on the memories of Americans for generations. On that terrible day when terrorists killed thousands of innocent people, we began to realize the true depths of evil in the human heart, and the uncertainty and fragility of life itself. What lesson would we learn from such an appalling tragedy? For the first time, many faced the shallowness and emptiness of their lives and turned to God. Millions came together to pray. But where are they now? Life has always been uncertain; this day only made it more apparent. Billy Graham shared these words:

We've always needed God from the very beginning of this nation, but today, we need Him especially. We're facing a new kind of enemy involved in a new type of warfare, and we need the help of the Spirit of God. The Bible's words are our hope: "God is our refuge and strength, an ever-present help in trouble. Therefore, we will not fear, though the earth give way and the mountains fall into the heart of the sea.

On this day, we pause to remember the events of September 11 and their profound impact on our world.

Therefore, since we are receiving a kingdom that cannot be shaken, let us be thankful and so worship God acceptably with reverence and awe.
Hebrews 12:28

WHO'S ON YOUR LIST?

Many times a year, you receive invitations to attend breakfasts, luncheons, and dinners. Some of these invitations spark no interest in us, while others are so compelling and close to our hearts that we respond with an enthusiastic, Yes! In Luke 14, a wealthy man sent invitations to a dinner party he was hosting. To get a personal invitation during this age signified a distinct honor. When the dinner was ready, he sent his servant out to notify all the guests, and that's when the unthinkable happened. His guests showed no respect for His invitation by making excuses as to why they could not attend the dinner. You would think the host might cancel the dinner, but he didn't. He sent out more invitations to the streets and alleys where the outcasts of Israelite society were found, to the country lanes, and behind the hedges where the Gentiles lived. In short, the servants were sent to persuasively invite the unwanted, the unfit, and the unworthy of society to the feast until the tables were full of guests. This brief but essential story reveals a beautiful truth about God: He values all of humanity—exceptionally the less fortunate. The message of salvation is fundamentally an invitation to everyone. How can we live this out?

So his master said, Go out into the country lanes and behind the hedges and urge anyone you find to come, so that the house will be full.
Luke 14:23

CHILDREN ARE IMPORTANT

In the gospel of Matthew, Jesus emphasizes the importance of children in the eyes of God. His call to welcome and care for them reflects His boundless love and compassion. In today's world, many children face hunger and lack of necessities. This reality presents us, as Christians, with both a challenge and an opportunity to live out the teachings of Jesus. When we talk about hungry children, it goes beyond physical nourishment. It ensures they can access education, emotional support, and spiritual guidance. Each child deserves a bright future, and our role is to nurture and support them, echoing the example set by Christ. Action can be taken in various forms—donating to food banks, volunteering at local shelters, or advocating for policies that address child poverty. Our acts of kindness and service meet immediate needs and testify to the love and care that Jesus has for every child. Reflect on how you can make a difference in hungry children's lives. By doing so, you become a living testament of faith, extending the reach of God's kingdom to the most vulnerable among us. Remember, in lifting the least among us, we fulfill the call to embody the love of Christ in tangible, impactful ways.

But Jesus said, Let the little children come to me, and do not hinder them, for the kingdom of heaven belongs to such as these.
Matthew 19:14

September 14

YOU ARE AN OVERCOMER

Life often presents us with challenges that seem impossible. Financial worries, health issues, relationship struggles—each one can feel like a mountain too steep to climb. Yet, as Christians, we have assurance through our faith that we are not alone in these battles. Jesus, in His wisdom and love, reminded us that troubles are a part of life. However, He did not leave us without hope. John 16:33 is a powerful reminder that despite the trials we face, Jesus has already overcome the world. His victory is our victory. This means that we have the strength and courage to overcome whatever obstacle lies before us because He is with us. Our struggles do not define us; our identity in Christ does. Overcoming doesn't mean our problems disappear instantly. Instead, it signifies our ability to face them with faith, knowing that God equips us with all we need to conquer what lies in our path. In our weakness, His power is made perfect, enabling us to rise above adversity. The next time you encounter a difficult situation, remember this promise. Jesus has already paved the way for you to be an overcomer. Take heart and walk confidently in your identity, knowing that His peace is yours to claim.

I have told you these things so you may have peace in me. In this world, you will have trouble. But take heart! I have overcome the world.
John 16:33

September 15

MAKE A DIFFERENCE

The call to make a difference resonates louder than ever in a world that often seems overshadowed by darkness. The scriptures invite us to be the light that illuminates the paths of others, reflecting the love of Christ through our actions. The verse from Matthew reminds us that our purpose is not self-serving but God-glorifying. Each good deed we perform is like a beacon that points back to the Father, inviting others to witness His presence in our lives. It challenges us to step beyond our comfort zones and into the active role of change-makers. Consider the small acts of kindness that ripple into more giant waves of transformation. A smile, a helping hand, or a word of encouragement can profoundly affect those around us. These acts are not just about being nice but about embodying the principles of Christ's teachings. Making a difference also requires courage. It means standing firm in our faith when the world pushes back. It involves making choices that reflect our values, even when they are unpopular or inconvenient. This courage is fueled by the assurance that we are not alone; God walks with us, empowering us to impact the world in His name. Reflect today on how you can be a light source in your community. Remember, the smallest flame can pierce through the darkness.

In the same way, let your light shine before others, that they may see
your good deeds and glorify your Father in heaven.
Matthew 5:16

September 16

STOP AND LISTEN

Taking a moment to pause can feel strange and counterintuitive. But this is precisely what God calls us to do. The invitation to "be still and know" is a powerful reminder that we are not defined by our busyness or accomplishments but by our relationship with God. Life can bombard us with noise—be it the demands of work, family, or technology constantly vying for our attention. It's easy to become overwhelmed, losing sight of God's presence and purpose. Yet, in the quiet moments, we often discover the peace and clarity we desperately seek. Stopping doesn't mean abandoning our responsibilities but rather allowing ourselves space to hear what God is trying to communicate to us. It's about cultivating a posture of listening, where we can discern His will and receive His guidance. When we stop and listen, we open our hearts to God's wisdom, strength, and love. The essence of being still is trusting God's sovereignty and plan for our lives. He is exalted in the quiet as in creation and worldwide. By taking time to listen, we affirm our faith in His timing and His perfect nature. This week, challenge yourself to find moments to stop and listen to God—and see how it transforms your perspective and renews your spirit.

Be still, and know that I am God; I will be exalted among the nations, I will be exalted in the earth.
Psalm 46:10

September 17

IT'S TIME TO CLEAR THE AIR

We often encounter situations where misunderstandings and conflicts arise. The air becomes thick with unspoken words and unresolved issues, clouding our relationship with God and others. Jesus, in His Sermon on the Mount, emphasizes the importance of reconciliation before worship. It's easy to ignore these unresolved matters, hoping they'll dissipate over time. But the reality is they linger, affecting our ability to fully experience the presence of God and the joy of fellowship with others. The call to clear the air is an invitation to address these issues head-on. Jesus teaches us to prioritize reconciliation over religious rituals. Before we present our offerings at the altar, we're urged to make amends with those we've hurt or who've hurt us. This is a powerful reminder that our relationships with others deeply impact our relationship with God. Clearing the air requires humility and courage. It means having open, honest conversations that can sometimes be uncomfortable. Yet, the peace that follows is invaluable. It opens the path for genuine worship and a deeper connection with God. Today, reflect on any unresolved conflicts in your life.

Therefore, if you are offering your gift at the altar and remember that your brother or sister has something against you, leave your gift there in front of the altar. First, go and be reconciled to them; then come and offer your gift.
Matthew 5:23-24

GOD WILL BLESS YOU

Walking in alignment with God's word is a deliberate and mindful choice. Psalm 1 paints a vivid picture of the blessed individual—one who consciously avoids paths of sin and instead finds joy in the teachings of the Lord. The promise here is profound yet beautifully uncomplicated. A life rooted in God's word brings stability, growth, and prosperity, much like a tree planted by nourishing streams. This imagery of a tree not only speaks of immediate blessings but also suggests long-term flourishing and resilience, regardless of external circumstances. Meditating on the law day and night, we cultivate a deep connection with our Creator. This relationship becomes a source of strength and guidance, enabling us to bear fruit in our lives and embody the virtues and character of Christ. Consider your own life. Are there areas where you're walking in step with the wicked or perhaps sitting in the company of mockers? Reflect on how you can turn towards God's word instead, allowing His teachings to direct your steps and shape your path.

Blessed is the one who does not walk in step with the wicked or stand in the way that sinners take or sit in the company of mockers, but whose delight is in the law of the Lord, and who meditates on his law day and night. That person is like a tree planted by streams of water, which yields its fruit in season and whose leaf does not wither—whatever they do prospers.
Psalm 1:1-3

ARE YOU A KNOW-IT-ALL?

Information is at our fingertips, and opinions are freely shared across social media; it's easy to fall into the trap of thinking we know it all. Our culture glorifies the self-made and those who have all the answers. But, as Christians, we are called to a different standard. Proverbs 3:7 cautions us against being wise in our own eyes. It reminds us to maintain a posture of humility and reverence towards God. The Scripture challenges us to recognize that our understanding is limited compared to the wisdom of God. When we acknowledge this, we open ourselves to divine guidance. Consider how often we rely on our knowledge and how that has impacted our lives. Have there been moments when leaning on your knowledge led to unforeseen consequences? Remember, God invites us to trust in His wisdom above our own. When we fear the Lord, it signifies a deep respect and awe for Him. It means acknowledging His sovereignty and seeking His guidance in every aspect of our lives. This reverence compels us to shun evil, turning away from actions and thoughts that lead us away from His presence. Reflect on areas where you might be acting as a know-it-all. Are you willing to surrender those areas to God, acknowledging His greater understanding? Allow His wisdom to guide you.

Do not be wise in your own eyes; fear the Lord and shun evil.
Proverbs 3:7

September 20

WORSE THAN GOSSIP

The fine line between gossiping and betrayal often blurs. Gossip, though harmful, is typically surface-level chatter that erodes trust and damages relationships. However, betrayal cuts deeper, severing once foundational bonds. Consider the story of Jesus and Judas Iscariot. Despite the whispers among the disciples, Judas's betrayal led to Jesus's arrest. While gossip may spread rumors, betrayal is the dagger at the heart. Judas's act wasn't just a breach of trust but a complete reversal of allegiance. When we reflect on our lives, betrayal can manifest in various forms. It might be a broken promise, a confidante sharing secrets, or a trusted friend acting against you. What makes betrayal feel worse than gossip is the intimacy of the relationship. Proverbs 16:28 reminds us that while gossip can drive a wedge between friends, betrayal goes further. For Christians, the challenge is to guard our hearts and actions. We must strive to be faithful in our relationships, avoiding the temptation to gossip and the treachery of betrayal. In our walk with God, we are called to emulate Jesus, who forgave even those who betrayed Him. This doesn't imply that betrayal doesn't hurt, but it invites us to seek reconciliation and healing, trusting that God can mend even the most broken of bonds.

A perverse person stirs up conflict, and a gossip separates close friends.
Proverbs 16:28

September 21

BEING IN CONTROL

The urge to control every detail of our lives can be overwhelming, yet it often leads to stress and anxiety. Instead, Scripture invites us to trust God completely, releasing our need to control and rely on His infinite wisdom. Being in control doesn't mean taking charge of everything but recognizing that true control lies in surrendering to God's will. When we lean not on our understanding, we open ourselves to divine guidance, which is more profound and far-reaching than we can imagine. Submitting to God is not about giving up; it's about gaining peace and clarity. When we acknowledge Him in all our ways, He promises to straighten our paths that may seem crooked or unclear from our limited perspective. This divine promise reassures us that God is orchestrating our journeys for good even when life feels chaotic. Consider areas of your life where you're holding on too tightly. Is it your career, relationships, or plans? Trusting God with these concerns means inviting His perfect plan to unfold. This week, take steps to release control, trusting that God will guide you with love and purpose. Remember, being in control is not about holding the reins but about trusting the One who does.

Trust in the Lord with all your heart and lean not on your own understanding; in all your ways, submit to him, and he will make your paths straight.
Proverbs 3:5-6

September 22

WHEN YOUR EYES OPEN

Mornings often become a mad rush of to-do lists and responsibilities. Yet, there's profound wisdom in giving God the first moments of your day. Before the demands of life set in, create a sacred space to align your heart with His word. The verse from Matthew reminds us of the importance of prioritizing our relationship with God. When we seek His kingdom first, everything else falls into place. Think of your morning time with God as an anchor, setting a peaceful and purposeful tone for the rest of your day. It may mean waking up just a few minutes earlier to read Scripture or meditate on His teachings. It might involve sitting quietly in His presence, allowing His peace to wash over you. During these moments, invite God into every aspect of your life. Share your hopes, fears, and gratitude with Him. Your morning with God is a powerful reminder that He is the center of everything you do. It cultivates a sense of trust, knowing that you are rooted in His love and guidance no matter what the day brings. As you prioritize these first moments with Him, watch how your perspective shifts. Challenges become growth opportunities, and mundane tasks transform into acts of worship. Start your day by seeking His presence, and witness the transformation it brings to your life.

But seek first his kingdom and his righteousness, and all these things will be given to you as well.
Matthew 6:33

September 23

LEAVING IT BEHIND

The pursuit of wealth and success often overshadows life's more profound questions. We accumulate, we strive, and we achieve, often equating our worth with our possessions. Yet, the apostle Paul reminds us in his letter to Timothy of an undeniable truth—our earthly gains won't accompany us into eternity. This Scripture challenges us to reconsider our priorities. While there's nothing inherently wrong with wealth and possessions, they should not define our identity or dictate our values. Instead, what truly endures are the spiritual riches we cultivate through our relationship with God and the love we extend to others. In Matthew 6:19-21, Jesus teaches us to store treasures in heaven, where rust and moth cannot destroy them. These treasures are found in acts of kindness, faithfulness, and the impact we make in the lives of others. They are the legacy of love and faith that we leave behind—not in material wealth, but in the seeds of hope and grace we plant in the hearts around us. Reflect today on where your true treasure lies. Are you investing in what will last beyond this lifetime? Consider how you can shift your focus from temporary gains to eternal rewards. Remember, while we may not take our possessions with us, the love and faith we cultivate will follow us into eternity.

For we brought nothing into the world, and we can take
nothing out of it.
1 Timothy 6:7

September 24

ARE YOU AT PEACE?

It's easy to get caught up in chaos and confusion. We find ourselves yearning for a sense of calm amidst the storm. But what does it indeed mean to be at peace? For Christians, peace is not just the absence of conflict or trouble, but a profound sense of tranquility that comes from a relationship with God. The peace that Jesus offers us differs from any peace the world can provide. It is not fleeting or dependent on external circumstances. Instead, it's a deep and lasting peace that resides within our hearts, given to us through the Holy Spirit. Consider the peace Jesus had, even in the face of adversity. His unshakeable trust in the Father allowed Him to remain calm, offering us a powerful example of how we can live our own lives. When our hearts are anchored in Him, we no longer need to be troubled or afraid. Reflect on your own life. Are you experiencing this divine peace? If not, think about what might be blocking it. Is it anxiety about the future, concerns over daily struggles, or unresolved conflicts? Take time to bring these burdens to God, trusting Him to help you find peace. Remember, true peace is a gift from God. It's a promise that we can remain steadfast and assured in His love regardless of what happens around us. Are you ready to accept this peace today?

Peace I leave with you; my peace I give you. I do not give to you as the world gives. Do not let your hearts be troubled, and do not be afraid.
John 14:27

September 25

INSTANT SUCCESS?

The allure of instant success is both tempting and misleading. Many believe that success can be achieved overnight, but Scripture offers a different perspective, emphasizing patience, perseverance, and faith. The Bible consistently teaches that success is not about quick gains but steady, diligent work. The wisdom found in Proverbs 21:5 makes it clear that diligent planning and hard work are the true pathways to success. It warns us against hasty decisions, often resulting in failure or unfulfilled promises. Consider the story of Joseph, who experienced a significant delay in his rise to power in Egypt. His path to success was filled with trials and waiting periods. Yet, his faithfulness and dedication eventually led him to a position of influence and authority, fulfilling God's purpose for his life. In the same way, our spiritual growth and life's accomplishments are often the result of time, effort, and divine timing. While seeking God's guidance, we are encouraged to develop patience and trust in His plan. When tempted by the allure of instant success, remember that God values faithfulness and integrity over immediate results.

Rely on Him, be diligent in your efforts, and trust He will lead you to true success in His perfect time. Success, according to God's plan, is a marathon, not a sprint—the plans of the diligent lead to profit as surely as haste leads to poverty.
Proverbs 21:5

UNDERSTANDING THE BIBLE

It's easy to feel overwhelmed when reading the Bible. With its vast history, poetic language, and profound teachings, it can be challenging to grasp its meaning. Yet, understanding the Bible is not beyond our reach. It requires patience, study, and prayer, but God desires to speak to us through His Word. The Bible serves as a guide for our lives. The Scripture from 2 Timothy reminds us that God inspires every part of the Bible. It's designed to teach us what is true and help us realize what is wrong in our lives. By reading and reflecting on these words, we are trained in righteousness and equipped for every good work. Begin by approaching the Bible with an open heart. Set aside preconceived notions and ask God to reveal His truth. Start with a passage, like the Gospels, where you can learn about Jesus' life and teachings. Use study tools like commentaries or Bible dictionaries if needed. They can provide context and clarity, making complex passages more understandable. Remember, it's a process. Understanding grows over time as we immerse ourselves in Scripture. Trust that God will honor your efforts to seek Him through His Word. Keep reading, reflecting, and allowing the Holy Spirit to guide you.

All Scripture is God-breathed and is useful for teaching, rebuking, correcting, and training in righteousness so that the servant of God may be thoroughly equipped for every good work.
2 Timothy 3:16-17

BE A MAGNET FOR OTHERS

In a world where darkness often overshadows the light, being a beacon is not just a responsibility but also an opportunity. Jesus calls us to be the world's light, illuminating the path for those around us. When we embody Christ's teachings and live in a way that reflects His love and grace, we naturally draw others toward us. But what does it mean to be a magnet for others? It means living authentically, showing kindness, and displaying integrity in our daily actions. It involves standing firm in our faith, even when faced with challenges, and allowing God's love to shine through us in every interaction. By doing so, we create an inviting space for others to explore their spiritual journeys. Our lives testify to God's goodness, encouraging others to seek and glorify Him. Remember, it's not about being perfect but genuine in our love for God and His people. Let's strive to positively influence our communities, drawing others closer to God through our words, actions, and love. By being a magnet for others, we fulfill our calling to spread His light in every corner of the world.

You are the light of the world. A town built on a hill cannot be hidden. Neither do people light a lamp and put it under a bowl. Instead, they put it on its stand, giving everyone in the house light. In the same way, let your light shine before others, that they may see your good deeds and glorify your Father in heaven.
Matthew 5:14-16

FASTING

Have you ever considered fasting? Fasting is an ancient spiritual discipline that Christians have practiced for centuries. It serves as a time of reflection, self-denial, and spiritual growth. In this guide, we'll explore what the Bible says about fasting and its importance in strengthening our relationship with God. Fasting is an act of humility and devotion meant to draw us closer to God and away from worldly distractions. Jesus instructs us to approach fasting sincerely, not seeking attention or recognition from others. Instead, fasting should be a private matter between us and God, an opportunity to deepen our faith and reliance on Him. It can be a powerful tool to refocus our priorities and align our hearts with God's will. By denying ourselves physical sustenance, we create space for spiritual nourishment. Consider integrating fasting into your spiritual routine to enhance your Christian walk. Reflect on what God may call you to surrender to grow closer to Him.

When you fast, do not look somber as the hypocrites do, for they disfigure their faces to show others they are fasting. Indeed, I tell you, they have received their reward in full. But when you fast, put oil on your head and wash your face, so that it will not be evident to others that you are fasting, but only to your unseen Father; and your Father, who sees what is done in secret, will reward you.
Matthew 6:16-18

September 29

SINFUL DESIRES

Sinful desires can be likened to small and seemingly insignificant seeds but with the potential to grow into something much larger and more destructive. In James 1:15, we see a powerful illustration of how unchecked desires can lead to sin and spiritual death. Often, these desires begin subtly—a fleeting thought, a momentary longing—and can seem harmless at first glance. Yet, as Christians, we are reminded of the importance of vigilance. Recognizing these desires early and taking steps to address them aligns with our commitment to live a life that honors God. Consider how the world around us frequently normalizes or even glamorizes certain desires. From material wealth to personal gratification, these desires can easily distract us from our true purpose. We must actively choose to avoid these worldly temptations and focus on God's word and promises. One approach is to immerse ourselves in Scripture, allowing God's truth to reshape our hearts and minds. Doing so replaces sinful desires with a hunger for righteousness and a deeper relationship with Christ. Challenge yourself today to identify any areas where unchecked desires might take root in your life. Reflect on how you can cultivate godly desires through prayer.

Then, after desire has conceived, it gives birth to sin; and sin, when it is full-grown, gives birth to death.
James 1:15

September 30

LET'S GO TO CHURCH

Attending church can sometimes feel like another item on the busy to-do list. However, gathering together as a community of believers is essential for spiritual growth and encouragement. These verses remind us of the power of fellowship and the importance of supporting each other in our Christian walk. Gathering together allows us to share our joys, bear each other's burdens, and grow stronger in faith. Attending church is about being part of a family—a community of believers who motivate and inspire each other to live out their faith in everyday actions. Church is a place to learn, grow, and find encouragement to impact the world positively. If you've been feeling disconnected or overwhelmed, take a moment to reflect on the joy and support that comes from being part of a church community. There's a unique strength found in worshiping together, hearing God's Word, and forming meaningful relationships that help us stay accountable and focused on our spiritual journeys. Commit to prioritizing church attendance, knowing that your presence enriches your lives and strengthens the body of Christ.

And let us consider how we may spur one another on toward love and good deeds, not giving up meeting together, as some are in the habit of doing, but encouraging one another—and all the more as you see the day approaching.
Hebrews 10:24-25

October 1

YOU ARE NEVER ALONE

In moments of silence and solitude, when it feels like the world has turned its back on us, we can find profound comfort in knowing we are never truly alone. The Bible is filled with reminders of God's enduring presence. Deuteronomy 31:6 offers powerful assurance that God is always with us, regardless of our challenges or fears. Consider the story of Joshua, who took the mantle of leadership from Moses. Leading the Israelites into the Promised Land was daunting, filled with uncertainty and formidable foes. Yet, God's words to Joshua, and by extension to us, were clear and reassuring. God promised His accompaniment every step of the way, urging Joshua to be strong and courageous. Like Joshua, we are encouraged to confront our challenges head-on. From personal struggles to global uncertainties, it's easy to feel overwhelmed. However, the promise of God's presence can transform our fear into faith. It provides a foundation to build courage, knowing that the Creator of the universe walks beside us. We might not always see God's presence, but His promises are unwavering. He is with us in the quiet moments, the busy seasons, and the trials of life. Remember, you are never alone.

Be strong and courageous. Do not be afraid or terrified because of them, for the Lord your God goes with you; he will never leave you nor forsake you.
Deuteronomy 31:6

WHO ARE YOUR ENEMIES?

We often encounter people who challenge us in ways that test our patience and faith. Whether they are co-workers, neighbors, or even family members, these individuals can be perceived as enemies. However, Jesus' teachings in Matthew 5 urge us to redefine our understanding of enemies. Rather than harboring resentment or ill will, we're called to love them—a radical shift reflecting God's heart. Why should we love our enemies? Firstly, it aligns us with God's nature. Our Heavenly Father loves unconditionally, providing for the righteous and the unrighteous. When we extend love to those who oppose us, we mirror God's grace and mercy, showcasing an alternative way of living that defies worldly norms. Loving our enemies does not mean we condone their actions, nor does it imply submission to harmful behavior. Instead, it challenges us to respond with a spirit of kindness and understanding, fostering peace rather than escalating conflict. This perspective invites us to see the humanity in others, even those who have wronged us, and to remember that we are recipients of God's boundless grace.

But I tell you, love your enemies and pray for those who persecute you, that you may be children of your Father in heaven. He causes his sun to rise on the evil and the good, and sends rain on the righteous and the unrighteous.
Matthew 5:44-45

October 3

ARE YOU NEGATIVE?

Negativity is like a slow poison that seeps into your soul, distorting your perspective and affecting your daily walk with Christ. Philippians 4:8 challenges us to focus on what is good and uplifting. But how often do we find ourselves dwelling on the negative? Life's challenges can make it easy to fall into negative thinking patterns. The news cycles constantly bombard us with conflict, disaster, and despair stories. Social media amplifies voices of criticism and complaint. These influences can cloud our hearts and minds, leading us to overlook the beauty and goodness around us. Paul's letter to the Philippians offers us a powerful antidote. We can combat negativity by intentionally focusing on what is true, noble, right, and pure. This doesn't mean ignoring the world's problems but choosing to view them through hope and faith. Consider how you spend your time. Are the books you read, the shows you watch, and the conversations you engage in lifting or dragging you down? Take moments throughout your day to pause and shift your focus to God's goodness. Imagine how your life could change if you consistently practiced positive thinking.

Finally, brothers and sisters, whatever is true, whatever is noble, whatever is right, whatever is pure, whatever is lovely, whatever is admirable—if anything is excellent or praiseworthy— think about such things.
Philippians 4:8

October 4

WE ARE ONE BODY

It can be easy to forget the profound unity we share as believers. The Apostle Paul uses the metaphor of the body to illustrate this truth. Just as the human body is composed of various parts working together, so is the church—a diverse community united by faith in Christ. Each member of the body has a unique role. Some serve through teaching, others through acts of compassion, and still others through prayer and encouragement. No role is inferior or superior; all are vital for the health and functioning of the body. When one part suffers, every part suffers; when one part is honored, every part rejoices with it (1 Corinthians 12:26). This analogy reminds us that differences in culture, background, or social status should not divide us. Instead, these differences enhance our collective strength by bringing varied perspectives and gifts. Our shared identity in Christ supersedes all earthly distinctions. Are you actively contributing your gifts or holding back due to comparison or insecurity? Through our interconnectedness, we reflect Christ's fullness to the world.

Just as a body, though one, has many parts, but all its many parts form one body, so it is with Christ. For we were all baptized by one Spirit to form one body—whether Jews or Gentiles, enslaved person or free—and we were all given the one Spirit to drink. Even so, the body comprises not one part but of many.
1 Corinthians 12:12-14

IT WON'T LAST FOREVER

Life brings storms into our path—trials that seem endless and burdens that feel too heavy to bear. But as Christians, we hold onto a profound truth that brings hope and reassurance in the midst of turmoil. This truth is simple yet powerful: it won't last forever. The Apostle Paul, who knew suffering firsthand, encourages us in 2 Corinthians to view our troubles as "light and momentary." This perspective shift is not meant to belittle our struggles but to remind us of the eternal glory that awaits beyond the present hardships. We are encouraged to lift our gaze from the temporary pains of this world and focus on the eternal promises of God. When life overwhelms us, let's remember to anchor our hearts in the knowledge that God provides. Our trials have a purpose: refining and drawing us closer to Him. They are shaping our character and preparing us for an eternity where pain and sorrow will be no more. Today, if you find yourself weary from your challenges, hold onto this promise—what you're going through is temporary. Fix your eyes on Jesus, the author, and perfecter of our faith, and allow His peace to fill your heart.

I pray that you may prosper in all things and be healthy, just as your soul prospers.
3 John 1:2

DO YOU FEEL OVERWHELMED

Life often presents us with moments where the weight of our responsibilities, worries, and emotions seem too much to bear. Yet, in these times of feeling overwhelmed, we are invited to lean into our faith and find solace in God's unwavering presence. Today's Scripture is a powerful reminder of God's boundless compassion and Invitation to surrender our burdens. When we feel overwhelmed, it's easy to isolate ourselves, thinking we must bear our struggles alone. However, God calls us to trust Him with our fears and concerns, knowing He is always ready to support us. Consider the areas in your life where you feel most overwhelmed. Is it work, family, or personal challenges? Take a moment to breathe deeply and bring these concerns before God in prayer. Try setting aside a few minutes daily to journal your thoughts and prayers. Write about what overwhelms you and any small victories or moments of clarity. Don't allow your busy day to make you feel overwhelmed. Allow this practice to become a refuge, a space where you can see God's hand steadying your heart. In the midst of chaos, may you find comfort and strength in His eternal love.

All these things shall be added to you.
Matthew 6:33

ARE YOU SELFISH?

A mother was preparing pancakes for her sons, Kevin, 5, and Ryan, 3. The boys began to argue over who would get the first pancake. Their mother saw the opportunity for a moral lesson. If Jesus were sitting here, He would say, Let my brother have the first pancake; I can wait. Kevin turned to his younger brother and said, Ryan, you be Jesus today. Selfishness is defined as the state of being overly concerned with one's self. On a scale of one to ten, how often do you think about the needs of others and try to meet them? Before you answer, read this: "If anyone has material possessions and sees a brother or sister in need but has no pity on them, how can the love of God be in that person?" God is not asking us to sacrifice for others to the point where we jeopardize our own health and mental wellbeing and then end up resentful for doing so. Nor does He expect us to meet every need that comes our way. He's challenging what's in it for me, an attitude of our age in which self-gratification, self-improvement, self-enlightenment, and self-indulgence are increasingly being promoted. Selfishness dies hard, but it's a stronghold we must break to experience the peace and joy that give life meaning.

How can the love of God be in that person?
1 John 3:17

SATAN'S SECRET

We often underestimate Satan's cunning strategies. The Bible reminds us that Satan is not just a symbolic figure but a real adversary who actively seeks to derail our faith. Understanding his tactics is crucial for every believer determined to live victoriously in Christ. Satan's secret? Subtlety. His most effective ploys are not overt and obvious but those that slip quietly into our lives, often unnoticed. He delights in sowing seeds of doubt, fear, and discontentment. He whispers lies that distort our perception of ourselves and our understanding of God's truth. One of his favorite tactics is deception. Satan loves to twist Scripture and manipulate truth, much like he did with Eve in the Garden of Eden. He aims to make us question God's goodness and faithfulness. When we're unaware of his deception, we risk falling into traps of discouragement and disobedience. However, we are not defenseless. Ephesians 6 encourages us to "put on the full armor of God." This means equipping ourselves daily with truth, righteousness, faith, and the Word of God. By actively engaging in spiritual disciplines such as reading Scripture and meditating on its truths, we fortify our hearts and minds against Satan's schemes. Satan's power is limited, but God's power in us is boundless.

Put on the full armor of God so that you can take your stand against the devil's schemes.
Ephesians 6:11

SMALL GROUPS

In a world that often emphasizes individual achievement and personal success, the biblical model for growth and support through small groups shines as a beacon of strength. The early church was built on the foundation of believers coming together in large gatherings and intimate settings where they could encourage and uplift one another. Small groups provide a place for believers to experience an authentic community where support and accountability become the norm. They offer a unique opportunity for members to share their stories, pray for one another, and study God's Word deeply and personally. Through such interactions, faith is nurtured and actively lived out. The beauty of small groups lies in their ability to reflect the diverse body of Christ. Each person brings unique insights and experiences that enrich the collective understanding of Scripture. Everyone has a voice in these settings, and each contribution helps others grow in their walk with God. Yet, small groups are more than just a spiritual exercise; they are vital to individual wellbeing. In times of need or joy, having a close-knit group of believers to turn to is invaluable. The support system built within a small group can offer comfort, celebration, and spiritual guidance. We are called to be in community with one another.

For where two or three gather in my name, there am I with them.
Matthew 18:20

October 10

GOD'S APPOINTMENT?

We often face disappointment. Plans don't manifest how we envision, and paths we thought were clear suddenly become obstructed. Yet, as Christians, we are called to trust that God's plan surpasses our understanding. The words of Proverbs 19:21 remind us, "Many are the plans in a person's heart, but it is the Lord's purpose that prevails." Consider the story of Joseph, who was sold into slavery by his brothers. Betrayed, imprisoned, and forgotten, Joseph's disappointment was profound. However, his story did not end there. Through his trials, God placed him in a position to save Egypt and his family during a famine. When faced with disappointment, it's easy to feel lost and question God's love. But these moments invite us to deepen our faith and surrender control. In Romans 8:28, we find reassurance, "And we know that in all things God works for the good of those who love Him, who have been called according to His purpose." God's timing and ways are perfect, though they may differ from ours. He sees the bigger picture and acts out of love and for our ultimate good. The challenge lies in trusting His timing. Subsequent times, disappointment strikes, so pause and pray.

Be strong and courageous. Do not be afraid or terrified because of them, for the Lord your God goes with you; he will never leave you nor forsake you.
Deuteronomy 31:6

YOUR PRAYER ROOM

We all find prayer hard. With noise and distractions, finding a dedicated space for prayer can be both a refuge and a powerful tool for deepening your faith. As Christians, we understand the importance of cultivating a personal relationship with God, and having a prayer room can be an integral part of that spiritual practice. Why a Prayer Room?

The concept of a prayer room is rooted in the idea of creating a sacred space, free from life's distractions, where you can commune with God. It's a place to lay down your burdens, offer thanksgiving, and seek guidance. Jesus Himself sought solitude in prayer, withdrawing from the crowds to be alone with the Father (Luke 5:16). By having a designated prayer room, we follow His example, making space for intimacy with God. In creating a prayer room, you're not only setting aside physical space but also affirming your intention to prioritize your relationship with God. Whether it's a few minutes or an hour, use this time to listen, reflect, and grow closer to Him. Do you have a prayer room? If not, consider creating one today and experience the peace and strength it can bring to your spiritual life.

But when you pray, go into your room, close the door, and pray to your Father.
Matthew 6:6

October 12

FIRST IMPRESSIONS

First impressions are powerful. They can shape our perceptions and influence our decisions. Yet, as 1 Samuel 16:7 reminds us, God's view is often contrary to our own. When Samuel was sent to anoint a new king, he was initially swayed by appearances. However, God instructed him to look beyond the surface. In our daily lives, we may be tempted to judge others based on their looks, attire, or demeanor. This inclination is natural, but it can prevent us from seeing the true essence of a person— their character, intentions, and Spirit. God's perspective invites us to dig deeper, see beyond external facades, and recognize each individual's divine image. Consider the times you've been judged based on first impressions. How did it make you feel? Conversely, reflect on instances where you've made snap judgments about others. Did those assessments hold over time? Adopting God's approach requires intentionality. It calls us to pause, reflect, and seek to understand the hearts of others. By doing so, we align ourselves with His way of seeing the world and open ourselves to richer, more authentic connections. Challenge yourself to move beyond initial impressions.

Do not consider his appearance or height, for I have rejected him. The Lord does not look at the things people look at. People look at the outward appearance, but the Lord looks at the heart.
1 Samuel 16:7

October 13

HURRY UP!

The phrase hurry up is ingrained in our daily lives. We rush from one commitment to another, barely pausing to reflect on where we're going or why. But what does the Bible say about our whirlwind of activities? Ecclesiastes 3 reminds us that there is a divinely appointed time for everything. It challenges us to examine whether our hurried pace aligns with God's timing or is a product of worldly pressures. Are we rushing through life, missing the beauty in the everyday moments because we're so focused on what's next? Jesus often took time to withdraw from the crowds and seek solitude in prayer, demonstrating the importance of aligning our actions with God's purpose. The account of Mary and Martha in Luke 10 also highlights this principle. While Martha was busy with preparations, Mary chose to sit at Jesus' feet and listen to His words. Jesus commended Mary's choice, teaching us the value of prioritizing spiritual growth over busyness. The next time you feel the urge to hurry up, pause and consider what is truly important. Ask yourself if your activities draw you closer to God or distract you from Him. Remember, God's timing is perfect, and His plans for you are always worth the wait. May you find peace and purpose every moment, trusting that God's timing is the best.

There is a time for everything and a season for every activity
under the heavens.
Ecclesiastes 3:1

WHY BAD THINGS HAPPEN

In the midst of life's trials, it is natural to question why bad things happen. For many Christians, these experiences challenge and refine faith. Understanding that suffering is part of the human condition can be daunting and comforting. Jesus acknowledged the presence of trouble in the world, yet He also offered hope by proclaiming His victory over it. The Bible recounts numerous stories of individuals who faced adversity —Job, Joseph, and Paul, to name a few. Their journeys reveal that while suffering is accurate, it is not the end of the story. Each story showcases God's faithfulness and the ultimate victory of His purpose for those who trust Him. Bad things may happen because we live in a fallen world marred by sin. However, God's sovereignty means He can use the darkest moments to produce something good. Romans 8:28 reminds us, "And we know that in all things God works for the good of those who love him, who have been called according to his purpose." Take heart and hold on to faith. In times of suffering, seek God's presence, lean into His promises, and remember that through Christ, we are more than conquerors. Whatever you face is temporary, and God's love and purpose for you are eternal.

In this world, you will have trouble. But take heart! I have overcome the world.
John 16:33

October 15

A TIME TO CRY AND LAUGH

Life comprises a series of seasons, each marked by distinct emotions and experiences. Ecclesiastes 3:4 reminds us that sorrow and joy are integral to our lives. Understanding this concept can help us better appreciate the ebb and flow of our emotional and spiritual journeys. Tears can be a powerful expression of grief, disappointment, or overwhelming joy. In moments of sadness, crying can bring healing and release, allowing us to process our feelings and draw closer to God. This period of weeping may also deepen our empathy for others, strengthening our capacity to offer compassion and support to those around us. Conversely, laughter is a gift that lightens our hearts and brings us together. It is often through laughter that we experience the warmth of God's love and the joy of fellowship with one another. When we find ourselves in seasons of laughter, it is essential to cherish these moments, allowing them to reinforce our faith and renew our spirits. As Christians, recognizing the divine timing in our emotional experiences can help us maintain balance and find purpose in our tears and smiles. By trusting in God's plan, we can rest assured that each season will contribute to our growth and understanding, leading us closer to the abundant life He has promised.

A time to weep and a time to laugh, a time to mourn,
and a time to dance.
Ecclesiastes 3:4

October 16

THE WAY IT USE TO BE

There was a time as children when we rode our bikes without helmets
and rode on roller coaster rides with our hands in the air. Each goal was
attainable. Then the doubters dissuaded us from going after our
dreams… You're crazy… it's too hard… play it safe… dreams weren't
meant for people like us. They instilled their insecurities in us… and
with so many people saying we can't… and so few saying we can, we
let fear into our lives. We're afraid of losing what we have that we don't
go after what we want. It's easy to feel paralyzed by fear or indecision.
Yet, the Bible offers countless examples of God encouraging His people
to step out in faith, assuring them of His unwavering presence. God is
with us and goes before us, clearing the path for our steps. Consider
Peter when he stepped out of the boat and walked on water towards
Jesus. He began his walk in faith, eyes fixed on Christ, defying the
natural laws of fear and uncertainty. It wasn't until he shifted his focus
to the winds around him that he began to sink. Similarly, we are called
to move beyond our comfort zones and take bold steps, trusting in the
divine guidance that accompanies our obedience. Just going for it means
more than taking risks; it's about aligning our hearts with God's purpose
and acting in faith, even when the path isn't clear.

The Lord is the strength of my life.
Psalm 27:1

ARE YOU SERVING OTHERS?

It's easy to get caught up in our own lives, forgetting the impact we can have on others. But as Christians, we are called to reflect Christ's love through service and selflessness. The question "What are you doing for others?" prompts us to look beyond ourselves and consider how we might serve those around us. Jesus taught us that the greatest commandment is to love God and our neighbors as ourselves (Matthew 22:37-39). This means showing compassion, kindness, and selflessness in our daily lives. By helping others, we enrich their lives and deepen our connection with God. Consider how you can serve in your community or church. It's volunteering at a local shelter, reaching out to a friend in need, or simply offering a listening ear. These acts of kindness may seem small, but they carry the power to transform lives—including your own. Take time today to reflect on ways you can make a difference. Pray for guidance and courage to step out in faith and serve others. Remember, it's not about the size of your deeds but the love behind them. How can you actively contribute to the wellbeing of those around you? Challenge yourself to identify one practical way to serve someone this week, and trust that God will use your efforts in extraordinary ways.

Honor one another above yourselves.
Romans 12:10

October 18

TIME TO MOVE ON

In life, we often find ourselves holding onto what was like a ship anchored in the harbor, reluctant to set sail into the open seas. However, there comes a time when God calls us to move on, release the past, and step into His promises for our future. Consider the story of Abraham in Genesis 12. God called him to leave his country, his people, and his Father's household to go to a land He would show him. It was a call to leave behind the familiar and step into the unknown, relying solely on faith and trust in God's promises. Abraham's obedience led to blessings for himself and generations to come. Similarly, there are seasons in our lives when God prompts us to move on, whether from past hurts, failures, or successes that have served their purpose. Philippians 3:13-14 encourages us to "forget what is behind and strain toward what is ahead," pressing on toward the goal God has set. Moving on requires faith, courage, and a willingness to trust God with the unknown. It involves laying down our plans for His and believing His ways are higher than ours. Today, reflect on what God might be asking you to release. Trust Him to guide you as you step forward, knowing that His plans for you are good, filled with hope and a future (Jeremiah 29:11).

Forgetting those things which are behind and reaching forward to those things which are ahead.
Philippians 3:13

HOW BAD DO YOU WANT IT?

It's easy to lose sight of what truly matters. We often find ourselves pursuing goals with lukewarm enthusiasm, distracted by the noise around us. We must ask ourselves, How bad do you want it? This question challenges us to examine the depth of our desire and commitment in all that we undertake—especially our relationship with God. Colossians 3:23 reminds us to put our whole hearts into our endeavors, working as if for the Lord. This means approaching our personal, professional, and spiritual lives passionately and passionately. Half-hearted efforts often lead to unfulfilled dreams and missed opportunities. But when we genuinely want something—and pursue it with the enthusiasm God calls us to—our work becomes an act of worship. Consider what it truly means to desire a deeper connection with God. How does this desire manifest in your daily routine? Are you investing time in Scripture, seeking His presence, and aligning your actions with His teachings? Or are you allowing distractions to dilute your focus? Reflect on your current pursuits and assess their alignment with your spiritual values. Do you approach your tasks with the zeal of someone working for the Lord, or have you become complacent?

Whatever you do, work at it with all your heart, as working for the Lord,
not for human masters.
Colossians 3:23

ADJUSTING YOUR ATTITUDE

The attitude we carry can shape our experience and impact those around us. Romans 12:2 offers profound guidance on adjusting our attitudes by renewing our minds. Instead of allowing external circumstances or worldly patterns to dictate our moods, we are encouraged to seek transformation from within, aligning our thoughts and actions with God's will. Consider the moments when you've felt disheartened or frustrated. Often, these feelings stem from focusing on negative aspects or conforming to societal pressures. However, when we shift our perspective to see through God's lens, we tap into a source of strength that transcends our immediate surroundings. Renewing your mind is not a one-time event; it's a continual process of aligning with God's truth. Are there areas where you feel you need more support or more critical? Challenge these thoughts with the perspective offered by Scripture. God's word provides a roadmap for positive change, encouraging us to view challenges as opportunities for growth. By adjusting our attitudes, we invite peace and clarity into our lives. This transformation allows us to discern and follow God's will more effectively.

Do not conform to the pattern of this world, but be transformed by renewing your mind. Then, you can test and approve God's will—his good, pleasing, and perfect will.
Romans 12:2

YOUR ATTITUDE IS ESSENTIAL

The importance of attitude cannot be overstated. Our perspective and mindset shape how we interact with the world and significantly impact our spiritual lives. When Paul wrote to the Philippians, he urged them to adopt an attitude mirroring Christ's — one marked by humility, obedience, and love. Jesus' life exemplified an unwavering commitment to serving others selflessly. He set aside divine privileges not to seek His glory but to uplift and redeem humanity. This calls us to reflect on our approach to life's challenges and relationships. Does self-interest drive us, or do we genuinely seek to serve and love others? Adopting Christ's attitude requires intentional focus and daily effort. It means choosing gratitude over complaint, patience over impatience, and love over indifference. When we align our thoughts and actions with the example set by Jesus, we allow His light to shine through us, impacting those around us for the better. Consider how your attitude today can be molded to reflect Christ's heart. In every interaction and task, endeavor to embody His grace and humility. By doing so, not only do we honor God, but we also become beacons of His love in a world that deeply needs it.

Remember, our attitude is essential. Choose to make it one that mirrors Christ's. Your attitude should be the same as that of Christ Jesus.
Philippians 2:5

FOLLOW YOUR HEART?

We often hear the phrase, Follow your heart. It sounds empowering and true to our desires, but as Christians, should we heed this advice unthinkingly? The Bible tells us something crucial about the human heart; it's not always the reliable guide we might hope for. Jeremiah's words remind us that our hearts, while passionate and sincere, are susceptible to deceit and confusion. Our emotions can sometimes lead us astray, clouding our judgment with desires that may not align with God's will. Instead of following our hearts, we are encouraged to seek God's wisdom and word as our guide. Proverbs 3:5-6 advises, "Trust in the Lord with all your heart and lean not on your understanding; in all your ways submit to him, and he will make your paths straight." God, who knows us intimately, offers a better path. When we trust Him, our choices and paths align with His greater plan for our lives. Following the heart might seem tempting, but true fulfillment lies in aligning our hearts with God's will. Reflect on when your heart has led you astray and how seeking God's guidance would have altered your path. How can inviting God into your decisions change your outcomes? Consider these thoughts as you seek to align your heart with His divine purpose.

The heart is deceitful above all things and beyond cure. Who can understand it?
Jeremiah 17:9

WHAT IS YOUR MINISTRY?

Every believer has a unique ministry gifted by God. While we may not all stand on a pulpit, our calling is woven into the fabric of our daily lives. Paul reminds us in Romans that these gifts are different, but each is essential in the body of Christ. Whether you're prophesying by speaking God's truth, teaching the next generation, or encouraging a friend through difficult times, your ministry is vital to God's plan. Service can take many forms—from helping at a local food bank to simply being a listening ear. Teaching might happen in a formal setting or casually over coffee. Reflect on where you find joy and fulfillment. Perhaps you take delight in organizing events or have a knack for making people feel included and valued. These moments of joy often point towards the ministry God has planted in you. Understanding your ministry involves recognizing and using these gifts to serve others and glorify God. Seek opportunities to develop these gifts, and trust that God will guide you in your ministry.

We have different gifts according to the grace given to each of us. If your gift is prophesying, then prophesy in accordance with your faith; if it is serving, then serve; if it is teaching, then teach; if it is encouraging, then give encouragement; if it is giving, then give generously; if it is leading, do it diligently; if it is showing mercy, do it cheerfully.
Romans 12:6-8

HOW IMPORTANT IS FAITH?

Faith is the foundation of a Christian's spiritual life. It's the lens through which we view the promises of God and the unseen realities of the divine. Hebrews 11, often referred to as the Faith Chapter, highlights how faith has been integral to the lives of key biblical figures. In the New Testament, Jesus emphasized the importance of faith repeatedly. In Matthew 17:20, He says, "Truly I tell you, if you have faith as small as a mustard seed, you can say to this mountain, Move from here to there, and it will move. Nothing will be impossible for you." This illustrates that even a small amount of genuine faith can accomplish great things when placed in God's power. Faith isn't merely belief; it's active trust. It's the confidence that God is who He says He is and that He will fulfill His promises. This assurance allows us to face challenges with peace and hope, knowing that God is in control. Hebrews 11 speaks of individuals who faced unimaginable trials yet remained steadfast because their faith anchored them. For Christians today, faith is just as crucial. It reassures us in times of doubt, empowers us to act according to God's will, and connects us to His eternal promises. Reflect on your faith today and consider how it shapes your actions and beliefs.

Faith is confidence in what we hope for and assurance about what we do not see.
Hebrews 11:1

October 25

LIFE CAN BE CONFUSING

Life often feels like a maze without an exit, with twists, turns, and dead ends. Confusion can be overwhelming, leaving us yearning for clarity and guidance. It's easy to feel lost when our paths are cluttered with uncertainty and doubt, but Proverbs offers us a way through. The Scripture invites us to relinquish our reliance on our understanding and instead place our trust in God. The call to trust with all our hearts suggests surrendering control, acknowledging that our finite minds cannot always comprehend the grand tapestry God is weaving in our lives. Leaning on our understanding can lead to disillusionment, but we open ourselves to divine guidance when we submit to God's will. This submission is not a passive act but an active decision to follow His lead. It's about acknowledging that while life might feel confusing, God's perspective is far greater than ours. It's a comforting reminder that God promises to straighten our paths even amid chaos. When we surrender the need for all the answers, we allow Him to guide us towards His perfect plan. Reflect on areas in your life where confusion reigns. Are you trying to resolve them on your own? Consider inviting God into those spaces.

Trust in the Lord with all your heart and lean not on your understanding; in all your ways submit to him, and he will make your paths straight.
Proverbs 3:5-6

PEOPLE ARE DIFFERENT

People are different. Someone's comfortable temperature is someone else's sweltering heat. Someone's loud music is someone else's perfect volume. Someone's tasty snack is someone else's source of nausea. We are all different and were made that way— on purpose. It is important to remember that our differences are not barriers but blessings that enrich our collective walk with God. They allow us to support each other in ways that wouldn't be possible if we were all the same. Our diversity reflects God's creativity and wisdom in the church, at work, or in our homes. When we encounter someone who thinks, acts, or believes differently than we do, it can be tempting to dismiss them or feel superior. However, God calls us to love one another deeply and to seek unity in diversity. This doesn't mean we need to agree on everything, but rather that we approach each other with genuine curiosity and respect. Consider how God might be calling you to celebrate the differences around you. How can you learn from others' perspectives and experiences? Ask God to open your heart to the richness of His creation and help you love those who are different with the same love He has shown you.

God has placed the parts in the body, every one of them, just as He wanted them to be.
1 Corinthians 12:18

ARE YOU THANKFUL?

The Bible reminds us in 1 Thessalonians 5:18, "Give thanks in all circumstances; for this is God's will for you in Christ Jesus." This verse calls us to cultivate a heart of gratitude, not just in the extraordinary moments but also in the mundane. Did you pause to appreciate the warmth of the sun on your face or the laughter shared with a friend? Gratitude transforms the ordinary into extraordinary, giving us a new lens through which to view the world. It invites us to focus on what we have rather than what we lack, opening our hearts to God's grace and mercy. Challenge yourself today to start a gratitude journal. Jot down three things you're thankful for each day. This act of reflection can deepen your awareness of God's presence in your life, nurturing a spirit of thankfulness that extends beyond mere words. Pray with gratitude, thanking God for His countless gifts. Ask Him to give you eyes to see His blessings in every corner of your life and the courage to express your thankfulness. May your heart overflow with gratitude, transforming your perspective and bringing you closer to God. Remember, a thankful heart is a joyful heart. Are you thankful?

Be thankful in all circumstances; this is God's will for you.
1 Thessalonians 5:18

October 28

ARE YOU TOO BUSY?

Do you wear busy as a badge of honor? Staying busy helps people feel needed and significant, but there is no reward or scholarship for burning ourselves out. In today's fast-paced world, it's easy to find ourselves overwhelmed by endless to-do lists and commitments. Despite our best intentions, we may put our spiritual life on the back burner, thinking we'll return to it when things settle down. But as life keeps moving, we must ask ourselves—are we too busy for God?

In Luke 10:38-42, we find the story of two sisters, Mary and Martha. While Martha was preoccupied with preparing a meal for Jesus, Mary chose to sit at His feet, listening intently. Martha, feeling overwhelmed, asked Jesus to tell Mary to help her. However, Jesus gently reminded Martha that Mary's choice to spend time with Him was better and would not be taken from her. This passage encourages us to evaluate our priorities. Are we more like Mary, devoted and attentive to our relationship with Christ? Or do we resemble Martha, so consumed with tasks that we miss the opportunity to connect with the Savior? Today, challenge yourself to pause and reflect. Carve out intentional time to sit quietly in God's presence. Pray, read Scripture, and listen for His voice. These moments will refresh your Spirit and realign your priorities, reminding you of what truly matters.

When Jesus heard him, He stopped.
Luke 18:40

October 29

PRAYING FOR HIS WILL

It is easy to approach prayer as a list of demands or desires. However, the true essence of prayer is not about insisting on our outcomes but aligning ourselves with God's purpose. When we pray for His will, we engage in an intimate dialogue with our Creator, seeking His wisdom and guidance instead of simply pushing forward our plans. The Scripture from 1 John 5:14 offers us profound assurance. It tells us that God hears us when we ask according to His will. This doesn't mean we should refrain from sharing our needs and desires, but it does encourage us to remain open to His direction. By seeking His will, we open ourselves to possibilities far more significant than we can imagine, trusting that His plans are for our best. Praying for His will requires humility and patience. It invites us to wait on the Lord, knowing His timing is perfect. This posture of surrender does not come naturally but is cultivated through faith and practice. By focusing on God's will, we learn to trust He is at work in every circumstance, crafting a story of redemption and grace. Reflect on how you can incorporate this practice into your daily life. Consider the areas where you might need to yield control and ask for God's guidance to align with His divine purpose.

This is our confidence in approaching God: if we ask anything
according to his will, he hears us.
John 5:14

A TIME TO DIE

In life, Ecclesiastes reminds us that there is a divine rhythm, a time for every purpose under heaven. Death, often considered a somber subject, is integral to this God-ordained cycle. It's a transition, not an end, embraced within the broader scope of eternity. For Christians, death is not a defeat but a passage to eternal life with our Savior. Jesus Himself spoke of this in John 11:25-26, saying, "I am the resurrection and the life. The one who believes in me will live, even though they die, and whoever lives by believing in me will never die." This assurance calls us to view our earthly end not with fear but with hope. Acknowledging a time to die encourages us to live fully in the present, appreciating each breath as a gift from God. It inspires us to nurture relationships, pursue God's calling, and prepare our hearts for the eternal kingdom. Death also invites us to lean into God's comfort and promises. In times of loss, His presence becomes our anchor, His word—our consolation. Isaiah 41:10 comforts us, "Do not fear, for I am with you; do not be dismayed, for I am your God." In understanding there is a time to die, we are reminded of life's transient nature and the eternal hope we hold in Christ.

There is a time for everything and a season for every activity under the heavens... a time to be born and die, a time to plant and uproot.
Ecclesiastes 3:1-2

October 31

FALLING OUT OF LOVE

Divorce is a challenging topic for many Christians, touching on personal loss, spiritual questions, and community dynamics. The Bible acknowledges the pain and complexity that can accompany marital dissolution. Jesus' teaching in Matthew 19 emphasizes the sacredness of marriage yet recognizes the reality of divorce. While marriage is designed as a lifelong covenant, there are circumstances where separation might occur.

The verse highlights the importance of unity in marriage, where two individuals become one entity, joined by God. When this bond is broken, it can leave emotional and spiritual wounds. It's essential to remember that Jesus spoke about compassion and understanding. In such hardship, the Christian community is called to support each other with empathy and love. The Bible doesn't overlook the strains that can lead to the end of a marriage. For those experiencing divorce, seeking healing and restoration through prayer, Scripture, and fellowship with believers is crucial. Remember, God's love and mercy are steadfast, offering comfort and guidance through life's most challenging transitions. If you're navigating the path of divorce, know that you are not alone. Allow God's word to be a source of strength and hope.

So they are no longer two, but one flesh. Therefore, what God has joined together, let no one separate.
Matthew 19:6

November 1

KEEPING SUNDAY HOLY

Sundays hold a special place in the hearts of Christians—it's a day set apart to rest in the presence of God and reflect on His goodness in our fast-paced world, where every day seems to blur into the next with endless tasks and responsibilities, keeping Sunday holy can become more of a challenge than a routine. Yet, honoring the Sabbath is not just a commandment; it's a gift from God designed to refresh our spirits and renew our focus on Him. The Sabbath is an invitation to pause and reprioritize, allowing us to shift our gaze away from worldly concerns and toward divine purpose. It's a chance for families to gather, worship together, and create lasting memories centered around faith and gratitude. We acknowledge God's sovereignty over time and our lives by dedicating this day to rest and worship. To keep Sunday holy, consider starting your day by attending a church service that fills your heart with joy and peace. Spend time with loved ones, engage in activities that nourish your soul, and reflect on the week's blessings and challenges.

Remember the Sabbath day by keeping it holy. You shall labor and do all your work in six days, but the seventh day is a sabbath to the Lord your God. On it, you shall not do any work, neither you, your Son or daughter, your male or female servant, your animals, or any foreigner residing in your towns.
Exodus 20:8-10

November 2

EMPTY NEST

The transition to an empty nest can be both challenging and rewarding. It's a time of new beginnings, fresh opportunities, and personal growth. Through Scripture, we can find comfort and guidance as we adjust to this new phase of life. As your children leave home, it's natural to feel a range of emotions—from pride and excitement to loss and uncertainty. But this season is also a chance for God to do something new in your life. Isaiah 43:19 reminds us that God is always at work, creating new pathways and providing refreshment even in barren times. During this transition, consider the open doors God is presenting. Perhaps it's a renewed focus on your marriage, the chance to pursue a forgotten passion, or the opportunity to serve in ways previously unimaginable. Trust that God's plan is unfolding in your life, and be open to the new things He is doing.

- What new opportunities is God presenting in this season of your life?
- Take one step toward exploring a new interest or serving in a new capacity.

This stage of life is not an ending but a beginning to a deeper, more personal relationship with God and His unfolding plan for you.

See, I am doing a new thing! Now it springs up; do you not perceive it? I am making a way in the wilderness and streams in the wasteland.
Isaiah 43:19

CHALLENGING STRUGGLES

Substance abuse is a challenging struggle that many people face, affecting not only the individual but their loved ones and community as well. For Christians, tackling this battle involves turning to faith and drawing strength from God's promises. The Scripture in 1 Corinthians 10:13 is a powerful reminder that no temptation, including substances, is beyond what we can bear with the Lord by our side. Often, we might feel isolated in our struggles, believing that no one understands the depth of our pain or the grip of addiction. Yet, God assures us that these temptations are not unique to us—they are common to mankind. This knowledge alone can provide comfort, knowing that we are not alone in our battles, and many have successfully navigated the same path with God's guidance. God's faithfulness means he will not allow us to face more than we can handle. He provides us with the strength to endure and overcome substance abuse. Importantly, God offers a way out—a path towards recovery and healing. This path might come in different forms, such as support groups, therapy, or strengthening relationships with those who encourage positive change.

No temptation has overtaken you except what is common to humanity. And God is faithful; he will not let you be tempted beyond what you can bear. But when you are tempted, he will also provide a way out so that you can endure it.
1 Corinthians 10:13

November 4

TIME TO STEP UP

It's easy to get caught up in the hustle and bustle of daily life, overlooking the divine purpose that God has set before us. Today's Scripture, Ephesians 2:10, reminds us that we are not just aimlessly walking through life. We are God's handiwork, crafted with intention and purpose to fulfill good works. This verse speaks directly to the heart of our theme—it's time to step up! God has uniquely equipped us with talents, gifts, and opportunities to impact the world around us positively. The good works mentioned aren't just grand gestures or monumental achievements but can be found in the small, everyday actions of kindness and love. Consider what God might be calling you today. Is there a neighbor who needs encouragement, a friend who could use a listening ear, or a community project needing your talent? Each day presents new opportunities to align our actions with God's purpose in our lives. Stepping up doesn't mean knowing every detail or outcome. It's about trusting in His path and taking the first step in faith. We honor God's creativity and the intentional design He has placed within us by stepping up. Let's challenge ourselves to see beyond the ordinary and recognize where God calls us to make a difference today.

For we are God's handiwork, created in Christ Jesus to do good works, which God prepared in advance for us to do.
Ephesians 2:10

THE BLOOD OF CHRIST

The concept of blood as a source of life permeates the Scriptures, culminating in the sacrifice of Jesus Christ. In the Old Testament, God established the sacrificial system, highlighting the importance of blood for atonement. The animals' blood temporarily covered the people's sins, pointing forward to the ultimate sacrifice. Enter Jesus Christ, whose blood shed on the cross offered a perfect and eternal atonement. Unlike the temporary sacrifices of old, He was sufficient once and for all. Hebrews 9:12 tells us, "He did not enter by means of the blood of goats and calves; but he entered the Most Holy Place once for all by his blood, thus obtaining eternal redemption." This profound act of love enables Christians to live in freedom and grace. Through His blood, we are cleansed from sin and reconciled to God. The blood of Christ signifies the new covenant—a promise of forgiveness and eternal life. Consider the power and significance of the blood of Christ in your own life. Reflect on how this eternal sacrifice impacts your daily walk with God. Are there areas where you need to accept His grace more fully? Remember, it's through His blood that we find peace and reconciliation.

For the life of a creature is in the blood, and I have given it to you to make atonement for yourselves on the altar; it is the blood that makes atonement for one's life.
Leviticus 17:11

DO YOU HAVE TO BE RIGHT?

In our daily lives, we are often confronted with situations where we feel the need to assert our correctness. Whether it's a heated discussion at work, a disagreement with a family member, or a debate on social media, the desire to be right can be overwhelming. Pursuing being right may seem harmless, but it can lead us down a path of judgment and pride. When we insist on our correctness, we risk placing ourselves as judges over others, forgetting that we are all fallible and need grace. Jesus reminds us in Matthew 7 that judgment is not ours to wield. Judging others can distort our perspective and create barriers in relationships that mirror Christ's love. Instead of focusing on being right, consider approaching conversations with humility and understanding. Listening with empathy and acknowledging the value of others' viewpoints does not diminish our beliefs. It opens doors for genuine connection and growth. Reflect on situations where you've felt the urge to insist on being right. How might choosing empathy over judgment change the outcome? We can foster unity and peace by relinquishing the need to be right, reflecting Christ's love and mercy.

Do not judge, or you too will be judged. For in the same way you judge others, you will be judged; with the measure you use, it will be measured to you.
Matthew 7:1-2

November 7

SKIPPING CHURCH

It's easy to see Sunday as a day to catch up on rest or personal errands. However, the Scripture from Hebrews gently reminds us of the importance of not neglecting our gatherings. It's about more than just tradition; it's about community and spiritual growth. Church isn't just a building or a service—it's a vital gathering of believers where faith is nurtured and strengthened. When we skip church, we miss out on the collective encouragement from worshipping with others. We miss the opportunity to share our lives, struggles, and victories with a community that genuinely cares. Gathering together is crucial for spiritual accountability. It's where we learn, grow, and develop our spiritual gifts. It's a place where we can offer support and receive guidance from fellow believers. Meeting together helps us stay grounded in our faith and align with God's life path. Consider how you might prioritize gathering with your church community this week. Think about the relationships that enrich your life and how you can encourage others. In doing so, you'll find your faith deepening and your sense of belonging growing stronger.

Let us consider how we may spur one another on toward love and good deeds, not giving up meeting together, as some are in the habit of doing, but encouraging one another—and all the more as you see the day approaching.
Hebrews 10:24-25

ARE YOU A FAN?

Being a fan is often as simple as a click of a button—a like, a follow, or a share. But what does it mean to be more than just a fan and truly follow Christ? In John 12, we encounter leaders who believed in Jesus, yet their desire for human approval concealed their faith. They admired Jesus from a distance but hesitated to declare their allegiance openly. This passage challenges us to reflect on our walk with Christ. Are we content to be admirers, tucked comfortably in the crowd, where belief costs us nothing? Or are we willing to step into the arena of true discipleship, where allegiance might cost us the world's approval but earn us the commendation of God? In an environment that often values popularity over truth, following Christ requires courage. It means prioritizing God's praise over human applause. It involves living out our faith boldly, unashamedly, and consistently, even when it may not align with societal norms. Today, consider the depth of your relationship with Christ. Are you merely a fan or committed to being a devoted follower? Reflect on ways you can live out your faith more openly.

Yet, at the same time, many, even among the leaders, believed in him. However, the Pharisees would not openly acknowledge their faith for fear of being put out of the synagogue, for they loved human praise more than praise from God.
John 12:42-43

DEALING WITH PRIDE

Pride is often seen as a barrier to our spiritual and personal growth. It entices us to elevate ourselves above others, skewing our perception of self-worth and leading us away from humility. The Bible reminds us that pride can be destructive, distancing us from God and meaningful relationships with those around us. In Philippians 2, the Apostle Paul offers a corrective to the prideful heart. He encourages believers to act not out of selfish ambition or vain conceit but to adopt an attitude of humility. This involves valuing others above ourselves and considering their needs alongside, or even before, our own. Such an attitude reflects the nature of Christ, who humbled Himself for the sake of humanity. When we struggle with pride, reflecting on the life and teachings of Jesus can be helpful. His acts of service and sacrifice are a model for us to follow. We open ourselves to more authentic and enriching relationships by choosing humility over pride. We become more attuned to the needs of others and more willing to serve, echoing the love and humility that Christ embodied. Challenge yourself today to identify areas where pride may take root.

Do nothing out of selfish ambition or vain conceit. Instead, in humility, value others above yourselves, not looking to your interests but each of you to the interests of the others.
Philippians 2:3-4

November 10

NEED MORE STUFF

In today's consumer-driven world, messages of instant gratification and endless acquisition are constant. From advertisements promising happiness with the latest gadgets to social media posts showcasing curated lifestyles, the pressure to accumulate more is relentless. But as Christians, we are called to a different standard of contentment and trust in God's provision. Hebrews 13:5 offers a profound reminder that the love of money and possessions can never fulfill our deepest needs. Instead, true contentment comes from understanding that God is our ultimate provider, and He promises never to leave us or forsake us. This assurance surpasses any material possessions we might achieve or desire. Living free from the love of more stuff means reevaluating our desires and focusing on what truly matters. It involves gratitude for what we already have and trusting that God knows our needs even before we ask. When we shift our perspective from accumulating to appreciating, we open our hearts to genuine peace and joy. Reflect today on areas where you may feel the pull of wanting more. Remember that in God's economy, contentment isn't found in what we possess but in recognizing that we are already blessed.

Keep your lives free from the love of money and be content with what you have because God has said, 'Never will I leave you; never will I forsake you.
Hebrews 13:5

SHARING THE GOSPEL

The Great Commission, found in Matthew 28, is a powerful reminder of our calling as Christians to share the Gospel with others. Jesus entrusted us with the mission to spread His teachings and bring the light of His love to every corner of the world. This task can seem daunting, yet it's also gratifying. Sharing the Gospel isn't just about preaching in a church setting. It's about living your faith daily, letting your actions reflect your beliefs, and seizing opportunities to speak about Jesus in your everyday interactions. Whether through words of kindness, acts of service, or sharing your own story of faith, each moment counts as a testimony to His grace. Consider how you can share the Gospel in your unique circumstances. It could be a conversation with a neighbor, a helping hand offered to a colleague, or a simple invitation to your community group. Remember, even the smallest gesture can spark profound change. Jesus assures us that we are not alone in this mission. His promise to be with us until the end of the age gives us the courage and strength to step out and share His message with confidence and love.

Therefore, go and make disciples of all nations, baptizing them in the name of the Father, Son, and the Holy Spirit, and teaching them to obey everything I have commanded you. And indeed, I am with you always, to the very end of the age.
Matthew 28:19-20

November 12

GIVING IT BACK

Tithing is more than just a financial transaction; it is an act of faith and obedience. As shown in Malachi 3:10, the concept of tithing invites believers to trust God with their finances by giving back a portion of what He has provided. This act demonstrates our reliance on God and an acknowledgment of His provision. At its core, tithing is about prioritizing God in our lives. When we choose to tithe, we're making a tangible commitment that our trust lies not in material wealth but in God's abundant blessings. It is a reminder that everything we own is ultimately from Him, and by tithing, we fulfill our role as stewards of His resources. God's promise in Malachi is clear—when we bring our tithe into His storehouse, He will respond with blessings beyond measure. These blessings come in various forms, not only financially but also through spiritual growth and deeper reliance on His provision. Tithing is a practice that shapes our hearts and aligns us with God. It's a powerful reminder of His promise and our place within His plan. By trusting Him with our resources, we position ourselves to receive His overflowing blessings.

Bring the whole tithe into the storehouse, that there may be food in my house. Test me in this, says the Lord Almighty, and see if I will not throw open the floodgates of heaven and pour out so many blessings that there will not be enough room to store them.
Malachi 3:10

DEALING WITH LUST

Lust is a powerful emotion that can be both compelling and consuming. It often masquerades as desire or admiration, but its roots run deeper, aiming to take control and lead us astray from our spiritual path. Within Christian teachings, lust is not merely about physical attraction but about the unchecked desire that can distance us from God's love and purpose for our lives. 1 Corinthians 6:18 advises us to flee from sexual immorality, underscoring the importance of actively avoiding situations where lust could take hold. By doing so, we protect our physical bodies and our spiritual integrity. Lust can cloud judgment, leading to actions that contradict the core values taught by Christ. In today's world, where temptation seems omnipresent, it's crucial to remain vigilant and mindful of our thoughts and actions. This doesn't mean suppressing natural feelings entirely but channeling them in ways that honor ourselves and God. Setting boundaries and seeking accountability within your community can provide additional support. Remember, the battle against lust isn't fought alone; God walks with you, providing strength and guidance. Through prayer and Scripture, we can overcome the grip of lust.

Flee from sexual immorality. All other sins a person commits are outside the body, but whoever sins sexually sins against their own body.
1 Corinthians 6:18

BEING TRUTHFUL

Truth can often seem negotiable. We are surrounded by messages urging us to bend the truth for convenience, gain, or acceptance. However, as Christians, we are called to a higher standard—to embody the truth in everything we do. Proverbs 12:22 reminds us that God delights those who speak the truth. Lying lips may make things easier or smoother momentarily, but they ultimately lead to broken trust and disconnection from God's will. On the other hand, being truthful fosters trust builds strong relationships, and aligns us with God's character. Reflecting the truth is not just about avoiding falsehoods but also about living transparently and authentically. It means being honest not only with others but also with ourselves. When we commit to truth-telling, we demonstrate integrity, which God treasures. Living truthfully can be challenging. It may require us to confront uncomfortable situations, admit our mistakes, or stand up against deceit. Yet, in these moments of truth, we find strength and grace from God to uphold His values. As you reflect on this Scripture, consider areas where truth may be compromised. Ask yourself how to align more closely with God's desire for honesty. Remember, telling the truth is not just an act—it's a way of living that draws us closer to God.

The Lord detests lying lips, but he delights in trustworthy people.
Proverbs 12:22

FAKE FLATTERY

Flattery is often perceived as a harmless praise or commendation, yet the Bible warns us of its hidden danger. The Scripture in Proverbs 29:5 paints a vivid picture of flattery as a trap that can ensnare those who both give and receive it. Flattery differs from genuine encouragement in its intent. While encouragement seeks to build others up and inspire them to grow, flattery aims to manipulate and control by appealing to one's ego. It often serves the flatterer more than the person being flattered. Recognizing this distinction is vital for a Christ-centered life, as genuine interactions reflect the love and truth we are called to embody. In our daily walk, it's essential to be mindful of our words and the intentions behind them. Are we offering praise to uplift someone genuinely or gain favor? Similarly, are we discerning when receiving compliments, understanding whether they stem from a sincere heart or an ulterior motive? Reflect on your interactions today. Seek to encourage with sincerity and be wary of flattery, which can lead to misunderstanding and false perceptions. Remember, as followers of Christ, our words should be aligned with truth and love, fostering genuine relationships that honor God and uplift one another in faith.

Whoever flatters a neighbor is spreading a net for their feet.
Proverbs 29:5

OUTWARD APPEARANCE

In a world that often judges by appearances, remembering that God sees beyond what is visible is reassuring. Society places immense value on how we present ourselves externally—our clothes, hairstyles, and even how we carry ourselves. However, the Lord invites us to focus on what lies beneath the surface. This Scripture from 1 Samuel reminds us of the story of David's anointing. While his brothers were tall and strong, fitting the human criteria for kingship, David's heart caught God's attention. God chose David for his integrity, humility, and faithfulness— attributes that outward appearance couldn't discern. For Christians, this serves as a profound lesson. We are encouraged to develop inner qualities that reflect God's nature—love, patience, kindness, and faithfulness. These attributes glorify God and make us truly beautiful in His sight. Let's strive to cultivate the heart God sees and values. While caring for our physical appearance is not wrong, let's prioritize our spiritual growth. The world's standards do not determine our worth but the richness of our spirit and the purity of our intentions.

But the Lord told Samuel not to consider his appearance or height, for I have rejected him. The Lord does not look at the things people look at. People look at the outward appearance, but the Lord looks at the heart.
1 Samuel 16:7

WHAT HUSBANDS WANT

With countless expectations and societal norms, understanding what husbands truly want can feel overwhelming. However, the Bible provides timeless wisdom that can help us cultivate loving and meaningful relationships. The desire for mutual respect and understanding is at the heart of many Christian marriages. When we turn to Ephesians 5:25, we see a clear directive for husbands to love their wives as Christ loved the church. This love isn't simply about feelings; it's an active commitment to selflessness and sacrifice. Husbands often long for appreciation and acknowledgment of their efforts and love. They desire a partnership where both individuals can grow together in faith and purpose, supporting one another through life's challenges. Beyond words, actions often speak volumes—valuing their input, making time for meaningful conversations, and nurturing a home where they feel respected and understood. Understanding these needs can lead to a stronger, more harmonious relationship. By aligning our actions with biblical principles, we can foster an environment of trust and love. It's not about grand gestures but the consistent, everyday acts of kindness and support that fulfill what husbands want.

Husbands love their wives, just as Christ loved the church and gave himself up for her.
Ephesians 5:25

November 18

WHAT WIVES WANT

In understanding what wives genuinely want, the Apostle Paul provides profound insights into the heart of marriage through his letter to the Ephesians. At the core of every wife's desire is a longing for love that reflects Christ's selfless and sacrificial love for the church. Such love involves a deep commitment, transcending emotion, and moving into action and devotion. This passage challenges husbands to love their wives with the same care and attention they give to themselves. It suggests that the love wives yearn for is genuine sacrifice and honor, echoing Christ's ultimate sacrifice for the church. When husbands prioritize their wives' spiritual and emotional well-being, they create a bond reflective of divine love. While many books and guides attempt to decode the complexities of a woman's heart, Scripture simplifies it by setting the example of Christ's love. Following this blueprint, husbands can foster relationships where both partners grow in faith and love.

Husbands love your wives, just as Christ loved the church and gave himself up for her to make her holy, cleansing her by the washing with water through the word, and to present her to himself as a radiant church, without stain or wrinkle or any other blemish, but holy and blameless. In this same way, husbands should love their wives as their bodies. He who loves his wife loves himself.
Ephesians 5:25-28

November 19

LOSING SOMEONE CLOSE

Losing someone close is one of life's most painful challenges, leaving us with a profound sense of emptiness and loss. It's natural to feel overwhelmed, as if the world has become harsher. However, as Christians, we have the assurance that we are not alone in our grief. God walks with us through every dark valley. The Bible speaks directly to our hearts with comforting words. Matthew 5:4 reminds us that those who mourn will be comforted. This verse promises that God is attentive to our sorrows, offering solace and hope even in the deepest moments of despair. It's an invitation to lean on His understanding and to find refuge in His unwavering love. Additionally, it's important to remember that mourning is a process, not a moment. Permitting ourselves to grieve in our own time while also seeking community and support can help us heal. Sharing memories and talking about our loved ones keeps their spirit alive within us, providing comfort and a sense of connection. For wives who have lost a partner, understanding what is truly needed in times of loss can be challenging. Many desire the acknowledgment of their pain, the freedom to express their grief, and the support of a compassionate community.

Blessed are those who mourn, for they will be comforted.
Matthew 5:4

WHAT ARE YOUR PRIORITIES?

Where does God rank on your list of priorities? For many, the day begins with an overwhelming to-do list—work commitments, family responsibilities, and personal goals—all seemingly vying for the top spot. Yet, Jesus provides a simple yet profound directive in Matthew 6:33. He urges us to seek His kingdom and righteousness first, promising that everything else will fall into place. This verse invites us to assess our daily choices and align them with divine principles. It's a call to place God at the center of everything we do. When we prioritize our faith, we experience a transformation in how we handle life's challenges. Our perspective shifts; worries about material needs or worldly success diminish when we trust God's provision. Consider what it means to seek His kingdom first. It's about dedicating time for scripture study, worship, and living out His teachings. By focusing on spiritual growth, we become more equipped to face life's complexities with grace and wisdom. Reflect on your own life. Are there areas where God might not be first? How can you shift your focus to prioritize His kingdom? Remember, when God is placed at the forefront, He shapes our desires and influences our actions, guiding us to a life rich in purpose and fulfillment.

But seek first his kingdom and righteousness, and all these things will also be given to you.
Matthew 6:33

PRAY FOR OUR COUNTRY

In a world of uncertainty and change, Christians need to pray for our nation. Our country is a tapestry woven with diverse backgrounds, faiths, and dreams, yet united by the values and principles we hold dear. When we pray for our country, we invite God's wisdom, peace, and protection to guide our leaders and citizens. This Scripture reminds us of the importance of praying for our leaders and those in positions of authority. By lifting them in prayer, we seek God's guidance and discernment for decisions that impact our nation and its people. Though written during exile, Jeremiah's message is clear—our well-being is intertwined with our nation's. When we pray for the peace and prosperity of our country, we align ourselves with God's desire for our community and future. Consider setting aside time daily to pray for our country, its leaders, and its people. Whether in moments of silence or spoken words, your prayers can become a powerful force for positive change. Through prayer, we seek to bring God's light into every corner of our nation, fostering unity and understanding amidst our differences.

First, I urge that petitions, prayers, intercession, and thanksgiving be made for all people—for kings and all those in authority- so that we may live peaceful and quiet lives in all godliness and holiness.
1 Timothy 2:1-2

November 22

GIVING THANKS FOR FAMILY

Family is often the first community we belong to. It's where we learn about love, support, and faith. In the hustle and bustle of daily life, we can sometimes overlook the tremendous gift family truly is. Ephesians 5:20 reminds us to continually thank God for everything, including the family He has placed in our lives. Whether it's the family we're born into or the one we choose, these relationships are part of God's design for us. Each family member, with their unique traits, contributes to the tapestry of our lives. Reflect on the moments when your family has supported you, celebrated with you, and even challenged you to grow. These are the times that knit hearts closer together, allowing the love of Christ to manifest in our everyday interactions. Consider how you can express gratitude for your family today. A simple "thank you" or a small gesture of kindness can go a long way in showing appreciation. When we cultivate a heart of thankfulness, we honor those we love and acknowledge God's work in our lives. In recognizing the value of family, we align ourselves with God's purpose, enriching our spiritual walk and strengthening our bonds with those we cherish. Let's make it a daily practice to give thanks for the family we've been blessed with, cherishing each moment spent together.

We always thank God the Father for everything, in the name of our Lord Jesus Christ.
Ephesians 5:20

GIVING THANKS FOR CHURCH

It's easy to overlook the simple act of gratitude. Yet, the Bible consistently reminds us of its importance. One of the most profound ways we can express our gratitude to God is through our participation in church life. Whether we are singing hymns, serving in ministries, or simply being present in fellowship with other believers, each act can be an expression of thanks to our Creator. Attending church gives us a dedicated space to pause and reflect on the blessings we often take for granted. It's an opportunity to gather with others who share our faith and rejoice in God's goodness. This communal experience strengthens our bond with God and deepens our appreciation for His enduring love. Consider how often you enter the church with a heart prepared to give thanks. Are you mindful of the blessings in your life that God has provided? It's the community that surrounds you, the lessons you learn, or the peace that comes from worship. Before attending church, take a moment to list the things for which you are grateful. Reflect on how these blessings can motivate you to participate more fully in church activities. Gratitude is not just about saying thank you—it's about living a life that reflects the goodness and love that God has shown you.

Give thanks to the Lord, for He is good; His love endures forever.
1 Chronicles 16:34

November 24

DIFFICULT PEOPLE

Encountering difficult people is an inevitable part of life. Whether it's a challenging coworker, a demanding family member, or someone who seems to push all the wrong buttons, these individuals can test patience and faith. However, as Christians, we're called to respond in ways that reflect God's love and grace. Romans 12:14 advises us to "bless those who persecute you; bless and do not curse." This verse challenges us to rise above our immediate reactions of frustration or anger. Instead of retaliating or harboring resentment, we are encouraged to extend kindness and compassion. This doesn't mean we accept harmful behavior; instead, we choose a higher path that aligns with the teachings of Christ. Dealing with difficult people becomes an opportunity to practice empathy and understanding. It allows us to grow in patience and demonstrate a love beyond what might seem reasonable. It's about seeing the person beyond their actions and realizing that they are loved by God and worthy of grace. When dealing with complex individuals, remind yourself of Jesus' example. He faced immense opposition yet responded with forgiveness and love. By emulating His example, we become a living testament to His teachings, showing that love can overcome adversity.

Bless those who persecute you; bless and do not curse.
Romans 12:14

DEALING WITH CRIME

Crime, in its essence, is an act against the laws that govern society. For Christians, there is a deeper layer of understanding—crime is not just a breach of human laws but an act against God's ordained order. Romans 13 reminds us of the divine purpose behind authorities and laws. Understanding this means we acknowledge that God places these structures to maintain peace and justice. Crime can take many forms today—from theft and deception to corruption and violence. While the temptation may arise to engage in or overlook these acts, believers are called to a higher standard. Recognizing that God establishes authorities encourages us to respect laws and live righteously. Furthermore, as Christians, we are responsible for advocating for justice and integrity, reflecting God's love in our communities. By doing right, we honor the laws of the land and witness the transformative power of faith. Today, consider how you can be an agent of peace and justice, living in accordance with both God's law and the laws of your community.

Let everyone be subject to the governing authorities, for there is no authority except that which God has established. God has established the authorities that exist. Consequently, whoever rebels against the authority is rebelling against what God has instituted, and those who do so will bring judgment on themselves.
Romans 13:1-2

IS HELL A REAL PLACE?

In today's culture, hell is often depicted as a mere metaphor or a concept used only to instill fear. However, the Bible presents hell as an authentic place. Jesus spoke about it multiple times throughout the New Testament, emphasizing its reality and the gravity of its consequences. Matthew 25 vividly depicts the final judgment scene, where the righteous are separated from the unrighteous. Jesus' words remind us that hell was not initially intended for humanity but for the devil and his angels. Yet, the reality of sin and the rejection of God's grace leads to this separation. This passage urges believers not to take the notion of hell lightly or dismiss it as an outdated idea. Understanding the seriousness of hell amplifies the depth of God's love and the sacrifice of Jesus Christ. God's desire is not for anyone to perish. Still, for all to come to repentance (2 Peter 3:9). This awareness should inspire Christians to live with greater urgency and compassion towards others, sharing the Gospel and the hope in Christ. Hell's reality challenges us to reflect on our lives, ensuring our faith is genuine, and our hearts are aligned with God's truth. Remember that God's grace is immeasurable, and He offers redemption to all who seek Him earnestly.

Then he will say to those on his left, Depart from me, you who are cursed, into the eternal fire prepared for the devil and his angels.
Matthew 25:41

SEPARATING FROM OTHERS

Seclusion might seem like a luxury or even an oddity. Yet, for Christians, it holds a vital place in spiritual growth and communion with God. Jesus often withdrew to solitary places to pray and reconnect with the Father. Seclusion is not avoidance; it's time set aside to deepen our relationship with God without distractions. When we choose seclusion, we're intentionally stepping away from the noise of life to focus on our inner spiritual dialogue. In these quiet moments, we can hear God's voice more clearly, receive guidance, and find peace. This practice allows us to reflect on Scripture, contemplate its meaning, and earnestly listen for God's direction. Seclusion isn't just physical; it's a state of heart and mind. It's about creating space within to welcome God's presence. Whether it's a few minutes during a lunch break or an hour in the evening, the importance lies in the intentionality of seeking God's presence. Consider how you can incorporate moments of seclusion into your daily routine. Use this time to reconnect, refresh, and realign your heart with God's purpose for you. Remember, your Father who sees what is done in secret will reward you, not just with answers, but with His peace and presence.

But when you pray, go into your room, close the door, and pray to your unseen Father. Then your Father, who sees what is done in secret, will reward you.
Matthew 6:6

November 28

IT'S IMPORTANT TO LAUGH

Daily, we often find ourselves caught in the hustle and bustle, burdened with responsibilities and challenges. It's easy to forget one of the simplest yet profound gifts God has given us—laughter. Laughter is a remarkable antidote to stress, pain, and conflict. It lightens burdens, inspires hope, connects us to others, and keeps us grounded, focused, and alert. Proverbs 17:22 reminds us that a cheerful heart is not just beneficial, but it acts as medicine. This Scripture highlights the power of joy and laughter as essential elements for a healthy life. When we laugh, we experience a release of physical tension and stress, leaving our muscles relaxed for up to 45 minutes. It elevates our mood and can even improve our immune system by releasing endorphins, the body's natural feel-good chemicals. In the Christian walk, laughter is more than just a physical response; it is a reflection of inner joy and peace from knowing Christ. This joy is not dependent on our circumstances but is rooted in the eternal promises of God. Sharing a laugh with others builds community and fosters relationships, creating bonds that help us through tough times. Today, take a moment to find joy in the small things and laugh with those around you.

A cheerful heart is good medicine, but a crushed spirit
dries up the bones.
Proverbs 17:22

November 29

DISASTERS / DESTRUCTIONS

In a world often marked by disasters and destruction, both natural and man-made, it's easy to feel overwhelmed and question where God is in these moments. However, the Bible offers reassurance and perspective that can help Christians find peace and purpose amidst chaos. This verse reminds us that God is not distant in our darkest times. Instead, He is a refuge—a place of security and protection. While disasters and destruction might shake the foundations of our physical world, they cannot undermine the spiritual truths that God is unchanging and always present. Our faith calls us to look beyond the immediate devastation and to trust that God has a plan, even when we can't see it. The Bible is filled with narratives of people who faced incredible turmoil yet emerged stronger and more faithful. These stories encourage us today to persevere with hope and faith. During times of disaster, we are also reminded of the importance of community. Christians are called to be the hands and feet of Christ, reaching out to help those in need and spreading His love. In doing so, we can become vessels of hope and healing in a broken world. While we may not have all the answers, we trust in a God who does. We find our strength and refuge in Him, knowing that His plans for us are good, even amidst life's most significant challenges.

The Lord is a refuge for the oppressed, a stronghold in times of trouble.
Psalm 9:9

ARE YOU KIND TO OTHERS?

Kindness is a simple yet profound act that can transform lives. In today's fast-paced world, where everyone is often caught up in their own concerns, the act of showing kindness can be a breath of fresh air—a reminder of God's love and grace in action. Reflect on how Jesus lived His life. He exemplified kindness in everything He did, from healing the sick to breaking bread with sinners. His actions were expressions of divine love, teaching us how to treat others. When we extend kindness, we follow His example and spread His love, creating ripples of compassion in our communities. Consider your interactions with others. Does kindness characterize them? In moments of stress or frustration, it can be challenging to remain kind. However, these are the instances when kindness can make the most impact. A gentle word or a small gesture can uplift someone's spirit, revealing God's love tangibly. Challenge yourself today to be intentionally kind. Look for opportunities to serve, listen, and show empathy. Remember that kindness is not about grand gestures but consistent, heartfelt actions that reflect the heart of Jesus. In embodying kindness, you draw closer to God and become a beacon of His love in a world that so desperately needs it.

Be kind and compassionate to one another, forgiving each other, just as in Christ, God forgave you.
Ephesians 4:32

December 1

HOME SWEET HOME

We often picture a place of comfort, security, and love when we think of home. It's where we feel understood and welcomed, a sanctuary from the chaos and uncertainties of the world. For many of us, home is where family and cherished memories reside. Yet, as believers, we are reminded that our ultimate home is not here on earth but with Christ in heaven. The Apostle Paul writes to the Philippians, reminding them that their true citizenship is not of this world but of heaven. This perspective shifts our earthly concerns and ambitions, guiding us to live with eternity in mind. Our everyday struggles, the pressures of life, and even our victories are seen in a new light when we recognize they are temporary compared to the eternal home awaiting us. Living with an awareness of our heavenly citizenship encourages us to reflect on God's love and grace in our daily interactions. It instills hope, especially during difficult times, reassuring us that our current circumstances are not our final destination. Instead, we have a home prepared for us by a loving Father, filled with joy and peace beyond our understanding. In our earthly homes, we strive to create environments of warmth and welcome. Similarly, as citizens of heaven, we are called to extend that same hospitality and love to those around us, reflecting the heart of Christ.

But our citizenship is in heaven. And we eagerly await a Savior from there, the Lord Jesus Christ.
Philippians 3:20

December 2

IT'S HALFTIME

Halftime in a game is more than just a break; it's a moment to pause, reflect, and refocus on what lies ahead. In our spiritual lives, we are often presented with halftime moments—times of transition that call us to reassess where we are and where we're headed. In 2 Corinthians 5:17, Paul speaks to the transformation available through Christ. Just as a sports team uses halftime to adapt their strategy, we too have the opportunity to recalibrate our lives in Christ. The old ways, marked by sin and separation from God, are replaced by a new identity rooted in Him. This transformation isn't just a change of tactics but a complete renewal of being. Do you feel like you're at a halftime in your life? Maybe it's a new job, a change in family circumstances, or a shift in your spiritual walk. Consider what the new looks like for you. Are old habits or thought patterns holding you back from fully experiencing this new creation? Take this moment to re-evaluate your current path. Just as halftime provides a fresh perspective, allow this season a time of renewal and growth. Trust in God's plan and purpose, knowing He molds you into something new and beautiful. Remember, halftime is not the end; it's a pivotal point that prepares you for what's next. Halftime always leads to new beginnings.

Therefore, if anyone is in Christ, the new creation has come: The old has gone, the new is here!
2 Corinthians 5:17

ETERNITY IS REAL

The concept of eternity is woven throughout the tapestry of the Christian faith. It invites us to look beyond the transient nature of our worldly experiences and focus on the promise of everlasting life with God. Daily, it's easy to become overwhelmed by difficulties and challenges. Yet, as Paul writes in his letter to the Corinthians, these troubles are "light and momentary" compared to the eternal glory that awaits. Eternity is not just a distant future but a present reality that shapes how we live today. We align our lives with God's eternal purposes by focusing on the unseen. This perspective empowers us to face trials with courage and conviction, knowing they are temporary and serve a greater purpose in God's plan. Imagine eternity not as an endpoint but as an ongoing relationship with the Creator that begins now and endures forever. This mindset changes everything. It shifts priorities, influences decisions, and fills our hearts with hope. Consider how this perspective might alter your response to them. Remember, while our earthly troubles may seem significant, they are fleeting in the grand scheme of God's promise.

For our light and momentary troubles are achieving for us an eternal glory that far outweighs them all. So we fix our eyes not on what is seen but on what is unseen since what is seen is temporary, but what is unseen is eternal.
2 Corinthians 4:17-18

December 4

FEELING ABANDONED

Abandonment is a profound emotion, often leaving us feeling isolated and unsupported. In times of feeling forsaken by friends, family, or society, it is crucial to remember that God's presence is unwavering. Through the lens of Psalm 23, we are reminded of God's promise to guide and comfort us, even in our darkest times. David, the psalmist, knew the reality of abandonment and isolation firsthand. Yet, he expressed unwavering trust in God's presence. The imagery of the "darkest valley" illustrates the challenging seasons we all face but underscores that we are not alone. Abandonment can tempt us to close off our hearts, yet it is during these times that God gently calls us to lean into His love. Rather than succumbing to despair, we are invited to draw closer to Him, allowing His "rod" and "staff" to guide us. His rod represents protection, and His staff signifies guidance, ensuring we are never truly left to wander alone. God's promise is not merely to accompany us but to offer comfort and direction. May we find solace in knowing that abandonment is never the end of our story when our trust is placed in the Lord?

Even though I walk through the darkest valley, I will fear no evil, for you are with me; your rod and your staff comfort me.
Psalm 23:4

December 5

ARE YOU SURE?

Uncertainty can be overwhelming. Many of us face daily challenges that leave us questioning our choices and the paths we've taken. Pursuing certainty often leads us to rely on our understanding, trying to control outcomes and predict the future. However, the Bible offers a different approach. Proverbs 3:5-6 invites us to place our trust wholly in the Lord. It calls us to abandon the need to lean on our limited understanding and instead submit our ways to Him. This submission is not surrendering to chaos but a conscious choice to trust God's wisdom and guidance. When faced with life's uncertainties, we are reminded that God's plans are more significant and His perspective is far-reaching. He promises to make our paths straight if we align our decisions with His will. This requires faith—believing in what we cannot see and trusting that God has a plan for our lives. Consider the areas in your life where you are seeking certainty. Are you relying solely on your understanding, or are you allowing God to lead? Trusting in the Lord doesn't eliminate life's uncertainties, but it does shift the burden of control off our shoulders and onto His.

Trust in the Lord with all your heart and lean not on your understanding; in all your ways, submit to him, and he will make your paths straight.
Proverbs 3:5-6

December 6

LEARNING TO SAY NO

Learning to say no can feel like a daunting task. Yet, it's a crucial skill for maintaining our spiritual and emotional well-being. Jesus taught us the importance of simplicity and honesty in our commitments with His words in Matthew 5:37. Saying no is not a sign of weakness or lack of generosity; instead, it reflects wisdom and discernment. We must evaluate each request through the lens of our priorities and God's calling in our lives. When we overcommit, we risk diluting our effectiveness and losing sight of our purpose. We create space to say yes to what's truly important by saying no to certain things. It allows us to focus on our relationship with God, our family, and the tasks He entrusted us. This selective commitment aligns our actions with our values and strengthens our faith. Consider the areas of your life where you've struggled to say no. Reflect on how these commitments impact your ability to live a Christ-centered life. Ask the Holy Spirit to guide you in making wise decisions about where to invest your time and energy. Remember, saying no doesn't mean you're closing doors permanently. It may be postponing for a future time when you can give more fully. Trust in God's guidance.

All you need to say is yes or no; anything beyond this comes
from the evil one.
Matthew 5:37

ARE YOU DISAPPOINTED?

Disappointment is a feeling familiar to us all. Whether it's a missed opportunity, a failed relationship, or a life plan that didn't unfold as expected, disappointment can leave us feeling lost and disheartened. However, as Christians, we have a unique perspective on how to handle these moments. In Romans 8:28, we find a powerful reminder of God's sovereignty and goodness. The verse tells us that in all things—yes, even in our disappointments—God is at work, orchestrating events for our ultimate good. This doesn't mean that everything we encounter is inherently excellent or enjoyable. Instead, it assures us that God can redeem every situation, using even our setbacks as stepping stones toward His more excellent plan for our lives. Perhaps you've prayed fervently for a particular outcome, only to see it crumble. It's easy to question God's presence during such times. Yet, it is in these moments that our faith is tested and strengthened. God invites us to trust Him, even when we cannot see the whole picture. He calls us to lean into His promises, knowing that He is weaving a tapestry far more beautiful than we could imagine. When disappointment strikes, remember Romans 8:28. Trust that God is at work, transforming your trials into testimonies.

And we know that in all things God works for the good of those who love him, who have been called according to his purpose.
Romans 8:28

December 8

MINDING YOUR BUSINESS

In an era where distractions are plentiful, and boundaries are often blurred, the wisdom found in 1 Thessalonians 4:11 serves as a refreshing reminder for Christians. We are called to lead a quiet life and focus on our growth and responsibilities. In writing to the Thessalonians, the apostle Paul encourages believers to concentrate on their own spiritual and personal development rather than meddling in the affairs of others. Minding your own business is not about being indifferent to the needs of others but about understanding your role in God's plan and respecting the boundaries of others. It's about prioritizing your spiritual growth and living a life that reflects God's peace and love. By focusing on your path, you can better support and inspire those around you, leading by example rather than through interference. As mentioned in the Scripture, working with your hands emphasizes the value of honest, diligent work. It's about using the talents and abilities God has given you to contribute meaningfully to your community. When you focus on nurturing these gifts, you fulfill your potential and enhance the lives of those around you. The call to lead a quiet life is an invitation to peace in a world of noise.

Make it your ambition to lead a quiet life, mind your own business, and work with your hands, as we told you.
1 Thessalonians 4:11

December 9

YOU NEED TO RELAX

The idea of taking time to relax can feel almost impossible. Yet, the Bible consistently encourages rest and relaxation to rejuvenate our bodies and spirits. This passage from Matthew highlights Jesus' invitation to find solace in Him. When we are overwhelmed by life's demands, it is essential to remember that proper rest comes from trusting in God's strength and provision. Jesus invites us to exchange our burdens for His peace. In Psalms, David also emphasizes the importance of rest by declaring, "In peace, I will lie down and sleep, for you alone, Lord, make me dwell in safety" (Psalm 4:8). This verse reassures us that God is our ultimate protector, allowing us to relax in His watchful care. Practically speaking, relaxing might mean setting aside time for prayer, reflection, or simply enjoying God's creation without distractions. It involves surrendering our anxieties to God and trusting He is in control. By prioritizing relaxation, we align ourselves with God's design for a balanced life. Remember that taking time to unwind isn't just beneficial; it's necessary for spiritual health. Allow yourself the grace to pause, breathe, and reconnect with God.

Come to me, all weary and burdened, and I will give you rest. Take my yoke upon you and learn from me, for I am gentle and humble, and you will find rest for your souls.
Matthew 11:28-29

December 10

AN UNBELIEVING FAMILY

The desire to see our families walking in faith can often drive many of our daily actions. We dream of peaceful meals where conversations naturally bend toward gratitude and faith, of moments where love and understanding prevail. At the same time, every family member finds their unique place in God's grand tapestry. Joshua's declaration, "But as for me and my household, we will serve the Lord," is a powerful reminder of our role in spiritually leading our families. Leadership begins with us. It starts when we set a godly example through our actions and attitudes, showing unconditional love, patience, and forgiveness, just as Christ has shown us. In reaching our family, engaging them with kindness and without judgment is essential, creating an environment where they feel safe to explore their faith questions. Share your personal faith stories and how the scriptures have impacted you. Encourage open dialogue and listen more than you speak; a sincere ear can often open hearts to spiritual truths. Building a family rooted in faith is a daily endeavor. It involves intentional living and making room for God in our homes through studying and reflecting on His word together. Stand firm in your faith, and trust that God will work through you to reach your family.

But as for me and my household, we will serve the Lord.
Joshua 24:15

December 11

WHEN GOD DOESN'T ANSWER

Waiting on God's answer can be one of the most challenging aspects of faith. It's in our nature to want immediate solutions and clarity. However, God's perspective is infinitely broader than ours. His silence does not indicate indifference or absence; rather, it's a space where He invites us to trust His wisdom. Consider the story of Job, a man who faced immense suffering without any clear response from God for a time. Yet, through his trials, Job came to a deeper understanding of God and himself. This narrative reminds us that God's silence can cultivate growth, patience, and a profound trust in His plan. When we pray for guidance or deliverance and hear nothing, it's essential to remember that God may be working behind the scenes in ways we cannot yet comprehend. His timing is perfect, even if it's not aligned with our desired schedule. This waiting period might also be a test of faith, teaching us to rely on His promises rather than our understanding of the situation. Trust that God is orchestrating something more significant than we can envision. In these quiet moments, meditate on His word and hold onto the assurance that God is always with you, even when He seems silent.

My thoughts are not your thoughts, nor are your ways my ways, declares the Lord. As the heavens are higher than the earth, so are my ways higher than your ways and my thoughts than your thoughts.
Isaiah 55:8-9

December 12

TO BUSY TO BE HAPPY

Many of us constantly rush from one task to another, barely pausing to catch our breath. Life becomes a series of to-do lists, meetings, and obligations that can overwhelm and exhaust us. In the hustle and bustle, we often miss out on the simple joys and blessings God has placed in our lives. The central message of Psalm 46:10 is to "be still" and recognize God's presence and sovereignty. It's a call to pause amidst our hectic schedules and take a moment to regain perspective. When we prioritize busyness over stillness, we may feel distant from God and disconnected from His intended happiness. Being busy isn't inherently wrong, but it can overshadow our relationship with God when it becomes our sole focus. We must make conscious choices to slow down and spend quiet moments with Him, acknowledging His role as the source of true joy and contentment. Consider setting aside time each day to disconnect from your daily tasks and reconnect with God. Reflect on His word, appreciate His creation, and listen for His guidance. By intentionally creating space for God, you open yourself to experiencing His perfect peace and happiness.

Be still, and know that I am God; I will be exalted among the nations and exalted in the earth.
Psalm 46:10

December 13

WHEN MONEY IS TIGHT

Financial strains are common and can weigh heavily on our hearts.
Whether unexpected expenses or dwindling savings, money woes can
leave us anxious and uncertain. Yet, as Christians, we are reminded that
God's provision transcends our earthly limitations. Paul's letter to the
Philippians assures us that God is aware of our needs and fully capable
of meeting them. The promise in Philippians 4:19 is not simply about
material wealth but a testament to the abundance found in Christ. It is a
reminder that God's resources are infinite, and His generosity knows no
bounds. When finances are tight, it's easy to slip into a scarcity mindset.
However, this verse calls us to shift our focus from lack to trust. Trust
that God sees our situation, understands our needs, and will provide for
us in ways we may not anticipate. Consider the lilies of the field and the
birds of the air. They do not worry or toil, yet our Heavenly Father
sustains them. In the same way, we are encouraged to lean into the
assurance of God's provision. During times of financial difficulty, we
can find solace in knowing that we are not alone. God is with us,
providing and guiding us through every trial. His grace is sufficient, and
we have all we truly need in Him.

And my God will meet all your needs according to the riches of his glory
in Christ Jesus.
Philippians 4:19

December 14

BREAKING BREAD TOGETHER

In the early church, breaking bread was not merely a meal. It was a powerful act of fellowship and unity among believers. When they gathered, it wasn't just to satisfy hunger but to share life and faith. This simple act represented a deep commitment to one another and the teachings of Christ. In today's fast-paced world, it's easy to view meals as just another task in our busy schedules. However, the early Christians provide us with a beautiful model of how breaking bread can be a time of spiritual significance. Sharing meals can be a sacred space for connection, where we can nurture our relationships and strengthen our bonds with others in faith. Imagine a table where stories are shared, encouragement is given, and laughter fills the air. This is not just a meal; it's a chance to engage deeply with those around us, to listen, and be heard. It's about building a community that reflects the love and teachings of Jesus. Breaking bread together is an invitation to pause, to remember, and to celebrate the grace we have received. It's a chance to acknowledge that we are more robust and unified in our pursuit of love and understanding. Make time to gather, break bread, and create meaningful moments with those in your community.

They devoted themselves to the apostles' teaching, fellowship, the breaking of bread, and prayer.
Acts 2:42

December 15

FAMILY TIME TOGETHER

Finding time for family can feel like a challenge. Work commitments, school schedules, and extracurricular activities often pull us in different directions. However, the Bible reminds us of the value and strength found in family unity. Proverbs 27:17 vividly depicts how relationships grow through interaction and mutual support. Just as iron sharpens iron, our families sharpen and refine us. Spending quality time together isn't just about being physically present; it's an opportunity to learn from one another, grow in faith, and strengthen bonds. Consider the story of Mary, Martha, and Lazarus. In their home, Jesus found a place of welcome and friendship. Similarly, when we open our homes and hearts to each other, we create spaces where faith and love flourish. Family time can be simple. It could be as simple as sharing a meal, discussing Scripture, or enjoying a walk together. These moments allow for meaningful conversations and sharing life's joys and challenges. Reflect on ways your family can carve out intentional time together this week. Whether it's a weekly game night, a Sunday afternoon walk, or reading a chapter of the Bible together, find what resonates with your family and make it a cherished tradition. In prioritizing these moments, we fulfill God's design for community and support.

As iron sharpens iron, so one person sharpens another.
Proverbs 27:17

December 16

LISTENING TO OUR CHILDREN

Parents often need more time for meaningful conversations with their children. Yet, listening to our children is essential to nurturing their spiritual and emotional growth. When we genuinely listen to our children, we convey a message of love and importance. It reassures them that their thoughts and feelings are valued. This act mirrors how God listens to us, His children, with patience and understanding. As we seek His guidance through prayer and reflection, children look to their parents for comfort and wisdom. James 1:19 urges us to listen intently and speak with care. This Scripture challenges us to adopt a posture of humility and attentiveness—qualities that foster open communication. We build a foundation of trust by being fully present, putting away distractions, and allowing our children the space to express themselves freely. Listening goes beyond just hearing words; it involves understanding the emotions and intentions behind them. When our children express joy, fears, or confusion, we have an opportunity to guide them spiritually, sharing biblical truths that align with their experiences. You have the time; listening is essential.

Everyone should be quick to listen, slow to speak, and slow to become angry.
James 1:19

GIVING THINGS AWAY

Giving things away is not just a physical act of parting with material possessions; it is a spiritual exercise that aligns our hearts with God's kingdom. In Matthew 6, Jesus instructs us to focus not on earthly wealth, which is fleeting, but on heavenly treasures, which are eternal. This teaching challenges us to consider what we truly value and where our hearts dwell. The call to give things away can seem counter-cultural in a world that often equates success with accumulation. Yet, through giving, we discover the joy of releasing our grip on material things and freeing ourselves from the bondage of possessions. We practice generosity and faith each time we choose to give, trusting that God will provide all our needs. Consider what you might give away today: clothing, food, time, or talents. Whatever it is, know that God sees and values every act of kindness. By focusing on what we can give rather than get, we nurture a heart that reflects God's love and compassion. Remember, true riches are not measured in what we keep but in what we are willing to share.

Do not store up for yourselves treasures on earth, where moths and vermin destroy and where thieves break in and steal. But store up for yourselves treasures in heaven, where moths and vermin do not destroy, and where thieves do not break in and steal. For where your treasure is, there your heart will be also.
Matthew 6:19-21

December 18

MAKING ROOM FOR JESUS

Our schedules can become cluttered with endless tasks, obligations, and distractions. Amid this chaos, it's essential to remember that Jesus stands patiently at the door of our hearts, waiting for us to make room for Him. Just as we prioritize work, family, and social commitments, we are called to carve out space for our relationship with Christ intentionally. Jesus' invitation to dine with us is both intimate and profound. Dining together isn't just about sharing a meal; it's an act of fellowship, connection, and communion. It signifies openness, trust, and a readiness to receive His love and guidance. When we make room for Jesus, we invite peace, wisdom, and a renewed sense of purpose into our lives. To make room for Jesus, consider setting aside specific times each day to read Scripture, meditate on His word, and reflect on His presence in your life. Find moments in your daily routine to acknowledge His handiwork, whether through the beauty of creation or acts of kindness around you. Doing so fosters a deeper, more meaningful relationship with Christ, allowing His light to shine brightly in our hearts and lives. Remember, when we open the door to Jesus, we open ourselves to transformation and abundant life.

Here I am! I stand at the door and knock. If anyone hears my voice and opens the door, I will come in and eat with that person, and they will be with me.
Revelation 3:20

December 19

THE SEASON

The Christmas season is here, and we're often swept up in the whirlwind of festivities, such as decorating homes, exchanging gifts, and gathering with loved ones. However, amidst the hustle and bustle, we must pause and reflect on the valid reason for the season. The birth of Jesus Christ marks a pivotal moment in history, not just as a significant event but as the embodiment of God's love for humanity. Sent to bring salvation and hope to a world in need, Jesus is more than just a figure from the past; He is the Wonderful Counselor guiding our hearts, the Mighty God who empowers us, the Everlasting Father who provides eternal care, and the Prince of Peace offering tranquility amidst life's storms. Consider how the birth of Christ impacts your life today. Do you seek His counsel in times of confusion? Do you rely on His strength when you feel weak? Is your relationship with Him personal, grounded in the understanding that His birth was the beginning of a path leading to grace and redemption? This season, take time to deepen your relationship with Jesus. Reflect on His attributes and how they manifest in your life. The actual celebration lies not in the external trappings of the season but in the internal transformation of the birth of Jesus.

For us, a child is born; to us, a son is given, and the government will be on his shoulders. And he will be called Wonderful Counselor, Mighty God, Everlasting Father, Prince of Peace.
Isaiah 9:6

INTERRUPTIONS

Interruptions are as inevitable as they are frustrating. We plan our days, setting our agendas, and then life happens—unexpected phone calls, last-minute requests, or sudden changes in circumstances. Yet, these disruptions often hold greater purpose than we initially perceive. Consider the ministry of Jesus. His life was entirely of interruptions. He was on His way to heal Jairus's daughter when a woman touched His cloak, seeking healing. Jesus could have ignored her to maintain His schedule, but He stopped, engaged with her, and commended her faith (Mark 5:25-34). Interruptions can be divine interventions. They are opportunities for growth, service, and unexpected blessings. When our plans are halted, we can pause and seek God's purpose in the deviation. In Proverbs 16:9, we are reminded that while we plan our paths, the Lord establishes our steps. This calls for a shift in perspective from seeing interruptions as obstacles to viewing them as divinely orchestrated moments that align us with God's will. Next time you face an interruption, ask yourself, What is God inviting me to learn or do now? This mindset transforms how we experience daily disruptions and opens our hearts to the unexpected ways God can work through them.

Humans plan their course in their hearts, but the Lord
establishes their steps.
Proverbs 16:9

December 21

DO YOU LIKE SURPRISES?

Life is full of surprises, both welcome and unwelcome. Surprises can come in many forms, from an unexpected visit from a friend to a sudden change in plans. But have you ever thought about the surprises God might have for you? Ephesians 3:20 tells us about a God whose plans exceed our wildest dreams. His ability is beyond our imagination, and He works through us to accomplish things we may never have considered possible. Sometimes, these divine surprises come when we least expect them, turning our lives in new and exciting directions. Think of Abraham and Sarah. They were well beyond childbearing years when God surprised them with the promise of a son. Or consider Joseph, who went from being sold into slavery to becoming second in command in Egypt. These stories remind us that God's surprises often carry more blessings than we could have envisioned. In our lives, unexpected challenges can lead us to grow spiritually, and unforeseen blessings remind us of God's abundant love. When faced with uncertainty or surprise, we can trust in God's more excellent plan, knowing He is at work in ways we cannot fully understand. Do you invite God's surprises into your life?

Now, to him, who can do immeasurably more than all we ask or imagine, according to his power at work within us,
Ephesians 3:20

December 22

MARY'S JOURNEY

Mary's story is a profound testament to faith, humility, and obedience. Mary's life was transformed from the moment the angel Gabriel visited her. Her journey offers lessons that resonate deeply within the Christian faith, illuminating the path of trust in God's plan. Mary was greatly troubled by his words and wondered what kind of greeting this might be. But the angel told her, "Do not be afraid, Mary; you have found favor with God. You will conceive and give birth to a son, and you are to call him Jesus. He will be great and called the Son of the Most High. The Lord God will give him the throne of his father David, and he will reign over Jacob's descendants forever; his kingdom will never end. Mary asked the angel how this would be since I am a virgin?" The angel answered, "The Holy Spirit will come on you, and the Most High power will overshadow you. So, the holy one to be born will be called the Son of God. Even Elizabeth, your relative, will have a child of her old age, and she, who was said to be unable to conceive, is in her sixth month, for no word from God will ever fail. I am the Lord's servant," Mary answered. "May your word to me be fulfilled. Then the angel left her." Mary's response to the angel's message exemplifies her unwavering faith.

The virgin's name was Mary. The angel went to her and said, 'Greetings, you who are highly favored! The Lord is with you.
Luke 1:26-38

December 23

NO ROOM IN THE INN

The story of Jesus' birth is filled with profound humility and simplicity. When Mary and Joseph arrived in Bethlehem, they found themselves without a place to stay. Due to the census, the town was bustling with travelers, and every inn was full. In this moment of great need, they were offered a humble stable. It was here, amid the animals, that Jesus, the world's Savior, was born. The "no room in the inn" message is a powerful reminder of how often the world overlooks what is genuinely significant. The King of kings was born not in splendor or comfort but in a manger. This setting underscores the radical nature of Jesus' mission on earth—His willingness to come as a servant to meet us in our most humble and needy state. Reflecting on this account encourages us to examine our own lives. Are there areas where we have no room for Jesus? Do our busy schedules, ambitions, or distractions crowd out His presence? Just as the inn was complete, our hearts can be filled with things that leave little space for the divine. This Christmas season, consider making room for the Savior in your life. Allow the simplicity and humility of Jesus' birth to inspire you to create space in your heart for Him.

She gave birth to her firstborn, a son. She wrapped him in clothes and placed him in a manger because no guest room was available for them.
Luke 2:7

December 24

THE BIRTH OF JESUS

The birth of Jesus marks a pivotal moment in the Christian faith. Imagine the shepherds tending their flocks under a starlit sky, suddenly bathed in divine radiance. An angel appears, proclaiming a message of joy and hope—a Savior is born! This isn't just any birth; it's the fulfillment of prophecy, the long-awaited Messiah. The angel's announcement encompasses everyone—"great joy for all the people." This inclusivity is integral to the message of Jesus. He did not come for one tribe, group, or nation but for all humanity. His birth signifies the start of a new covenant based on grace and love. The image of Jesus lying in a manger, wrapped in simple clothes, is profound. The King of Kings chose a humble beginning, emphasizing His accessibility. He meets us in the ordinary, transforming our lives with extraordinary love. The heavenly host's praise reflects the divine harmony Jesus brings —"peace to those on whom his favor rests." How does this divine gift redefine your understanding of peace, joy, and salvation?

Today, in the town of David, a Savior has been born to you; he is the Messiah, the Lord. This will be a sign: You will find a baby wrapped in clothes and lying in a manger. Suddenly, a great company of the heavenly host appeared with the angel, praising God and saying, Glory to God in the highest heaven, and on earth, peace to those on whom his favor rests.
Luke 2:11-14

December 25

CHRISTMAS DAY

Christmas Day is a celebration of hope realized. It marks the birth of Jesus Christ, the Messiah, who came to bring light into our world and offer salvation to all. This significant event in the town of Bethlehem was the fulfillment of prophecies and the answer to centuries of waiting for a Savior. The shepherds were among the first to hear the joyful news. Imagine their awe and wonder as the angel announced the birth of the Lord, filling the sky with heavenly light. Their immediate response to go and see the newborn shows the urgency and excitement that this news brought. For Christians, Christmas is more than just a day of festivities; it is a reminder of the profound love of God and His plan for redemption. The birth of Jesus signifies a new beginning and a promise fulfilled, encouraging us to reflect on the true meaning of this season. In the hustle and bustle of holiday traditions, take a moment to ponder the magnitude of this gift. Jesus came into the world humbly, yet his impact is immeasurable. His life and teachings inspire and guide us, reminding us of the joy, peace, and hope we can find in Him. As you celebrate Christmas today, may you be filled with the wonder of the shepherds, the joy of the angels, and the peace of knowing that our Savior has come?

Today, in the town of David, a Savior has been born to you; he is the Messiah, the Lord.
Luke 2:11

December 26

ANTICIPAITON

The theme of anticipation is woven throughout the Bible, often reflecting a deep trust and expectation in God's unfolding plans. To anticipate is to wait expectantly, believing that God's promises will come to fruition in His perfect timing. Jeremiah 29:11 offers profound comfort. It reminds us of God's intimate involvement in our lives. Despite our challenges, this verse assures us that God's plans are designed for our well-being and growth. Anticipation, therefore, becomes an act of faith. It's not passive waiting but active trust in the divine author of our life stories. Reflecting on anticipation invites us to examine our expectations. Are we placing our hopes in temporal outcomes, or are we anchored in the eternal promises of God? In moments of uncertainty, when the future seems unclear, this anticipation becomes our lifeline, guiding us back to the certainty of God's goodness. Consider how biblical figures like Abraham and Mary demonstrated anticipation. Abraham awaited the promise of descendants as numerous as the stars, and Mary embraced the angel's news with a heart full of trust. Their stories encourage us to maintain a posture of anticipation rooted in faith. Living in anticipation means aligning our desires with God's will.

For I know my plans for you, declares the Lord, plans to prosper you and not to harm you, plans to give you hope and a future.
Jeremiah 29:11

TIME TO GET EXCITED

Have you ever felt trapped in the monotony of daily life, where each day merges into the next without distinction or excitement? It's a shared experience, but it's time to break free. The message in Isaiah 40:31 encourages us to place our hope in the Lord and find renewed strength in Him. When we anchor our hope in God, something extraordinary happens. Our perspectives shift, and we begin to see beyond our immediate circumstances. The promise of soaring on wings like eagles is more than just poetic imagery; it signifies a life lifted above earthly concerns, driven by divine purpose and enthusiasm. They possess a unique ability to rise above storms, using the winds meant for adversity to lift them higher. Similarly, when we align our hopes with God's promises, we can rise above our struggles and find excitement. Today's invitation is to rekindle your excitement about God's plan for your life. Whether walking through seasons of quiet or running through times of busyness, remember that God offers strength and excitement for every step of your journey. Now is the time to get excited, to look forward with anticipation, and to trust that God has prepared a path filled with purpose and joy.

But those who hope in the Lord will renew their strength. They will soar on wings like eagles; they will run and not grow weary; they will walk and not be faint.
Isaiah 40:31

December 28

REVIEWING PAST DECISIONS

We reach a crossroads in life where decisions must be made. These moments can be both exhilarating and intimidating. Once created, decisions become part of our life's tapestry—each one influencing the next. Reflecting on past decisions allows us to learn and grow, which is essential for anyone walking in faith. In Proverbs 3, we are reminded to trust in the Lord with all our hearts. This trust extends into our decision-making process; it beckons us to involve God in our choices and to rely on His wisdom rather than merely our understanding. Looking back, we might see decisions that worked out beautifully and others that may have led to challenges or regrets. Through this review, we can discern patterns and recognize where reliance on God's wisdom was pivotal—and where it might have been lacking. Consider reflecting on a past decision that weighs heavily on your heart. With an open mind, ask yourself how you involved God in that process. Did you seek His guidance? Was there room for divine wisdom, or did human reasoning prevail? We gain valuable insight into how God has worked in our lives by revisiting these decisions in light of faith. This reflection strengthens our trust in God for future decisions.

Trust in the Lord with all your heart and lean not on your own understanding; in all your ways submit to him, and he will make your paths straight.
Proverbs 3:5-6

December 29

LOOKING FORWARD

It's easy to become bogged down by past events—those moments of failure or regret that linger in our minds. Yet, the Apostle Paul offers a powerful perspective in his letter to the Philippians. He reminds us of the importance of letting go of the past, urging us to focus on what lies ahead. The Christian life is a continual journey forward. When we cling too tightly to our past mistakes, we can hinder our growth and impede the fulfillment of God's purpose. Paul emphasizes looking forward with eager anticipation, pressing on to reach the ultimate goal—a deeper relationship with Christ and the heavenly prize that awaits. For many, this requires a conscious effort to release the weight of past failures. It demands that we trust God's divine plan, confident that He works all things for our good. By focusing on the future, we open ourselves to the new opportunities and blessings God has prepared for us. Thus, as we move through our days, let us keep our eyes fixed firmly ahead. May we strive for spiritual maturity, driven by the promise that our best days will still come in Christ.

Brothers and sisters, I do not consider myself yet to have taken hold of it. But one thing I do: Forget what is behind and strain toward what is ahead. I press on toward winning the prize for which God has called me heavenward in Christ Jesus.
Philippians 3:13-14

December 30

IT'S TIME TO PLAN

Living a life anchored in faith doesn't mean leaving our daily routines to chance. Planning is an essential part of fulfilling our God-given purpose. The Bible reminds us that when we commit our plans to the Lord, He can establish and guide them. Planning is not merely a secular task; it is a spiritual exercise. It begins with seeking God's wisdom and aligning our desires with His will. Throughout Scripture, faithful servants like Joseph and Nehemiah planned diligently, trusting that God would guide their steps. Their stories teach us that careful preparation and faith can lead to extraordinary outcomes. In our own lives, making plans can involve setting goals, prioritizing tasks, or simply organizing our day-to-day activities. Yet, it's crucial to remember that these plans should always be placed in God's hands. This means being open to His direction and ready to adapt when He redirects us. Perhaps you've hesitated to plan, fearing that doing so might limit God's work in your life. On the contrary, planning with God at the center can expand your horizons and open doors you hadn't considered. It's about partnering with the Creator, who knows the end from the beginning, to bring forth His purposes in you. Take some time today to reflect on your plans. Are they aligned with God's desires for your life?

Commit to the Lord whatever you do; he will establish your plans.
Proverbs 16:3

December 31

NEXT YEAR WILL BE GREAT

As we approach the close of this year and look toward the next, it's natural to reflect on our hopes and aspirations. The theme Next Year Will Be Great resonates profoundly, mainly when anchored in the truth of God's word. Jeremiah 29:11 reminds us that God has a path for each of us, one filled with hope, prosperity, and a bright future. The promise here isn't about avoiding difficulties but about trusting that God's plans transcend our challenges. Our daily lives might bring unforeseen trials, yet the assurance of God's guidance and purpose offers a sense of calm and certainty. Consider the significance of "plans to prosper you." This prosperity is not solely material; it encompasses spiritual growth, deeper relationships, and a peace that surpasses understanding. In God's plan, every step we take is an opportunity to align with His will and experience His blessings. This coming year, invite God into your planning process. Seek His wisdom in your decisions. Our confidence is not rooted in the shifting sands of circumstance but in the steadfast love of God. May we stand firm in the assurance that Next Year Will Be Great because our hope is anchored in an unchanging God who charts our course.

For I know my plans for you, declares the Lord, plans to prosper you
and not to harm you, plans to give you hope and a future.
Jeremiah 29:11

About the Author

Dr. Pettigrew received his undergraduate degree at the University of Tennessee, his Master's degree at Murray State University, and his Doctoral degree from the University of Memphis.

Joe has been a high school teacher, university professor, College Dean, and and the CEO for Leaderpoint Consulting Group. He has consulted with many of the most successful corporate leaders in the world and has close ties with many national Christian sports celebrities.

In 2008 he founded the national men's ministry, In The Zone. The ministry held in large arenas and churche was closed during Covid-19.

Joe has authored four books. and is currently the Pastor at Brownsville Presbyterian Church in Tennessee.

He has been married to Trudy for over 50 years, and together they have three children: Ashley, Tara, and Tyler. He also has seven grandchildren.

Thanks for reading My Daily Huddle.

For information about Joe speaking in your church or about ordering additional books, please contact info@inthezone.org.

May God Bless You.